MW01056358

A Fourth-Century Daoist Family

A Fourth-Century Daoist Family

The *Zhen'gao,* or *Declarations of the Perfected,* Volume I

Stephen R. Bokenkamp

UNIVERSITY OF CALIFORNIA PRESS

University of California Press
Oakland, California

© 2021 by Stephen Bokenkamp

Library of Congress Cataloging-in-Publication Data

Names: Bokenkamp, Stephen R., 1949- author. | Tao,
    Hongjing, 452–536. Zhen gao. | Tao, Hongjing,
    452–536. Zhen gao. English.
Title: A fourth-century Daoist family : The Zhen'gao or
    Declarations of the perfected, Volume 1 / Stephen R.
    Bokenkamp.
Description: Oakland, California : University of
    California Press, [2021] | Includes bibliographical
    references and index. | Text in English and Chinese.
Identifiers: LCCN 2020019228 (print) | LCCN 2020019229
    (ebook) | ISBN 9780520356269 (cloth) |
    ISBN 9780520976030 (ebook)
Subjects: LCSH: Tao, Hongjing, 452–536. Zhen gao. |
    Taoism—Relations—Buddhism. | Buddhism—
    Relations—Taoism. | Taoism—Sacred books—History.
Classification: LCC BL1900.T355 B65 2021 (print) |
    LCC BL1900.T355 (ebook) | DDC 299.5/1482—dc23
LC record available at https://lccn.loc.gov/2020019228
LC ebook record available at https://lccn.loc
    .gov/2020019229

Manufactured in the United States of America

30 29 28 27 26 25 24 23 22 21
10 9 8 7 6 5 4 3 2 1

Dedicated to my teachers:
Edward H. Schafer
Michel Strickmann

Contents

Acknowledgments   *ix*

Introduction   *1*

Contents and Background of the Work   6

Women and Goddesses   9

Mediumism in the Declarations   11

Buddhism in the Declarations   18

Prior Translations   24

Conventions of the Translation   25

Abbreviations   27

1) Tao Hongjing's Postface (DZ 1016, Chapters 19–20)   29

     Translation: Introducing the Declarations of the Perfected   33

     Translation: Account of the Perfected Scriptures from Beginning to End   53

     Translation: Genealogy of the Perfected Forebears   78

2) The Poems of Elühua   98

     Translation: The Poems of Elühua (DZ 1016, 1.1a–2a)   98

3) The Sons of Sima Yu   108

   Introduction   108

   Translation: The Sons of Sima Yu   114

4) "Eight Pages of Lined Text"   122

   a) *Introduction to the "Eight Pages of Lined Text"*   122

   b) *Introduction and Translation: Poems on Dependence
      and Independence*   129

   c) *Introduction and Translation: Han Mingdi's Dream*   141

   d) *Introduction and Translation of On Fangzhu*   145

   e) *Introduction and Translation of the Teachings and
      Admonitions of the Assembled Numinous Powers
      (= The Scripture in Forty-Two Sections)*   154

   f) *Related Fragments*   168

Works in the Daoist Canon   173
Works Cited   175
Index   183

Acknowledgments

This translation began as a wisp of aspiration in the winter of 1978 in Berkeley, California. It came about as follows.

Michel Strickmann had just arrived as a visiting professor in what was then called the "Oriental Languages Department." He had been invited from Japan by eminent scholar of Tang poetry and material culture Edward H. Schafer. As a visitor, Strickmann could not teach a seminar, so it was arranged that he teach an upper-division undergraduate course. Only newly arrived graduate students might take such a course for credit. I was one of two. My fellow student was "Doug," a graduate student who, perhaps more intelligent than am I, left to become a lawyer soon after our experience. Auditing the course, if memory serves, were Judith M. Boltz, Suzanne Cahill, Robert Chard, and Donald Harper—all advanced graduate students—and my primary instructor Edward Schafer himself. The topic of the course was the *Declarations of the Perfected*, which existed then only in the unpunctuated edition of the Ming-period Daoist canon.

The course was conducted as follows: As enrolled students, Doug and I would be asked to read aloud, breaking the Chinese text into sentences, and translate. Neither of us had seen a Daoist text before, and the result was what you might have expected. After we read, Strickmann kindly told us how the lines might actually be parsed and what they meant. After that, the "auditors" would discuss the passage for a while before turning to either Doug or me once more. The brilliant red periods and commas on my notes from that term show that I seldom parsed the text correctly. And despite my heroic dictionary work, my translations are each stricken out with a strong, and sometimes frustrated, pencil stroke.

The journey from then until now is too convoluted to recount here. Professors Schafer and Strickmann were—for thirteen years in the former case and five in the latter—my wonderfully inspiring teachers. The seeds they planted are responsible for the persistence with which I kept coming back to this text before it began working its own charm on me. I owe them a debt that cannot be repaid.

My concentrated work on the volume began with a grant from the John Simon Guggenheim Memorial Foundation in 2013 and was supported at key points by generous grants from the Institute of Advanced Study of Princeton as Edwin C. and Elizabeth A. Whitehead Fellow; the Chang Ching-kuo Foundation; the Max Planck Institute; the International Consortium for Research in the Humanities at Friedrich-Alexander-Universität of Erlangen-Nürnberg, Germany; Peking University; and Arizona State University.

But it takes more even than a village to bridge the distance between nineteenth- and twentieth-century America and fourth-century China. Beyond my teachers, I need to thank a veritable army of friends, students, and colleagues. First, my partner, Lisa Berkson, has demonstrably read more drafts (including a draft of this page, so that these sentences had to be added later) than any other person on the planet. I am blessed by her continued support of and faith in me. Second, I thank the classmates who audited Strickmann's first course. Beyond restraining their amusement at my early efforts, they remained supportive. Don Harper has even continued to read my manuscripts and provide advice down through the decades. A few more wonderful scholars have read and commented on drafts of this work: Robert F. Campany, Chang Ch'ao-jan 張超然, Terry F. Kleeman, John Lagerwey, and Mark Csikszentmihalyi. Lü Pengzhi 呂鵬志 even accepted a request to do a last check of the important final chapter of this volume. Since I have lived with the *Declarations* for so long, I have received help and inspiration from a number of students and colleagues. Third, and no less important, then, are those many who chipped in with helpful criticisms from time to time, sometimes without even realizing it, sometimes at my request: Yipaer Aierken, Bai Bin 白彬, Michael Stanley-Baker, Cheng Lesong 程樂松, Robert Joe Cutter, Albert Dien, Patricia Ebrey, Tyler

Feezell, Geoffrey Goble, Vincent Goosaert, Hsieh Shu-wei 謝世維, Stephan Kory, Paul W. Kroll, Lee Feng-mao 李豐楙, Li Jiangnan 黎江南, Li Jinglin 李景林, Liu Yi 劉屹, Min Sun Young 閔善映, Jan Nattier, Jonathan Pettit, Gil Raz, Anna Marshall Shields, Dagmar Schäfer, Sun Qi 孫齊, Timothy Swanger, Tang Qiaomei 唐巧美, Stephen F. Teiser, Franciscus Verellen, Wang Zongyu 王宗昱, Stephen West, Lucas Wolfe, Wu Wei 武薇, Wu Yue 吳嶽, Xu Liying 徐李穎, Stefano Zacchetti, Beverly Zhang, and Zhao Luying 趙鹿影. I thank you all.

The editors for the University of California Press—Reed Malcolm, Archna Patel, and Enrique Ochoa-Kaup—as well as the copy editor, Beth Chapple, and all the others I have worked with at the Press have been supremely kind and understanding. The level of annotation that presenting a translation such as this requires is daunting, to say the least, and they have worked hard to make the result easily navigable. I am grateful.

As you read these translations, you will come to understand something of the impossibility of the work I have tried to do here. When one cannot with full confidence interpret a letter written yesterday across town, it is not really a source of wonder that something written nearly seventeen hundred years ago is transcendentally difficult to understand. Add to this the fact that some of what was written was suppressed, as I hope to demonstrate, and you will know why those listed above cannot be held responsible in any way for anything I have written. In fact, some who have contributed the most actively disagree with aspects of my analysis. Those were helpful contributions as well, and I thank them all.

Introduction

This book is a translation and study of the transcripts of a fourth-century CE Chinese Daoist medium. The medium, Yang Xi 楊羲 (330–ca. 386), or rather those deities he channeled, wrote poems and instructions of such compelling literary excellence that they drew the attention of one of the foremost scholars of the early medieval period, Tao Hongjing 陶弘景 (456–536). Tao collected the autograph manuscripts based on calligraphy, then added a history of the participants and a scholarly apparatus explaining the texts. The resulting work was the *Zhen'gao* 真誥 (*Declarations of the Perfected*).

If we could imaginatively transport ourselves back to Yang Xi's oratory on Mount Mao, where he crafted his beautiful poetic visions of celestial scenes and human perfectibility, we would likely be disappointed. Yang describes his mountain meditation chamber as a thatched wooden hut roughly five by four meters in area and only two and a half meters high under the ridgepole. The hut had only a single door and a small window in the opposite wall. Within was a short bench long enough for Yang to lie down for meditations that required this posture. For decorations, there would have been an incense burner, a paper knife, an ink stone, brushes, and paper. What occurred within occurred inside the imagination of Yang Xi: Female deities appeared, their garments flashing with ethereal light, sometimes accompanied by scripture-bearing attendants. Divine refreshment was offered. Sometimes Yang's deities brought news from the darkest corners of the underworld, where infernal judges held stern sway; more often they told of flight as they moved effortlessly between one end of the cosmos and the other, swooping lightly back to their floating palaces in the seas off the eastern coast of the empire. All that and more we find not on Mount Mao, then or now, but in the pages Tao Hongjing so patiently patched together for us.

The *Declarations* arguably rivals in quality other world classics of imaginative literature. It is in many ways comparable to Dante Alighieri's (1265–1321) *Divine Comedy*. Both works deliver compelling visions of bright celestial realms and dark underworld regions; both present a political perspective on the important figures of their respective societies; both feature love portrayed as holy and ethereal; and both helped remake the literature to come through pushing the boundaries of poetry.[1] The major differences between the two works are three: Yang Xi's visions of other worlds were conveyed through the media of his deities and, as this infers, he did not claim to have written the work himself. Further, he did not in this work attempt a single, clear narrative. Rather, the work tells a number of tales at once, perhaps making it even more deserving of vertical reading than is the *Divine Comedy*.[2]

We might also compare the *Declarations* with the classics of religious literature. Unlike such influential works as the *Apocalypse of John*, the *Book of Mormon*, or the *Tractatus de Purgatorio Sancti Patricii*, however, the *Declarations* enjoyed the attentions of a textual scholar soon after its production.[3] We thus have not only a description of Yang Xi's procedures in contacting the divinities, but also an account of the realia surrounding the event. We learn the size and furnishings of his meditation chamber, the paper and calligraphy of the revelations, and so forth. We learn as well the justifications for these procedures, such as the elaborate explanations that the deities give when asked why they refuse to write anything in their own hands. For these reasons, we are informed

1. I will be unable to prove these claims. The scholarship on Dante is vast, exhaustive, and spans centuries, while that on the work of Yang Xi is sparse and begins to expand only in the 1930s. Dante scholars have begun to debate whether the literary nature of his work can be separated from its religious impetus. (See, for instance, Barolini, *Undivine Comedy*, and the reviews by Sowell (1998), Botterill (1994), and a host of others). We have scarcely begun to understand the religiosity of Yang Xi.

2. I refer, of course, to the remarkable series of essays collected in the Cambridge University open library project, *Vertical Readings in Dante's 'Comedy.'* (See Corbett and Webb, introduction, 1–12.)

3. For recent work on the realia surrounding the revelations accorded Joseph Smith, see Taves, "History and the Claims"; for an introduction to the *Tractus de Purgatorio*, see Barbezat, "He Doubted."

on the social and material background of Yang Xi's revelations in detail that far transcends what we can know of similar revelations from other cultures.

In the section on prior translations later in this introduction, I will discuss how I intend to exploit these aspects of the text, which will hopefully be of use to scholars dealing with the revelatory literature of other times and places. For now it is enough to note that the *Declarations*, both in their narrative accounts concerning the living and the dead and in the extensive annotation provided by Tao Hongjing over a century later, offer new and unexpected perspectives on the history of the period. The standard official history of the Jin 晉 dynasty is based on tale literature and is notoriously inaccurate.[4] Tao Hongjing's extensive citations of earlier lost histories supply much new information.

In comparison with other classics of early Daoism, the *Declarations* have long been regarded by scholars as a guide to the analysis of the scriptures and biographies that Yang Xi wrote, as well as to those his work influenced. Firmly dated, Tao Hongjing's collection was the primary temporal milestone that pioneering scholars used to navigate the undated morass of texts in the Daoist canon.[5]

The excellent work done on this text does not exhaust what it has to tell us. For instance, given the sharp disciplinary divisions and sectarian distinctions that formed our understanding of that period's religion, scholars tended to miss the ways that Yang Xi's Daoism also borrowed much from the foreign religion of Buddhism that was just coming into its own at that time (see the section on Buddhism). Today we know that Daoism was a shape-shifting religion intimately involved in the cultural history of China that did not organize itself around unalterable doctrine or creed in the ways we at first imagined. At the time of the *Declarations*, Daoists had just begun a full-scale adoption of various strategies brought in with the foreign religion—lengthy scriptures, description of postmortem destinations, new forms of religious vocation, and the like.

The *Declarations* further mark the moment in history when new forms of religiosity became popular with the literate aristocracy and became poised to influence Chinese cultural life in the centuries to come. The *Shangqing* 上清 (Upper Clarity) scriptures of Yang Xi, which are

---

4. I refer to Fang Xuanling's (579–648) *Jinshu*.

5. Particularly worthy of mention are Chen Guofu, Yoshikawa Tadao, Michel Strickmann, Mugitani Kuniō, and Isabelle Robinet, but many scholars contributed to this enterprise.

introduced in the *Declarations*, feature new, higher heavens and a new type of celestial being, all unknown to previous Daoists.[6] Yang Xi's triad of heavens—Grand Clarity, Upper Clarity, and Jade Clarity— restricted the previously-known *xianren* 仙人 (Transcendents) primarily to the lower heaven, while a new class of qi-formed beings, the Perfected 真人, reside in the middle heaven but might roam throughout.[7]

Beyond new celestial realms, Yang's informants provided him with the most detailed descriptions we possess of the lands of the dead as they were imagined before the arrival of Buddhism. Buddhism brought with it the concept of a hellish underworld filled with infernal torture camps, where the dead were made to suffer for impossible periods of time for transgressions they had committed during their lives, such as the consumption of meat. In these camps, a new class of fear-inspiring hell beings punished the dead before sending them off to be reborn as human or beast, with no regard for their original families. Judgment was visited not on families or social groupings, but on individuals, who were made to account for their personal sins. Fengdu 酆都, the underworld found in Yang's revelations, by contrast, is entirely family centered and bureaucratically organized. One might be demoted for a personal indiscretion, but the rest of one's family would be punished as well. Members of the terrestrial aristocracy typically could expect to hold positions in Fengdu similar to those they held in the sunlit world. They could remain there in the underworld for long periods of time, but with luck would eventually move through underground study centers to become Transcendents or, just possibly, Perfected. Promotions and demotions were thus, in this time when family welfare was still seen as intimately tied to the fate of the ancestors, a matter of intense concern to the consumers of Yang's revelations.[8]

The primary recipients of the communications assembled in the *Declarations* were members of a single gentry family. The Perfected directed Yang to pass their words on to Yang's patron, Xu Mi 許謐 (also named

6. Shangqing is also sometimes translated "Highest Purity," though it was not the highest of the heavens imagined in Shangqing writings. In addition, the scriptures are also sometimes referred to by the name of the mountain where Yang Xi received his revelations, Mao Shan 茅山. For an introduction to the Shangqing scriptures, see the Works Cited for works by Yoshikawa, Strickmann, and Robinet.

7. The Perfected are described as pure emanations of the Dao. For the best brief description of these beings, the gods that also inhabit their bodies, their relationship with the stars, their diet of mysterious minerals, and their place in Daoist cosmology, see Strickmann, "On the Alchemy," 177–92.

8. These ideas are explored in Bokenkamp, *Ancestors and Anxiety*.

Mu 穆, 303–73?) and to Xu Mi's sons, Xu Lian 許聯 (328–404) and Xu Hui 許翽 (341–ca. 370). But the Perfected also report on the religious progress (or lack thereof) made by a number of their acquaintances. Since the pursuit of Daoist Perfection was also, to a certain extent, a family affair, we learn much about these people, both from the Perfected and from Tao Hongjing. As a careful scholar, Tao continually checks the pronouncements of the Perfected against his own sources. Detailed political, social, and spiritual accounts of these men and, to a lesser extent, women, are provided in the accounts of Fengdu. Details on members of the extended Xu family are given in Tao's postface, translated in this volume.

Members of the Xu family were clearly enchanted by the exalted language that the Perfected used to write to them through Yang. They respond in the same idiom when they address communications to the deities through Yang. Further, as Tao Hongjing details, Yang's posthumous news of family members and self-cultivation methods circulated fairly widely. The *Declarations* thus influenced Chinese literature to a greater extent than we yet appreciate. Yang did not claim to be a poet, but the gods and goddesses he channeled were, and their untrammeled verse had a wide-ranging impact on later poetry.[9] It contributed in equally surprising ways to Chinese narrative. Yang Xi placed prominent statesmen and public figures in his bureaucratic underworld. He recounted their promotions and demotions in chilling detail, since the fates of these recently deceased ancestors directly affected the health of their living descendants, the immediate audience for Yang's writings. Some of these are lengthy enough that they feature in subsequent works of the *zhiguai* 志怪 ("strange tales") genre. In fact, Xu Mi for a while toyed with the idea of composing a supplement to the *Traditions of the Divine Transcendents* 神仙傳, employing "where are they now?"—type accounts from the Perfected.[10] In this way, Yang's accounts focus on some of the most prominent families of Eastern Jin society.

Many of these same people feature in the other major narrative work of the period, the *New Account of Tales of the World* 世說新語, translated by Richard Mather in 1976.[11] The complex interplay between social imaginings expressed in these two works remains largely

9. For excellent studies on some of these issues, see the works cited by Edward H. Schafer, Paul Kroll, and Zhao Yi 趙益.

10. On *zhiguai*, see Campany, *Strange Writing*; for the *Shenxian zhuan*, Campany's translation in *To Live as Long*.

11. Mather, *New Account*.

unexplored. But we can, perhaps, distinguish them roughly as being one public and one private in nature.

The *Tales of the World* is a collection of anecdotes. These are divided into chapters with titles that reflect the supposed personality types of the main characters appearing therein, such as "Virtuous Conduct" or "Cultivated Tolerance."[12] The events recorded are sometimes quite intimate, but they typically involve interactions with those outside the family, in the public realm. We thus might characterize these tales and anecdotes as "outside," public assessments. The sorts of character assessments often provided by the Perfected regarding members of the Xu family and their acquaintances are, by contrast, intensely private. Sometimes the Perfected even specify that their information on someone outside the circle of the family *not* be revealed to that person. It is therefore not an exaggeration to claim that the *Declarations* provide our sole intimate glimpse of family life from this period of Chinese history. Yang Xi's revelations were addressed to the quotidian concerns of the Xu family and buttressed with notes and written communications between the principals. The attentive listener can thus hear the voices of family members, including the female members of the family. This sort of intimate familial record is extremely rare, even in later periods of Chinese history.

CONTENTS AND BACKGROUND OF THE WORK

The *Declarations* contain several different types of material. Most important for Tao Hongjing, the editor whose work we will follow, were the references to the Shangqing scriptures. As we will see from his postface, Tao was intensely interested in the transmission and contents of the Shangqing scriptures and began collecting fragments of Yang Xi's calligraphy for that reason.[13]

Tao Hongjing was not the first to collect the autograph manuscripts of Yang and the Xus. An earlier collection, entitled *Traces of the Perfected* 真迹, was written by Gu Huan 顧歡 (fl. 420–479).[14] That work no longer survives. The extent to which Tao's work relied on this previous collection is unknown. Our only hints come from Tao's correction

12. On the chapter headings of the *Shishuo xinyu*, see Mather, *New Account*, xvi, and "Chinese Letters."
13. SKKY, iii–v.
14. Gu Huan is best known for his anti-Buddhist treatise, the Yixia lun 夷夏論, arguing that, as a foreign faith, Buddhism was appropriate only for foreigners. See Barrett, "Gu Huan."

of the errors he noticed in Gu's account. For one thing, the very title of Gu's work, Tao announces, is inaccurate. The Perfected beings left no traces. Indeed, they had Yang Xi write out what they dictated to him. As this critique shows, Tao Hongjing brought the habit of precise scholarship to his work. Most interesting are those passages in which Tao struggles with information passed on by the Perfected that contradicts what he finds in other sources.

Tao Hongjing divided the materials that he gathered in a very particular way. Michel Strickmann, in his dissertation, provided a useful characterization of the first six sections, the seventh being Tao's postface. (The way Tao Hongjing himself describes these six sections appears in chapter 1.)

1. Minutes of the visionary sessions particularly relevant to Yang and the Xus. (chapters 1–4)

2. More general counsels and admonitions, often highly philosophical in tone, and documents related to the cause and treatment of disease. (chapters 5–8)

3. Technical instructions concerning a variety of technical operations, including propitiation of the stars and absorption of astral essence, respiration, and massage. (chapters 9–10)

4. Revelations concerning the secret subterranean structure and the administrative hierarchy of Mao Shan. (chapters 11–14)

5. Particulars concerning the isle of the dead, Fengdu, in the far north, and its spectral denizens. (chapters 15–16)

6. Personal jottings of Yang and the Xus—and thus, properly speaking, not "declarations" at all. Here are included specimens of their correspondence, extracts they made from secular as well as sacred writings, memoranda with regard to the performance of certain sacred duties, and records of their dreams. (chapters 17–18)[15]

This organization poses challenges for the modern translator. Often, Tao Hongjing's placement of materials is more a matter of genre than of narrative continuity. In fact, Tao frequently complains that he has no sure way of reconstructing the order of the textual fragments he has

15. The text is from Strickmann's English-language typescript draft of the dissertation, p. 9. I have converted Strickmann's original Wade-Giles romanization to pinyin. For the published copy, see Strickmann, *Le Taoïsme*, 11–12.

recovered. Writings related to a single incident may thus appear in several sections of the work.

For example, one of the primary issues related to Yang Xi's early work on the Xu family centered around the death of Xu Mi's wife Tao Kedou 陶科斗. Following her death, several members of the family fell ill. Yang Xi's Perfected revealed to him that she was being held in her tomb by aggrieved shades who had been murdered by Xu Mi's uncle. Horrifyingly, but not unreasonably, she offered to bring living Xus into the underworld courts to answer the accusations. Her argument was apparently that, since in origin she was a Tao and not a Xu, there were others who might more properly answer the charge. Yang's job was to communicate with the otherworldly generals who might help to stop the underworld lawsuit, free Tao Kedou from her tomb, and save the living members of the Xu family from death.

Documents related to this affair appear primarily in section 2, since the lawsuit from beyond the grave in which Tao Kedou finds herself involved is the cause of illness in the family. But details concerning the dead involved in the lawsuit have been placed in section 5, and very informative communications in letter form between Yang Xi and Xu Mi, some containing advice from the Perfected, appear in section 6. Tao Hongjing sometimes provides cross-references between materials relating to a single incident. It seems clear to me that a modern reader will be better served by rearranging the work, with the goal of translating materials related to single incidents together.

This is where my translation differs from previous approaches to the work. Tao's cross-references provide a key to reorganizing the *Declarations* in a way that will be more familiar to Western readers and will aid future research. In one of the volumes of scholarship on the *Declarations* produced by a Kyōto University study group, Aramaki Noritoshi 荒牧典俊 identified clusters of documentation found in various parts of the text that related to incidents in the lives of Yang and the Xus prior to the main incidents related in the text.[16] This suggested to me the idea that I might follow Tao Hongjing's annotations and other clues to rearrange the material in the *Declarations* by incident or theme. I first tested the methodology in reconstructing the fascinating story of Tao Kedou in my book *Ancestors and Anxiety*.[17] Working this way, I learned, brought

16. See Aramaki, "Shinkō yizen."
17. Bokenkamp, *Ancestors and Anxiety*, 130–57.

aspects of the events into clearer focus, especially the concerns of family members whose objections the Perfected had to answer.

With Aramaki's identification of early incidents as a starting point, I have organized the rest of the *Declarations* according to the major events and themes to which Yang Xi's revelations responded. In some cases I have identified clusters of texts relating not to a single incident, but to a theme or topic. For example, one of Yang's goals was to convince the head of the Xu family, Xu Mi (Tao Kedou's husband), to leave his official post and pursue the Dao full time. As incentive, Yang offered Xu Mi the prospect of a young celestial bride who would join with him spiritually and aid his practice in enticing ways. But Xu Mi seems never to have responded to the call. His writings and the practices he did undertake were rather directed to stopping the march of time through improving his eyesight, turning his white hair black again, and curing the troublesome ailments of old age. The full story of Xu Mi becomes clear only when one follows Tao Hongjing's work closely through the various parts of the *Declarations*.

I am not as sanguine as Aramaki that I can recover a chronology of incidents when Tao Hongjing—a much better scholar than I—despaired of doing so. Even more discouraging is the fact that, as I discovered (see the section "Buddhism in the *Declarations*"), we do not even have the book as it left Tao's hands. Nonetheless, I think that the rearrangement that I have hit upon with the help of Tao's footnotes will help future scholars make fuller use of the text. In the introductions to each textual cluster, I will give my reasons for presenting the materials as one.

WOMEN AND GODDESSES

Tao Hongjing was fascinated by the fact that these fragments of text included accounts of Yang's own dealings with Perfected beings 真人. Some of these beings, while interacting with Yang in human ways, had never been human. Among those who had been human was the primary instructor of Yang Xi, Wei Huacun 魏華存. After ascension, she boasted the title Lady of the Southern Marchmount, Director of Destinies among the Higher Perfected 上眞司命南岳夫人. Before death, she was a Libationer for the Way of the Celestial Masters.[18] Her example, related

---

18. This is mentioned in Tao Hongjing's commentary to the *Dengzhen yinjue* (DZ 421, 3.5b–6a). On the evidence that she actually existed, see Zhou Ye, "Nanyue Weifuren."

in the *Declarations*, held out the hope that humans might also aspire to Perfected status.

Wei Huacun's interactions with Yang show precisely how such a pursuit might be successful. Among the methods of physical cultivation she proffered, the one that takes up the most space in the *Declarations* was known obliquely as *oujing* 偶景, which might be translated "mating of the phosphors." The "phosphors" were the glowing, perfected gods inhabiting the bodies of the two partners, one celestial and one human. Tao Hongjing, in his postface, refers to this joining of spiritual forces as "linked lapels and joined phosphors" 併衿接景, metaphorically portraying the practice as a marriage.[19] Given that the goddess and human vowed to remain together and, in describing it, Yang's Perfected employed many of the metaphors signifying human marriage in early medieval China, this is likely justified.[20] Another term we might employ is *hierogamy*, though in this case the union is between a divine woman and a human being.[21] The human partner in this case was not necessarily a prince or king in the mortal world, but was promised high rank in the next.

The description we find in the *Declarations* of this hierogamy is not, to my knowledge, common to other Daoist texts. Nonetheless, the context in which it is presented makes it clear that the hierogamy was meant to replace the widely practiced *heqi* 合氣 "merging of pneumas" ritual of early Celestial Master Daoism. This ritual, performed by living human participants through *coitus reservatus* accompanied by a complex program of massages and movements, was meant to balance the yin and yang qi of practitioners and to prepare them to pass unscathed through the cataclysms to come.[22] Yang Xi's Perfected do not deny the efficacy of this ritual, but they do emphasize repeatedly that *heqi* was easily performed incorrectly. The result of incorrect performance—a likely result since both participants were human seekers—was more dangerous than dancing on an axe blade. They thus explicitly replaced *heqi*, sometimes styled the "yellow and the red," with the deity-directed practice of mating of the phosphors.

19. See chapter 1, p. XX.

20. See Bokenkamp, *"Declarations."*

21. For the terminology I am using, see Pongratz-Leisten, "Sacred Marriage," 44. On how scholars have begun to reconsider the concept of sacred marriage, freeing it from the narrow definition by James George Frazer, who saw the *hieros gamos* as evidence of ancient fertility rituals, see Nissinen and Uro, *Divine Marriages*, 1–6.

22. See Kleeman, *Celestial Masters*, 159–62; on the details of the ritual, see Raz, "Way of the Yellow."

The actual women of the Xu household—who had likely been practicing *heqi* with their human partners—did not fare well in Yang Xi's estimation. The Perfected revealed to the Xu males that nearly every woman in their lives had threatening involvements in the courts of the underworld. I have recounted how Tao Kedou was held in her grave as a result of the misdeeds of a Xu forebear and how she sought to free herself by bringing her own grandchild into the tomb to answer the accusation. But, as we will see as we trace this event in a future volume, nearly every woman in the Xu household—and certainly the principal wives—had her own culpability. This was most often a result of the misdeeds of a recently deceased father or mother in their natal family. Most vulnerable in this regard was Xu Lian's wife, Hua Zirong 華子容. She is "accused by her father" and has her own "documents" in the courts of the Water and Earth Offices, the two lower courts of the Three Offices. Among the women we learn about, only Tao Kedou had any chance of becoming Perfected herself. By the end of the accounts, she has moved on to the study center meant for women within Mount Mao and is passing helpful information on to her husband, Xu Mi.

The poor treatment that the Perfected accord the majority of Xu family women is in perfect contrast to the care they lavish on description of celestial women. And, in fact, the descriptions of powerful and enticing Perfected women found in the *Declarations* would quite soon be exploited by female Daoist practitioners in their quest to make room in society for their own practice.[23]

MEDIUMISM IN THE *DECLARATIONS*

Throughout this introduction as well as in my previous publications on the *Declarations of the Perfected*, I have described Yang Xi as a Daoist "medium." It might be well to be a bit more precise about what I mean by the term, especially in that mediumism has been taken as one of the defining characteristics of shamanism. Scholars of China have argued over the presence of shamanism in early China for at least seventy years.[24] The classic definition of the shaman is that he or she leaves the body to experience other worlds. Often, the shaman is distinguished from the medium, who is possessed by an outside spiritual being who acts and

23. See Cahill, *Divine Traces*, and Bokenkamp, "Sisters of the Blood."
24. For the history of this controversy, centering on the term *wu* 巫, see Boileau, "Wu and Shaman," 350–78.

speaks through her.[25] I. M. Lewis, however, criticizes the distinction, which he traces to Mircea Eliade, between the medium who represents the descent of gods into the human realm and shamans who represent the ascent of humans to the realm of the gods. He argues instead that shamans are masters of the gods and often both embody them and travel with them. Thus, all shamans are mediums.[26] For Lewis, almost any spirit possession or even socially stigmatized behavior might count as mediumism, from Biblical accounts of those receiving the Holy Ghost to "dervish dancing, fire-walking, sword-eating, and transvestitism."[27]

Mediumism, thus construed, could not adequately describe Yang Xi. Even as popularly understood, the term *medium* does not quite apply to Yang Xi. We think of a medium as someone who communicates with the dead, while most of the Perfected who appeared to Yang Xi had never been human. Neither is there any evidence that Yang traveled with the celestials who appeared to him. Yang was a medium only in the sense that he provided a conduit for the words of the Perfected for his audience. But I think we can be even more precise. My goal here will not be to find a definition that will fit all sorts of mediumism, shamanism, and what Lewis calls "ecstatic religion," but rather to describe, as precisely as possible, the nature of Yang Xi's receipt of his revelations.

At first sight, the evidence seems sparse. In most cases, the Perfected are described by Tao Hongjing as having "descended" 降 to "transmit [writings]" 授 to Yang. More specifically, Tao notes that the scriptures and writings Yang Xi brought from his nightly visions were "dictated announcements" 口授之誥. Yang himself employs this terminology. His descriptions of the encounters make it quite clear that he sees and hears the Perfected with perfect clarity and for lengthy periods of time. Yang does not depict the deities as materializing gradually or as in any way immaterial or hazy in appearance. Instead, he describes them—and particularly their garb—in great detail. The Perfected are either portrayed as "descending" or simply as present, as in "on the night of ____, Lord Mao bestowed a text that said. . . ." But the only evidence that he has to show for these visits are his transcriptions of their words. When Tao Hongjing considers certain of the Perfected beings cited by Yang as too

25. For the classic definition, see Eliade, *Shamanism* and Bourguignon, "Hallucination and Trance."

26. Lewis, *Ecstatic Religion*, 50–57.

27. Lewis, "Spirit Possession," 307–8.

exalted to have actually descended to him, Tao opines that their words must have been relayed by other deities who *did* "meet" with Yang.[28]

Tao Hongjing discusses the fact that Xu Mi and Xu Hui could not receive transmissions from the Perfected, echoing the deities' pronouncement that this failure was due to their continued involvement in the affairs of the world. Thus, they were unable either to "receive the Perfected" 接真 or "personally receive the spoken words and commands" 親承音旨 of the deities.[29] Interestingly, Xu Hui's older brother was accused by the Perfected of lacking the perspicacity even to receive the words of the Perfected in dreams, so that they were reduced to appearing to him in the form of his younger brother.[30] This slighting reference makes it clear that Yang Xi himself did not normally receive the words of the Perfected in dream. But in fact, dreams were still important to him. One of the sections of the *Declarations* contains records of dreams written by Yang and the Xus. They are rather different than the meetings with the Perfected of the wakeful Yang and will be translated and discussed in a future volume.[31]

Signs of other sorts of interactions between Yang and the Perfected are few in number. In at least one instance, Yang describes the taste of a jujube given him by one of the Perfected.[32] On several occasions, he depicts himself as moving his body in certain ways, as for instance, in accepting the jujube. We have, however, no means of determining whether he actually moved within his meditation chamber or merely imagined himself moving. From Yang's descriptions, however, we do know that he did not visualize travel with them on the wondrous journeys that the Perfected describe for him.

Fortunately, recent scholarship on the role of cultural expectations in fostering religious visions give us another angle from which to consider Yang's revelations, opening vistas toward which we shall only be able to gesture here. The psychologist Richard Noll was one of the earliest to provide clinical and ethnographic evidence showing that what he styled "mental imagery cultivation" was not only possible but widespread in

28. See the introduction to the "eight pages of lined text" in chapter 4.
29. DZ 1016, 19.3b–4a.
30. Bokenkamp, *Ancestors and Anxiety*, 142–43.
31. A more comparative treatment of this material can be expected from the forthcoming Campany, *Dreaming*.
32. DZ 1016, 1.13a.

different societies.[33] He argued that visionary skills could be cultivated through a two-stage process of (1) gradual increase of focus on mental images and (2) training in the ability to increase the endurance of images.[34] Barbara Newman, applying these insights to the visionary culture of medieval Christianity, adds helpful distinctions between spontaneous waking visions, disciplined visions, aesthetic visions (the interplay of vision and art, to include both visual and stylized textual representation), and supernatural visions.[35]

The psychologist T. M. Luhrmann, through her fieldwork with contemporary evangelical Christian charismatics, brings in examples closer to our own times, as well as citing a number of clinical experiments on vision.[36] As she helpfully reminds us, seeing or hearing a deity "is technically a hallucination because divinity is immaterial. By nature, the divine is not a sensory stimulus."[37] Luhrmann distinguishes three types of hallucination, which can together be defined as the sense that what was seen or heard was not in the mind itself. She terms these: "sensory overrides," which are of short duration, rare and not distressing; "psychosis," of long duration, frequent, and quite distressing; and "Joan of Arc," the kind that will interest us, that tend to be of longer duration, frequent, but quite the opposite of distressing. Most impactful for our purposes is Luhrmann's finding that hallucinations of the Joan of Arc type might be cultivated through cultural expectation and training. She also improves on Noll's preliminary ideas about how this is accomplished, using "techniques that focus attention on the inner senses" and "those that train attention away from thought and sensation."[38]

Within the cultural milieu in which he learned his craft, Yang Xi's visions did not seem unusual, except in the excellence of their presentation, and so we are not told much about how they were cultivated.[39]

33. Noll et al., "Mental Imagery," 443–61.

34. Noll et al., 445.

35. Newman, "What Did It Mean," 3–6. Newman goes on to show the ways in which spiritual visions were valorized or seen as demonic and uncontrollable as visionary techniques spread beyond the cloister. For the somatic nature of medieval Christian visions, see Bynum, "Female Body," 160–219. For some of the literary aesthetics of vision, see Hamburger, "Speculations on Speculation," 383–408, and Cruse, "Matter and Meaning," 45–56.

36. Luhrmann, "Hallucinations," 71–85 and, for her field research, Luhrmann, *When God Talks Back.*

37. Luhrmann, "Hallucinations," 71.

38. Luhrmann, 79.

39. Celestial Master Daoists, the tradition to which Yang Xi belongs, received messages and scriptures from the very beginning of the movement. See Kleeman, *Celestial Masters,* 344–47.

Still, prompted by the studies outlined above, we can learn something of how this was done.

Judging from the texts he produced, Yang's hallucinations were visual, auditory, gustatory, and, to a certain extent, kinesthetic. The term he uses to describe his hallucinations is most often *cun* 存 "to retain sensorily, to actualize."[40] Less frequently, he employs the terms *cunsi* 存思 "to actualize in thought," *cunjian* 存見 "to actualize in vision," or *cunxiang* 存想 "to actualize in the imagining."

We will see in subsequent volumes of this translation that Yang was particularly intent on training the visionary capabilities of Xu Mi and his son, Xu Hui. Reading attentively, we notice some of the same didactic intent in the documents collected in this volume. Take, for instance, the necessity to "train attention away from thought and sensation." We find reference to this initial move even in the brief passages that Yang inserted into his version of the Buddhist *Scripture in Forty-Two Sections*. With regard to practicing Daoism, one must first and foremost "maintain clarity and stillness to actualize the Perfected, guard the mysterious to retain in thought their numinosity 清淨存其眞, 守玄思其靈."[41] "Clarity and stillness," drawn from the *Daode jing*, had by Yang's time become a Daoist term for specific methods of stilling thought and emotions.[42] The image is of dirty river water that, when allowed to sit unmoved in a vessel, clarifies. Throughout the *Declarations*, Yang and the Perfected who speak through him repeatedly emphasize the need to quiet all emotions and close off the irrepressibly galloping thoughts of the heart 心 (our "mind") in order to actualize and meet with the Perfected.

Yang's use of techniques that focus on the development of the inner senses and methods to make them persist are even clearer. Take, for example, his directions from a meditation for controlling the movements

---

40. This translation is suggested by Campany, "Shangqing jing," 30. As Edward Schafer noted some time ago, "the word [*cun*, translated here as visualize] means 'to make sensibly present,' 'to give existence to,' almost 'to materialize.'" ("Transcendent Vitamin," 28). Campany's "actualize" is not only closer to the actual denotation of the Chinese word than "visualize," which I used indiscriminately in previous publications, but also allows for the mobilization of multiple senses, which is clearly an important part of the process. In this work, I will use "visualization" to translate 存見 and "actualization" to translate 存 where it appears that multisensory images are meant.

41. See chapter 4, pp. XX–XX. The "Perfected" "numinous" of this passage may be the spirits resident in one's own body.

42. The term is more commonly written 清靜. Yang Xi apparently used the grapheme 淨 in a unique way. (See DZ 1038, 19.7a2.) The term appears in section 44 of the *Daode jing*. For early Daoist uses of the term, see Bokenkamp, *Early Daoist Scriptures*, 40–48.

of the *cloud-souls*, three *yang* elements of the person that tend to rove outside the body when one sleeps:

> Lie down to sleep facing upwards with a pillow beneath your head, your feet extended, and your arms crossed over your heart. Close your eyes and block your breath for the space of three normal breaths, knocking your teeth three times. Actualize a vermilion pneuma as large as a chicken's egg coming from within your heart and rising to emerge from between your eyes. After it emerges from between your eyes, this vermilion pneuma will become large enough to cover your body and will flow over the body to the top of your head. Transforming, it will become fire which wraps all around your body. Once the body is encircled, cause the fire to penetrate your body as if it were igniting charcoal. Once this is complete, you should feel slightly hot internally. When this happens, again knock your teeth three times and, envisioning them, call the three cloud-souls by name.[43]

Here we notice the combination of directions for physical control—body position, breathing, sometimes hand position—and for the mental creation of images described in terms of mundane sights and feelings—chicken's eggs, fire, heat, et cetera. Adepts are urged to make the images endure as they shift in form and take over the entire sense field. In other instances, deities are to appear from within the body. Yang suggests their age, dress, and appearance in just enough detail that the adept might fill in the rest from mundane experience, thus ensuring that the beings are at once marvelous and familiar.

The standard explanation among contemporary Chinese scholars for such actualization practice, as well as much else in early and medieval Daoism, is that it originated in ancient *wu* 巫 practice. Insofar as *wu* is often translated "shaman" and the ancient *wu* indeed functioned in ways similar to Siberian shamans, this brings us full circle but does not shed much light on Yang's practices. Yang Xi was clearly not reviving an ancient practice. Instead, he learned his craft in the fourth-century society of southern China.

I wish to suggest that this method of actualization was closely analogous to ancestral practice, historically a fairly ubiquitous practice among China's elite. Elsewhere, I have cited a passage from the *Record of Rituals* 禮記, a collection of ancient ritual directives compiled circa 50 BCE, that details how one should prepare for the practice of "feeding" one's ancestors. This passage describes how, during the preparatory purgation ritual, the performant should think 思 of their forebears who will be the

---

43. Translation adapted from Bokenkamp, *Early Daoist Scriptures*, 323.

recipients of the food offerings: "Think of their living place, think of their smiles and speech, think of their will and intentions, think of that which makes them happy, and think of what they liked to do." After three days of this, the performant is to see 見 all of this at the same time. And, on the day of the offering, perhaps not surprisingly, the performant is to see 見 the departed seated on the offering mats. Leaving the chamber, he will hear their sighs at being parted again.[44]

If this passage approximates normal ancestral practice among the elite, the cultivation of mental imagery must have been fairly widespread, at least among those with the resources to undertake the practice. It is only a short step from hearing the sad sighs of the departed to engaging in longer and more meaningful verbal exchanges with them. And, in fact, the actualization of spiritual beings was part of daily life in other ways as well, for fate calculation, the curing of disease, building construction, and the like.[45] These methods may be retraceable to the diviners and mediums who served the ancient Chinese kings, but by Yang Xi's time, spirit actualization was the norm among those of his milieu. Those who were able to bring back from their visions reports that were of the literary excellence and complexity of Yang Xi's were rare, but the practice itself was ubiquitous enough that Tao Hongjing felt no need to provide details.

Whatever its historical roots, Yang's revelations show marked affinities with the methods of image cultivation studied by Noll and Luhrmann. And we find this most clearly expressed in the actualization instructions that Yang passed on to his disciples. Allowing for cultural differences, we detect a version of the techniques Noll and Luhrmann discovered as necessary for the hallucinator—the suppression of external thought and sense impressions and inculcation of mental receptivity—even in the brief passages we have examined.

Taking his literary legacy in its entirety, then, it seems that Yang Xi has told us quite a bit concerning the methods he used to meet with Perfected beings. Not only that, he seems quite intent on teaching those of us who come into possession of his texts how to do so ourselves.[46]

44. *Liji*, ch. 47: SSJZS 1592c; see also Legge, *Li Chi* 2: 210–11. Translation my own.
45. We know this from Warring States and Han-period hemerological manuscripts (books of prognostication by the calendar) that were widely circulated. See Yan, "Daybooks and the Spirit World," 207–47; Bujard "Daybooks," 305–35.
46. Much more research must be done to demonstrate the methods by which actualization of the unseen was cultivated among Daoists. Unfortunately, we do not have the same sort of material evidence as that surrounding spiritualists such as Arthur Conan

BUDDHISM IN THE *DECLARATIONS*

Tao Hongjing's scholarly methodology will become clear as we examine his work on the *Declarations* more closely. There is one aspect of Tao's religiosity that bears preliminary exploration here, however, for it has a direct relation to the fate of his manuscript remains and the editions of the *Declarations* we have today.

The first of Tao's signature exegetical works, *Secret Instructions on the Ascent to Perfection* 登真隱訣, survives today only in truncated form.[47] This is strange. Tao Hongjing's writings were honored by contemporaries and carefully preserved. Two accounts of his life were written while he was yet alive. Even Tao's occasional writings survive, seemingly intact, in the Daoist canon.[48] Further, the *Secret Instructions* was a very important work, giving Tao's organization and understanding of the Shangqing scriptures, the texts that formed the basis for the first of the three sections of the nascent Daoist canon. So, why do we have only three of the twenty-four scrolls that once made up the *Secret Instructions*?

A possible answer to this question comes from the cached manuscripts found at Dunhuang 敦煌. I have recently shown that one of these fragments, corresponding to Dunhuang manuscripts S.4314, S.6193, P.2751, represents a missing part of the *Secret Instructions*.[49] This text contains Tao's annotation to the *Central Scripture of the Nine Perfected*, the received version of which is cited in the earliest Daoist collectanea, the *Wushang biyao*.[50] These two witnesses, when compared with the Dunhuang copy, show that in the seventy or so years following

---

Doyle, his wife, and their spirit guide, Pheneas, the modern Wei Huacun. See Faivre, "Sir Arthur Conan Doyle," and Thurston, "Summer Land." One promising line of research might be to follow up on the concept of "boundedness" of the self, "the degree to which presence external to the mind can be understood to participate within the mind," introduced by Luhrmann ("Hallucinations," 78–79) as a measure of the openness of cultures to accepting visionary experience. This might help explain why there were more Wei Huacuns in medieval China than Pheneases in our own time.

47. See Wang Jiakui, *Dengzhen yinjue*, 6–8 for textual history of the text. The number of *juan* 卷 (literally "scrolls," hereafter "chapters") seems to have remained fairly stable through the Song dynasty, but we have few citations of the missing portions beyond that at issue here.

48. Tao's literary collection is DZ 1050, *Huayang Tao yinju ji* 華陽陶隱居集.

49. Bokenkamp, "Research Note."

50. The canonical version of the Nine Perfected is DZ 1376, *Shangqing taishang dijun jiuzhen zhongjing* 上清太上帝君九真中經. On the composition of the circa 570 CE collectanea, the *Wushang miyao* (無上秘要, DZ 1138), see Lagerwey, *Wu-shang pi-yao*, 3–48.

Tao's completion of his annotations on the text, unknown editors had clearly seen Tao's notes, since they "corrected" several questionable references that Tao found in the scripture. More importantly, they purged the *Nine Perfected* of its references to Buddhism and, seemingly, repressed a part of his *Secret Instructions*.[51] For instance, the Dunhuang text of the *Nine Perfected*, the earliest version annotated by Tao, had the following passage:

> In the case of the Daoist Retreat, we call it "preserving stillness." In the case of the Buddhist Retreat, it is called "*danchen*." For the Daoist [practice of] stillness, one joins the hands on the two knees. For the Buddhist [practice of] *chen* (dhyāna?) one joins the palms before one's mouth.

> 道齋谓之守静，佛齋谓之耽晨。道静接手於兩膝，佛晨合手於口前。[52]

Both the canonical version of the *Scripture of the Nine Perfected* and the *Wushang biyao* replace this passage with four alternate names for the scripture. These names are followed by the phrase "while there are four names, they refer to but one precious writing." 雖有四名，故一寶書耳。[53] This reference to alternative celestial copies of the scripture not only leaves Buddhism out of the picture, it also provides deniability for the redactors. Other versions of the text, it allows, might exist, but this is the orthodox, collated edition. This evidence points to a widespread purgation of Buddhist elements from Daoist scripture by the scholars working at the Abbey of the Pervasive Dao 通道觀 who produced the *Wushang biyao*.[54]

Tao's annotations to the *Nine Perfected* are thoroughly saturated with assertions that Buddhist practice is but a variant of Daoist practice. He writes forthrightly:

> As a path, [the way of the] Buddha is but one practice of the Dao. When one forgets the body to maintain spirits, that is also the height of wondrous action. *Danchen* is what is today called "*dhyāna*." . . . The two Studies are similar. It is just that, in technique, there is internal and external; in doctrine, there are differences and similarities. At base, it is *not* a difference of Chinese/ Foreign or a distinction between refined and coarse. The border kingdoms'

---

51. For other examples of the fifth- to seventh-century purgation of Buddhist terms and concepts from Daoist scripture, see Bokenkamp, "Stages of Transcendence"; Maeda, *Shoki dōkyō*, 373–96.

52. *Ziwen xingshijue*紫文行事決, ZH, 2.357b16–17.

53. See DZ 1138, 30.2b5–9 and compare DZ 1376, 1.3a4–6.

54. See Lagerwey, *Wu-shang pi-yao*. Ironically, the collection was itself expurgated as a result of subsequent Buddho-Daoist debate.

[population] is strong, yet scattered, thus it is appropriate that they use massive scriptures. That of the Center is flexible and close-packed, thus they venerate the profound and subtle.

夫佛之爲道，乃道之一法。忘形守神，亦妙之極也。耽晨，即今所謂思禪者矣。。。兩學相若。此乃術有內外，法有異同。本非華戎之隔，精粗之殊也。而邊國剛疏，故宜用其宏經;中夏柔密，所以遵其淵微耳。[55]

From this, it seems that Tao Hongjing was one of the Chinese intellectuals of the fifth to sixth centuries who held that the teachings of Śakyāmuni (our Buddhism) were at base fully compatible with the teachings of the Dao (our Daoism). The views of Tao Hongjing on this issue, however, were not simple. When Xiao Yan 蕭衍, the Martial Emperor of the Liang Dynasty, (r. 502–549) held a series of discussions in preparation for his 504 ban on Daoism in favor of Buddhism, Tao responded forcefully to his friend Shen Yue's 沈約 (441–513) *Treatise on the Equality of the Sages*均聖論. Shen's treatise, perhaps written on imperial command, argued that Buddhism was entirely compatible with China's traditional teachings. Tao argued the opposite.[56] At the same time, Tao Hongjing took Bodhisattva vows and made a pilgrimage to what was said to be a relic of the Indian Buddhist king Aśoka's stupa-building activities located in what is now Zhejiang Province. During his residence on Mount Mao, he built a white pagoda, a shrine for Buddhist observances, and is said to have performed services to Śakyāmuni and to the Lords of the Dao on alternate days.[57] While all of this information is derived from sources in the Buddhist canon, it is lent credence by a find at the site of Tao's grave.

In 1986, the scholar Chen Shihua 陳世華 visited Mount Mao and made a significant discovery. Among the populace, he found some tiles clearly from Tao Hongjing's grave that had been looted during the Cultural Revolution. One gave the precise year of Tao Hongjing's death, and another identified the tomb as "the Dark Offices of XX Huayang" 華陽XX幽館. Given the location, the date, and Tao's sobriquet "Recluse of Huayang 華陽隱居," these artifacts clearly came from Tao

55. *Xingshi jue*, ZH ed., 2.357b2–9.

56. This dispute is recorded in Dao Xuan's 道宣 (596–667) *Guang hongming ji* 廣弘明集 T. 2103, 52.121–123. See Wang Jiakui, *Tao Hongjing*, 26–28. Wang is, in my opinion, too much focused on determining which ism the figures in these events might have upheld. In fact, the underlying issues deserve more nuanced treatment. Nonetheless, Wang does get to the emotional content of the discussion between these two scholars and provides compelling evidence that Shen Yue's contribution was written to please the emperor.

57. See Strickmann, *Le Taoïsme*, 30.

Hongjing's tomb. Interestingly, the tiles also identified the tomb occupant as both "Disciple of the Buddha Śākyāmuni" 釋迦佛陀弟子 and as a "Minister of the Most High Lord of the Dao" 太上道君之臣.[58] As Chen points out, these precise titles were first discovered when a Daoist studying on the mountain broke into the tomb looking for alchemical elixirs around 1086.[59]

But what sort of Buddhism did Tao favor? I will show that he practiced a form of Buddhism that had been "discovered" by Yang Xi. The evidence for this is necessarily scattered and partial. As the alterations to the *Scripture of the Nine Perfected* in the *Wushang biyao* show, the rewriting must have occurred between Tao's completion of the *Secret Instructions* around 500 and the completion of the collection that first cites the edited material, the *Wushang biyao* 無上秘要, released circa 580.[60] Most likely, this occurred as part of the anti-Buddhist proscriptions and thoroughgoing reformation of Daoist thought and practice instituted under the Northern Zhou emperor Yuwen Yong 宇文邕 (543–78) that resulted in the *Wushang biyao* itself.[61] The rearrangement and perhaps rewriting of passages in the *Declarations* likely occurred at about the same time. The few citations of the *Declarations* found in the surviving sections of the *Wushang biyao* do not allow us to draw conclusions.

Fortunately, the Dunhuang survival of Tao Hongjing's commentary on the *Central Scripture of the Nine Perfected* gives us some notion of what the Buddhist contributions to Yang's thought might have been. It also helps us to make sense of the importance of Buddhist practice among the Daoist Perfected who resided on Fangzhu, floating isles inhabited by Transcendents that legend had placed in the Eastern Seas since at least the third century BCE.[62]

58. Chen Shihua, "Tao Hongjing."

59. See Liu Dabin 劉大彬 (fl. 1317–28), *Mao Shan zhi* 茅山志, DZ 304, 8.6a–b.

60. On the *Wushang biyao* and preliminary discussion of its fragmented state, see Benn, "*Wushang biyao*."

61. Given the evidence Wang Jiakui provides as to bibliographical notices of the *Dengzhen yinjue*—editions of twenty-five chapters are recorded for the Tang down to the Southern Song—it is difficult to argue that this tampering occurred only once or that it solely involved deleting things from the text. (See Wang Jiakui, *Dengzhen yinjue*, 6–8.) Two points can be made here. First, Wang also cites notices of editions of thirty-five or sixty chapters, so one wonders if these bibliographers had even seen the text. Second, the evidence I give here shows early emendation, not deletion of content.

62. The better known mythical eastern islands are Penglai and Fusang. Noting that Fangzhu was named after the bronze mirror that was used to catch the dew of the new moon, Paul Kroll translates the term as "Square Speculum." See Kroll, "In the Halls," 79 and note 33. For a lively account of the early legends of floating isles, see Schafer, *Mirages*, 51–60.

In the midst of talking about the different postures of Buddhist and Daoist meditation, cited above, Tao lists several examples of Shangqing relations to Buddhism found in the *Declarations*:

> The Jade Luminary and *Liuqin* [= Krakucchanda] are both images born of the mysterious essences.[63] The Red Lord of the Southern Marchmount changed his garb to accord with his teachings.[64] In the realms of Fangzhu, those who honor [the Buddha] are half the population.[65] The disciples of the Three Perfected regard the two studies (Daoism and Buddhism) as equivalent.[66]

> 玉皇留秦，玄精同象， 南岳赤君，隨教改服。方諸者之境，奉之者半，三真弟子，兩學相若。

With the exception of Krakucchanda, fourth of the seven Buddhas of the past, who was compared to the deity Jade Luminary earlier by the Daoist Lu Xiujing 陸修靜, the remainder of the examples cited here are from the *Declarations*.[67] They refer to stories featuring Shangqing Perfected who practice a form of Buddhism, presumably that of the Lesser Fangzhu Isles of the east. Thus, we can conclude that Yang Xi knew, and perhaps himself practiced, versions of Buddhist ritual revealed by Perfected on the eastern and western isles of Fangzhu.

63. Krakucchanda is the fourth of the seven Buddhas of the past, more commonly known in later translations as 拘留孫佛. Most importantly, he was the first Buddha of our kalpa cycle, making him a cosmic deity on a par with the Jade Luminary 玉皇大帝. See Nattier, *Once upon a Future Time*, 19–20. For early translations using the transliteration 拘留秦佛, see T. 154, 3.78a 竺法護譯生經卷第一 and T. 559, 14.912b 支謙譯，佛說老女人經.。

64. In his annotation to the *Declarations*, Tao notes that "the central chapter of the *Mysterious Record of the Seven Sages* says that when the Red Lord brought down his teachings, he changed his traces to be a monk. He revealed his names to the world together with his six disciples." 《七聖玄紀中》云：赤君下教變迹作沙門，與六弟子俱皆顯姓名也。(DZ 1016, 14.19a)

65. The restored passage on the eastern and western isles of Lesser Fangzhu is translated on pages 148–150 of this volume. This reference, by the way, seems to confirm that the fragment I have found is also part of the original *Declarations*. Greater Fangzhu's inhabitants are all Daoist; those of *both* of the Lesser Fangzhu isles are Buddhist. For the interpolated passage, see Bokenkamp, "Research Note," 247–53.

66. The *Declarations* lists three Perfected who have Buddhist disciples and their numbers. Eighteen of thirty-four of the disciples of Lord Pei 裴, Perfected of Pure Numinosity 清靈真人, "study the Way of the Buddha 學佛道." For Lord Zhou 周, Perfected of Purple Yang 紫陽真人, the number is four of fifteen disciples, and for the Perfected of Mount Tongbo 桐柏真人, the number is eight of twenty-five. (DZ 1016, 14.7a–b; see also 2.7b). Significantly, one of the placards from Tao Hongjing's tomb discovered by Chen Shihua read "Practitioner of the Three Perfected of Shangqing" 修上清三真. (Chen Shihua, "Tao Hongjing," 55.)

67. For Lu Xiujing's comment, see *Sandong zhunang* 三洞珠囊, 2.3b, citing the now lost *Daoxue zhuan* 道學傳.

This form of Buddhism, as the lost commentarial passage of Tao Hongjing translated in this volume makes explicit, features Buddhists who play music on remarkable Chinese reed organs with thirty keys, rather than blowing conch shells and beating drums like those dusty Buddhists from the deserts of the Western regions. Eastern Buddhists represent the oldest, and presumably original, form of the teaching. Yang portrays them as chanting texts from the mythical Xia dynasty, dated to at least a thousand years before the earliest reported dates for the life of Śakyāmuni. The Fangzhu Buddhists seem to have existed since the beginnings of time on the pristine floating isles that the Chinese had long expected to harbor Transcendent beings. But it only came to light when human followers of Śakyāmuni redundantly introduced a foreign version. This was redundant in that the texts brought overland to China had been especially designed to meet the needs of *Hu* people. The differences between the two Buddhisms reflects the cultural prejudices that lay behind the *huahu* 化胡 ["Conversion of the Western Barbarian"] stories.[68] The music of Western Buddhists is not soothing to Chinese ears attuned to instruments like the reed pipe. More importantly, the Eastern Buddhists regard "life as blissful and death a calamity," while the foreign Buddhists of the West "take life to be an illusion and regard death as a joyful thing."

Further improvements Yang Xi's Perfected introduced into the teachings of Śakyāmuni to make them more compatible with contemporary Chinese sensibilities are clear from the version of the Buddhist *Scripture in Forty-Two Sections* granted Yang. Tao discusses a remarkable copy of this text that he was able to retrieve, written on lined paper in the fashion of Buddhist scriptures such as those found at Dunhuang. Tao's work on this remarkable document, too, was broken up by later editors. What survives is now found scattered in the received copies of the *Declarations*.

I will deal with my reconstruction of this document in my introduction to chapter 4, the "eight pages of lined text," preceding my translation. Suffice it to say here that this evidence, coupled with the Dunhuang fragments of Tao's *Secret Instructions*, allows us at least to glimpse a heretofore unremarked Daoist response to Buddhism and helps us understand the reasons behind Yang Xi's plagiary of the *Scripture in Forty-Two Sections*.

Taking this evidence as a whole, I think we can form the following rather strong hypothesis: Yang Xi, through his Perfected, learned of a

68. See Zürcher, *Buddhist Conquest* and, for an early Daoist version, Bokenkamp, *Early Daoist Scriptures*, 158, 169–70.

more ancient, more pristine, and not coincidentally more "Chinese" Buddhism that had existed since the beginnings of time on an isle floating in the Eastern Seas, one of those miraculous lands that the Chinese had long suspected to harbor the marvelous. The Perfected not only instructed Yang on the contours of this isle, Fangzhu 方諸, they also brought him at least one text from this land, a more authentic version of the *Scripture in Forty-Two Sections*.[69] At some point, a formal copy of this striking new evidence on the origins of Buddhism was made on eight or more sheets of lined paper, probably for presentation to the emperor. Tao Hongjing, for his part, practiced this more authentic form of Buddhism along with the other methods he learned from the Shangqing scriptural fragments.

Unfortunately, this "Dao-Buddhism" did not meet the approval of later Daoists. The guilty "Buddhist-seeming" material was removed from Shangqing scriptures, from Tao's *Dengzhen yinjue,* and from the *Declarations*. The first wave of purgation occurred during the Northern Zhou (557–81) and continued in later periods. If we are attentive to its altered state, the *Declarations* thus stands testimony to the role of religious competition in the development of one strand of Daoism and to the multiple ways that religion contributed to Chinese history and culture.

PRIOR TRANSLATIONS

To date, there has been only one attempt to translate the entire *Declarations*. This is the Japanese translation that is the product of a reading group held over a number of years at Kyōto University (SKKY). I was privileged to attend only one session of their reading group, but their translation has become a primary resource in my own work. The contributors have been my constant interlocutors, both through their individual work and in the blended voice of their translation. It would be tiresome (and likely double the bulk of the present work) were I to acknowledge each and every instance where I benefited from their work.

---

69. Scattered hints throughout the received *Declarations* that survived the redactors support the suspicion that the elisions have fundamentally altered our picture of Shangqing Daoism. For example, the Buddhists of Fangzhu seem to have spoken a language very similar to that of "foreigners"—most likely Buddhists in this context: "In foreign countries, they call the sun *yaoyaoluo*. The Perfected of Fangzhu call the sun *Yuanluoyao*. 外國呼日爲濯耀羅. 方諸眞人呼日爲圓羅曜." (DZ 1018, 9.25a3–4). We shall see more on the impact the languages of Buddhism, *fanwen* 梵文, had on Yang Xi's revelations in subsequent volumes.

There are, to my knowledge, two attempts to translate integral chapters of the *Declarations*. My classmate at Berkeley, Elizabeth Hyland, translated chapter 1 for her PhD dissertation.[70] Someday someone will do a computer-based source-critical study of published translations and will discover the extent to which our later translation idiom is based on this pioneering work. The only earlier work in English was that of Michel Strickmann, whose fine turn of phrase Hyland also exploited. The same procedure would not be kind to the second work, a recent translation of the first four chapters of the *Declarations* by Thomas E. Smith.[71] Where this work strikes out in new directions from previous, published work, it leads the reader astray. It is also flawed in not paying close enough attention to the annotations of Tao Hongjing.

There are numerous scholars who have studied the *Declarations*, translating and explicating passages in the process. Those in this category upon whom I have relied most extensively are Hu Shi, Michel Strickmann, Isabelle Robinet, Wang Jiakui, Paul Kroll, and Terry Kleeman. I shall only be able to acknowledge a portion of my indebtedness to this previous work. Where my translation differs, I will note the fact only when my interpretation differs widely.

CONVENTIONS OF THE TRANSLATION

This translation follows the following conventions:

1. The Chinese text following each translation is the received edition as it appears in the *Zhengtong daozang* 正統道藏 of the Ming Dynasty, which I have taken as my base text. Tao Hongjing's annotations and textual notes are set off by brackets. In some cases, my translation is based on variants found in other editions of the text. These are explained in the footnotes. In all cases, the punctuation is my own, though I have also consulted the Academia Sinica website, the *Zhonghua daozang*, and the work of Yoshikawa Tadao and Mugitani Kunio (see the following section).

2. Since Tao Hongjing's guidance is of such importance in understanding the *Declarations*, I have sometimes moved his substantive footnotes above the passages to which they refer. My translation of Tao's notes will be given in ten-point type and slightly

70. Hyland, "Oracles."
71. Smith, *Declarations.*

indented. I have also provided my own introduction to those passages that I think require further explanation. These will be in sans serif type and ended with the abbreviation "Trans."

3. As in any Chinese social setting, the persons appearing in the *Declarations* are known by a bewildering number of names and titles. Xu Mi, for instance, is also known as Xu Mu 穆, Sixuan 思玄, and as the Senior Officer 長史. Xu Hui is known as Daoxiang 道翔, Yufu 玉斧, Fu 斧, and as the Accounts Clerk 計掾. Some of these names are social, and some are used only within the family. There are times when Tao Hongjing himself is unable to pronounce with certainty to whom intimate family names apply. These names do, of course, make a difference. They indicate the relative status of the speaker to the person addressed, as well as attitude, seriousness, and the like. Nonetheless, they pose a problem of understanding. I have adopted two strategies. When I think that the name used is important in the context, I leave it in the text and place the name with which the reader will be more familiar in parentheses. In other cases, I have silently substituted the more familiar name, marking in a footnote when this name is the guess of Tao Hongjing.

4. Footnotes to the translation are of two types. The majority are meant for the general reader and will refer to publications listed in the bibliography by the name of the author and a short form of the title of the work. Footnotes to the Chinese text provide technical information on the location of a passage, parallel texts, and, when necessary, the rationale behind my acceptance of one variant over another. When I do not accept a variant, I simply list it in the footnotes. Since I have attempted to restore a few passages that are no longer part of the two received editions of the *Declarations*, the notes are necessary. I do signal my insertions in the translator notes, however.

5. Generally, I have followed the text-critical principle that the most difficult reading (*lector difficultor*) is likely the earliest. In this respect, my readings sometimes differ from those of the Japanese translation group, whose work is marked SKKY.

6. While their work is incredibly valuable, the Japanese translators often explicate Yang Xi's terminology through reference to later works that use his vocabulary. Since Yang Xi's writings had a marked and demonstrable impact on later writers, even when he

did not fully explain his terminology (as Tao Hongjing often admits), this is a dangerous methodology. I have, insofar as possible, refrained from citing later explications that are not glosses to the actual words of the *Declarations*. If I do cite later explanations of words that Yang Xi seems to have coined, I am careful to mark the fact.

ABBREVIATIONS

DZ   Scriptures in the Daoist canon 正統道藏, are cited according to their number in Kristofer M. Schipper's *Concordance du Tao Tsang* (Paris, 1975), preceded by the abbreviation DZ.[72] This abbreviation is followed by page and line number information in the form chapter.page (a = recto, b = verso), line number. All citations are from the *Zhengtong daozang* 正統道藏.

S   Dunhuang manuscripts collected by Aurel Stein

P   Dunhuang Manuscripts collected by Paul Pelliot

            The Dunhuang manuscripts cited in this work are collected in Ōfuchi Ninji, *Tonkō dōkyō zurokuhen.*

SKKY   *Shinkō kenkyū: yakuchū hen* 真誥研究: 譯注篇, ed. Yoshikawa Tadao 吉川忠夫 and Mugitani Kuniō 麥谷邦夫 (Kyoto: Kyōto daigaku jinbun kagaku kenkyūjō, 2000).

SKQS   *Siku quanshu* 四庫全書 ed. Ji Yun 紀昀 (1724–1805) et al. (Taibei: Wenyuan ge 文淵閣, 1986). Books in this series are cited by chapter and string-bound page number, *recto* (a) or *verso* (b).

SSJZS   *Shisan Jing Zhushu* 十三經注疏, 2 vols. (Beijing: Zhonghua, 1979).

T   Works in the Buddhist canon are cited by their number in the *Taishō shinshū daizōkyō* 大正新修大藏經, ed. Takakusa Junjirō 高楠順次郎, 100 vols. (Tokyo: Daizō shuppan kai, 1922–33). This number is followed by the volume, page and line number in the following form: volume:page#(+register a, b, or c.).line#.

YWLJ   *Yiwen leiju* 藝文類聚, compiled by Ouyang Xun 歐陽詢 (557–641) (Shanghai: Guji, 1965).

---

72. Brief descriptions of these texts, locatable by DZ number, are found in Schipper and Verellen, *Taoist Canon.*

Yu Edition   A small number of variants are found in the edition of
Yu Anqi 俞安期 (fl. 1596) as reported in **SKKY**.

ZH   Works not available in the *Zhengtong Daozang* are cited
as they appear in *Zhonghua Daozang* 中華道藏, ed.
Zhang Jiyu 張繼禹 (Beijing: Huaxia chuban she, 2010)
in the form: volume:page#(+register a, b, or c.).line#.

CHAPTER ONE

Tao Hongjing's Postface
(DZ 1016, Chapters 19–20)

The chapter that follows was added by Tao Hongjing as a postface to his work. While it is not structured in quite the same fashion as a modern preface, it provides information that is vital to our attempt to understand the *Declarations*. Tao provides a precise description of each section as he has divided the work, but the contents are not quite so orderly and tend to spill over the boundaries implied by Tao's subtitles. This is, after all, a collection of disparate fragments. Further, the text of the *Declarations*, as we have it today, is not the same as when it left Tao's hand. But Tao's postface does provide a rough overview to the work's contents and serves very well as an introduction. We gain vital information as to how Tao organized the manuscript materials that came into his possession.

Tao has divided his postface into discrete parts. First, there is a general introduction. This is followed by an account of the diffusion of the manuscript corpus. Finally, Tao gives a genealogy providing biographies of Yang Xi and the Xu family. He also provides what appears to be self-commentary throughout. There are, however, traces of at least one later editor. This unknown person divided the *Declarations of the Perfected* into its present twenty-chapter form. This new division of the text is highly unlikely to be by Tao Hongjing himself, as he shows himself inordinately proud of his division of the *Declarations* into seven chapters, the same number of divisions seen in two other works he admires, the *Lotus sūtra* and the *Zhuangzi*.

Given our own interests, we might further divide the three major sections into parts dealing with Tao's organization of the work, calligraphy, etc. I have thus interspersed commentaries as translator notes to guide our reading.

Tao's introduction is quite complete, providing for instance the only surviving biographies of the principals, Yang and the Xus, but it fails in one respect. It provides no introduction to Tao Hongjing himself. Fortunately, we have a complete biography in the Daoist canon. This is the *Intimate Traditions of Recluse Tao of Huayang* 華陽陶隱居內傳, completed by Jia Song 賈嵩 (ca. 830).[1] Jia's work is based on quite detailed earlier accounts written during Tao Hongjing's lifetime, one by Tao's nephew Tao Yi 陶翊 (n.d.) and another by Pan Yuanwen 潘淵文, one of Tao's disciples.[2] The following brief account, like other modern biographies of Tao, is based on those works.[3]

Tao Hongjing was born on 18 June 456. We can be so precise since he gives the date himself to demonstrate how to calculate one's destiny-day, important for Daoist ritual.[4] He descended from a distinguished family that moved south of the Yangzi River at the end of the second century CE when the fate of the Han dynasty became clear. Generations of his forebears served the southern kingdoms. Both his father and his grandfather were famed as calligraphers and had an interest in herbal lore, two pursuits in which Tao Hongjing would also excel.

Tao Hongjing himself served both the Liu-Song dynasty and the subsequent Qi dynasty in official posts. He served the Qi as secretary to several crown princes, but left his position as Left Palace guard on the death of his mother in 484.[5] During the three years of mourning, Tao

---

1. DZ 300. Jia Song is known as a *fu* poet and was a contemporary of Zhao Gu 趙嘏. See Ou-yang Xiu et al., *Xin Tangshu*, 66:1616.

2. Pan Yuanwen's account no longer survives as a separate work. Tao Yi's account is collected in the *Yunji qiqian* 雲笈七籤 (DZ 1032, 107.1b–11b). See Strickmann, "On the Alchemy," 142–43. The detailed attention given Tao Hongjing in these writings is perhaps best exemplified in the fact that his nephew notes that Tao had "ten small black spots on the inner side of his right buttock and the greater part of them formed in the shape of the seven stars [of the Big Dipper constellation] 右股內有數十細黑子, 多作七星形 (DZ 1032, 107.11a3–4). The fact that the "seven stars" formed a Dipper shape is made explicit in the account of Jia Song (DZ 300, 1.4a5). On the importance of physical signs in Shangqing Daoism, see Bokenkamp, *Early Daoist Scriptures*, 297–98.

3. See Mugitani, "Tō Kōkei"; Wang Ming 王明, *Daojia*, 80–98; and Wang Jiakui, *Tao Hongjing*.

4. Strickmann, "On the Alchemy," 138n40.

5. See Espesset, "Tao Hongjing" for more information on Tao's official and Daoist careers.

was instructed in Daoism by Sun Youyue 孫遊嶽 (399–489), a disciple of Lu Xiujing 陸修靜 (406–477) and head of the Abbey to Revivify the Age 興世館 in the capital.[6] Lu had completed a first listing of the scriptures and writings that would come to be known as the Daoist canon and Sun seems to have instructed Tao Hongjing in its contents. He also passed autograph manuscripts from Yang and the Xus on to Tao, though Tao mentions only a single title in his account of the diffusion of the Shangqing manuscript corpus. And that mention concerns the *Five Talismans of Lingbao*, a text that, Tao claims, Lu had kept secret in order to circulate his own version. Tao's remarks in this case indicate that the textual integrity of the manuscripts he began to collect at this time was even more important to him than his relations with his Master, who had studied under Lu Xiujing.

In 492, Tao retired from his official career and took residence at the structure he built on Mount Mao, where Yang Xi had worked.[7] It was here at the Abbey of Flourishing Yang 華陽館 that Tao Hongjing completed his three exegetical works. These include two important Daoist works, his annotated copy of the Shangqing scriptures, the *Secret Instructions on the Ascent to Perfection* 登真隱訣, and the present work.[8] These two exegetical works were likely completed by 499, though it is also probable that Tao continued to add material after this time. In addition, Tao is also known for his writings on pharmaceuticals and his annotation of the *Bencao gangmu*.[9]

As this indicates, Tao Hongjing was a scholar of the first order. His scholarly methods will become clear as we work through his struggles with the manuscript material he had collected. We will, for instance, have ample opportunity to see how he reacted to certain of the pronouncements of the gods he believed in when these contradicted what he knew from other reliable human sources. In this, as in many other respects, the *Declarations of the Perfected* proves a fascinating window into a world long gone, as well as into the thought processes of an intelligent individual who tried to make sense of that world.

6. Sun Youyue was one of the most successful of Lu Xiujing's disciples and the Master of Tao Hongjing. (See Mugitani, "Sun Youyue" and Bumbacher, *Fragments*, 263–64.) On Lu Xiujing, see Bokenkamp, "Lu Xiujing."

7. Mount Mao is in Jiangsu Province, about seventy kilometers east of the capital Nanjing.

8. Only three chapters of the *Secret Instructions* survive in the present Daoist canon (DZ 421).

9. The preface to this work was discovered at Dunhuang and is translated in Needham, *Science and Civilisation*, 6.1:243–48.

One striking aspect of this complex person—Tao Hongjing's attitudes toward the foreign religion of Buddhism--will be discussed below in relation to Yang Xi's citations from what would become the Buddhist *Sūtra in Forty-two Sections*. Suffice it to mention here that Tao several times refused to serve under Xiao Yan 蕭衍 (r. 502–549), the Martial Thearch of the Liang dynasty. In 504, Xiao Yan took Buddhist vows and issued an empire-wide proscription of Daoism that required Daoist priests to return to lay life.[10] Nonetheless, the emperor continued to patronize Tao Hongjing and even expected Tao to complete an elixir for him. Tao wisely made excuses and declined. The emperor's support of Tao even resulted in an imperial command that resulted in the construction of another Daoist establishment, the Abbey of Vermilion Yang 朱陽館, on Mount Mao. At the same time, Tao Hongjing, whose grandfather and mother had both been pious practitioners of Buddhism, is recorded as having taken Boddhisattva vows and practiced Buddhist ritual on Mount Mao as well as Daoist. Michel Strickmann has suggested that these signs of faith might have been strategic, meant to protect Tao's community of Daoists.[11] Wang Jiakui 王家葵 presents evidence that Tao venerated the Buddha throughout his life, but holds that he was forced to do so by pressure from the emperor.[12] While determining the true motives of historical actors is always dangerous, we will see that the answer to this question is likely yes and no. There is evidence that Tao did venerate one version of the teachings of the Buddha, while denigrating other versions.

The matter does not come up in Tao's postface to the *Declarations of the Perfected*. What is very clear from Tao Hongjing's account of his work is his devotion to the teachings of the Perfected. For example, he believes the predictions of the Perfected for the three principals in the revelations: Yang Xi, Xu Mi, and Xu Hui. He thus believes that they have ascended at the time of his writing and refers to them as "Lord" jun 君.[13] Further, the death dates he provides for them are those predicted by the deities.

10. For one sign of the effectiveness of this order, see Strickmann, "Taoist Confirmation."

11. Strickmann, "Taoist Confirmation," 471–72, particularly footnote 19.

12. Wang Jiakui, *Tao Hongjing*, 31–32.

13. Since I prefer using gender-nonspecific titles whenever possible, I have a hard time trying to translate this term. In traditional Chinese society, 君 referred primarily to men, but in the *Declarations*, it refers to both male and female Perfected. I will use the translation "lord" in all cases.

TRANSLATION: INTRODUCING
THE *DECLARATIONS OF THE PERFECTED*
Section One, Transmitting Subjects and Images 運題象[14]

In these chapters [the Perfected] both establish a discourse to express
their intentions and issue rhymed chants to fully make known their
meanings. They discuss how the fate calculations emanating from
the dark world move the spirits to pair with humans and to find
suitable matches for themselves. This section is divided into four
chapters.[15]

眞誥運題象第一。(此卷竝立辭表意, 發詠暢旨。論冥數感對, 自相儔會。
分爲四卷)

*Section Two, Verifying Destinies and Transmission
Recipients* 甄命授

In these chapters [the Perfected] both expound and lead those who
are engaged in the practice as students [of the Dao] and admonish
and scold those who transgress or are negligent. Moreover, they
inform those who have good allotments and outstanding moral
attainments, clearly issuing news of blame and blessing.[16] This
section is divided into four chapters.

眞誥甄命授第二。(此卷竝詮導行學,〈誡〉[誡] 屬愆怠。 兼曉諭分挺,
炳發禍福。 分爲四卷)

Section Three, Aiding Health and Prospects 協昌期

These chapters all express principles relating to cultivation practice
and the regulation of [drug and *qi*] ingestion. They are concerned
with the appropriate use of the multiple methods, and [the Perfected]
reveal their methods in response to actual situations.

眞誥協昌期第三。(此卷竝修行條領, 服御節度。 以會用爲宜, 隨事
顯法)

14. These three-word titles are extremely difficult to translate. As Tao relates, he was
thinking of the three-word titles of the *Zhuangzi* when he crafted them. Generally speaking, they all look to be verb-compound object constructions. I have thus taken them in
that way.

15. The division of the *Declarations* into twenty scrolls was accomplished by a later
editor who changed this postface to accord with this new arrangement. The final sentence
of each of these "section" introductions is thus likely not from the brush of Tao Hongjing.

16. "Blame and blessing" 禍福 most often refers to posthumous reward and punishment for deeds committed while alive. The palaces of Fengdu, land of the dead, described
in the *Declarations*, specifically contain offices where blame and blessing are meted out.
See DZ 1016, 15.3a.

Section Four, Investigating Pivotal Spiritual Locales 稽神樞

These chapters reveal the structure and inner connections of
mountains and rivers and expatiate on cavern residences. They
plumb the ranks and careers of the Perfected and the Transcendents
and what each administers, as well as vacancies. This section is
divided into four chapters.

眞誥稽神樞第四。(此卷竝區貫山水，宣敍洞宅。測眞仙位業，領理所
關。分爲四卷)

Section Five, Revealing the Hidden and Subtle 闡幽微

These chapters are on the Palaces and bureaus of the spirits, their
offices and clans. It demonstrates that the body and consciousness do
not perish and that good and evil deeds cannot be escaped.[17] This
section is divided into two chapters.

闡幽微第五。(此卷竝鬼神宮府，官司氏族。明形識不滅，善惡無遺。
分爲二卷)

Section Six, Grasping the Aid of the Perfected 握眞輔

These chapters contain personal notes written by the three Lords
[Yang Xi, Xu Mi, and Xu Hui] when they were alive as well as the
letters circulated among them.[18] These are not declarations of the
Perfected. This section is divided into two chapters.

握眞輔第六。(此卷是三君在世自所記錄，及書疏往來。非眞誥之例。
分爲二卷)

Section Seven, Aiding the Collation of Perfected Gleanings 翼眞檢

In these chapters I reveal the evidences of the Perfected lineages,
verifying the sources of their mysteries. All of it is narrated [by me],
the Recluse. These are not declarations from the Perfected. I have
divided these remarks into two chapters.

眞誥翼眞檢第七。(此卷是標明眞緒，證質玄原。悉隱居所述。非眞誥
之例。分爲二卷)

The previous pages record the contents of the *Declarations of the Perfected.*

17. That is to say, there are postmortem consequences for deeds committed during life.
18. Tao refers to the three as "Lords" 君 because he believes that they have ascended
as Perfected.

Anonymous note: Sixteen chapters were announced by the Perfected. Four chapters are records made in this world.[19]

右眞誥一蘊。(其十六卷是眞人所誥。四卷是在世記述)

Seeking into scriptures on the Way, we find that the higher chapters of the Upper Clarity [scriptures] serve to reveal fully the enterprises of the Higher Perfected.[20] The Buddhist scripture *Lotus Flower of the Wondrous Dharma* brings together logically the complete understandings of the single vehicle, and the Transcendent writings of the *Inner Chapters of Zhuangzi* thoroughly explore the meanings of the realms of those who abandon themselves to the mysteries. These three paths are sufficient to encompass the ten thousand images and embody all that is manifest and hidden.[21] And each of these is divided into seven chapters, probably to match *xuanji* [= the seven stars of the Dipper] and the seven regulators, in order to regulate the eight directions.[22] The *Secret*

19. This note depends on the current division of the *Declarations* into twenty chapters. It is clear, however, that Tao divided the text into seven chapters. In that case, the division would be five and two.

20. The Japanese translation team takes the phrase to mean "As for the upper chapters of Shangqing, they make complete the enterprises of the extremely lofty Perfected." (SKKY, 660–70). But Tao seems to be using a term that occurs first in Han Feizi's discussion of the *Daode jing* 58. Han Feizi describes the sage capable of rule as someone who completes the Dao so thoroughly that "he is able to cause others not to see the ultimate extent of his activities 能令人不見其事極.." (See *Hanfeizi*, SKQS ed. 6.8a.) Tao Hongjing uses the term in this sense in a letter comparing Buddhism and Daoism: "Transcendence is the ultimate in attainment achieved through [physical] molding and refinement; the [psychic] connection to underlying principles brought about by moving [the gods] and transformation" 仙是鑄鍊之事極, 感變之理通也. (See DZ 1050, 1.19a.) Here 極 and 通 are verbs meaning about the same thing, just as *ji* is a verb in the *Declarations* passage above. I thus take 事極 as a phrase meaning something like the "extreme/ultimate/highest in undertakings."

21. It is interesting that Tao writes of the "ten thousand images" 萬象. The more usual term is "ten thousand things" 萬物, but Yang Xi's Perfected informants pronounced the phenomenal world illusory (see chapter 4, p. 168), and Tao seems to have agreed.

22. While Kumārajīva's (334-413) translation of the *Lotus* sūtra, completed in 406, contains twenty-six sections, he seems to have completed a seven-chapter version of the text in 399. (See Sengyou's 僧祐 (445–518) references to the text, T. 2145, 55.10c19.) In so doing, he was probably following an earlier tradition. Fajing's 法經 (fl. 600) *Zhongjing mulu* 眾經目錄 (T2146, 55.177a6-7), also lists Dharmarakṣa's (233?-310?) version as having seven sections. Tao more likely is referring to this edition. The *Inner Chapters of Zhuangzi* also contains seven chapters. Xuanji 璇璣 is a name for the four stars forming the bowl of the Northern Dipper, but here stands for the Big Dipper as a whole. As rotating cosmic timekeeper, the seven stars of the Dipper point to all eight directions of horizontal space. (See Schafer, *Pacing the Void*, 49–52.) The term *seven regulators* first appears in the Shundian chapter of the *Shangshu* in a passage describing how the sage king constructed a kind of armillary sphere to regulate the cosmos according to these seven celestial bodies.

Instructions on the Ascent to Perfection, which I, the Recluse, compiled, is also divided into seven chapters.[23] Now, in relating these *Declarations* of the Perfected, it has also formed seven sections. Numerologically, five and seven are the completion of the inner principles of all matter.[24]

仰尋道經。上清上品，事極高眞之業。佛經妙法蓮華。理會一乘之致。仙書莊子內篇。義窮玄任之境。此三道足以包括萬象，體具幽明。而並各七卷者。當是璇璣七政，以齊八方故也。隱居所製登眞隱訣亦爲七貫。今述此眞誥復成七目。五七之數，物　理備矣。

The instructions of the Perfected are not titled in the same way as those of worldly [teachers]. I reverently modeled myself on the weft texts and prognostications, adopting their way of classifying by theme, and using three-word subject headings.[25] As for why the *Zhuangzi* is also like this,[26] presumably it was because of the "whispered words" of [Zhuangzi's teacher] Zhangsang Gongzi 長桑公子.[27] When common scholars

---

According to Kong Yingda 孔穎達 (574–678), the term refers to the sun, moon, and five naked-eye planets. Both groups of celestial bodies are seven in number.

23. Correcting 二十 to "seven" 七 on the basis of the *Yu* edition. This error by the copyist, who changed the number of scrolls to accord with the current division of the text into twenty scrolls but neglected to alter the surrounding text with its discussion of "sevens," allows us to be fairly certain about the original organization of the text. Tao Hongjing refers to himself by his style name, the Recluse 隱居. Hereafter, I will replace this style name with the first person pronoun.

24. While there are numerous permutations, in general five stands for space and seven for time. Five is, first of all, the four cardinal directions plus the center, aligned with the five phases or agents (*wu xing* 五行). According to Chinese correlative cosmology, the primal qi that vivifies the world moves through five states, which correspond to the five elements (wood, fire, metal, water, and earth), the seasons, directions, colors, tastes, internal organs—indeed all aspects of existence—linking them in a constant process of change. The number seven, as Tao states, refers primarily to the seven stars of the Dipper or to the sun, moon, and five naked-eye planets. The seven-day week eventually came to China through Buddhist texts but was not widely known in Tao's time.

25. The weft texts are apocryphal scriptures appended to the Confucian classics (the "warp" texts or *jing* 經) that deal with stellar omens and celestial intervention in human affairs. Tao follows the practice of referring to these books as "weft and signs" 緯候, the "weft writings and the Central Signs of the *Book of History*" 緯書尙書中候. (See Fan Ye, *Hou Hanshu*, 82A.2703.)

26. The *Inner Chapter* titles are, in the translation of A. C. Graham (Chuang-tzu), "Going rambling without a destination 逍遙遊," "The sorting which evens things out 齊物論," "What matters in the nurture of life 養生主," "Worldly business among men 人間世," "The signs of fullness of power 德充符," "The teacher who is an ultimate ancestor 大宗師," and "Responding to emperors and kings 應帝王."

27. As the Japanese translation team notes (SKKY, 670n10), the story of Zhangsang Gongzi's tutelage and naming of Zhuangzi was itself received from the Perfected. (DZ 1016, 14.14b8–10.)

notice these [three word titles], they don't understand the reason for them.

夫眞人之旨不同世目。謹仰範緯侯。取其義類。以三言爲題。所以莊
篇亦如此者，蓋 長桑公子之微言故也。俗儒觀之，未解所以。

The *Declarations of the Perfected* are the dictated announcements of the Perfected. It is similar to the way that Buddhist scriptures all say "The Buddha said: . . ." But Gu Xuanping 顧玄平 called these writings the *Traces of the Perfected*.[28] This would seem to refer to the written traces from the hands of the Perfected, but it could also refer to the "traces" of their activities. If he meant their handwriting, the Perfected never wrote in clerical [human] script; and if he meant traces of their activities, the activities described herein are not those of the Perfected. Moreover, those who wrote these records could not yet be called "Perfected" at the time of writing. Thus, the title [*Traces of the Perfected*] has no logical support and should not be applied to these revelations.

眞誥者眞人口授之誥也。猶如佛經皆言佛説。而顧玄平謂爲眞迹。當
言眞人之手書迹也。亦可言眞人之所行事迹也。若以手書爲言。眞人
不得爲隸字。若以事迹爲目。則此迹不在眞人爾。且書此之時、未得
稱眞。既於義無旨。故不宜爲號。

. . .

Having explored his reasons for dividing the work into seven sections and given his assessment of its value, Tao Hongjing next explores the dating of the revelations. This proves to be a somewhat complex process. Tao bases his estimates on internal evidence. In the course of this discussion Tao reveals much of interest concerning how the revelations were transmitted into the human world. –Trans.

. . .

The *Traditions of the Lady of the Southern Marchmount* records a Blue Register Text that says:[29]

28. Xuanping is the byname of Gu Huan 顧歡 (ca. 424–ca. 487), the first compiler of Yang-Xu manuscripts. For Gu's other contributions, see Barrett, "Gu Huan."

29. Tao here cites a passage from the *Traditions of Lady Wei* 魏夫人傳 that does not appear in the surviving fragments of that text. The *Traditions* is a revealed work, composed by Fan Miao 范邈 on the orders of Wang Bao 王褒, Perfected of Clear Vacuity. (See Chang, *Xipu*, 173–75.) The *Blue Register Text* 青籙文 is a type of mysterious prognostication in verse form. Chang provides further information confirming that scriptural transmission did actually begin in 364.

The year is in *jiazi*,
The first day of the month, *xinhai*,
On the morning of the First Farmer's feast,
Or between *jia* and *yin*, with its rain waters,[30]
Arising and bringing peace, the year begins
And the scriptures are for the first time transmitted.
Those who wish to achieve the Dao
Should practice these jade texts.

I respectfully calculate that, according to the Jin [dynasty] calendar, this is the first day of the first month, *xinhai*, of the second year of the Ascending Tranquility [reign period] of the Mourned Thearch [Sima Pi 司馬丕, r. 361–65], when the year was in *jiazi* (19 February 364) to the fourth day *jiayin*, rain water (22 February).[31] "Arising" means "ascending" and "bringing peace" means "tranquility" so [this line of the blue register text] obliquely refers to the name [of the Ascending Tranquility reign period]. From this, we can conclude that in the first month of the second year of Ascending Tranquility, the Southern Perfected [Wei Huacun] had already descended to bestow on Lord Yang [Xi] all of the [Shangqing] scriptures. Now, checking the earliest recorded year and month of Perfected transmissions [in the *Declarations*], I identify a question from the Certifier of Register [Mao Gu] on the twentieth day of the sixth month of the *yichou* year (24 July 365) as the earliest. From this date on there were increasingly numerous cases of the Perfected descending.

南嶽夫人傳載青籙文云。歲在甲子。朔日辛亥。先農饗旦。甲寅羽水。起安啓年。經乃始傳。得道之子。當修玉文。謹推按晉曆。哀帝興寧二年太歲甲子。正月一日辛亥朔。（曆忌可祀先農）四日甲寅羽水。（正月中炁。羽即雨也）起者興也。安者寧也。故迂隱其稱耳。如此則興寧二年正月，南眞已降授楊君諸經也。今檢眞授中有年月最先者、唯三年乙丑歲 六月二十日定錄所問。從此月日相次稍有降事。

---

30. *Jia* 甲 and *yin* 寅 are points on the diviner's compass to which the handle of the Dipper points at the beginning of the lunar year. See Major et al., *Huainanzi*, 124. Tao notes below that 羽水 should be 雨水. This brings the reference into accord with the *Huainanzi*.

31. Tao notes that, because of calendric taboos 曆忌, this was a time when sacrifices to the First Farmer 先農, patron of agriculture, could take place. For the sacrifices to the First Farmer during the southern dynasties, see Fang Xuanling et al., *Jinshu* 14.354. He also notes that *jiayin* 甲寅 is the first month and that the graph *yu* 羽 "feather" should be read *yu* 雨 "rain." I have translated as his notes suggest.

ADDITIONAL NOTES[32]

又按 The Lady Central Watchlord announced:[33] "Cause them to plant bamboo under the northern eaves in order to bring offspring."[34] She also said "Fuhe 福和 will have two sons. They will be overflowing in virtue and command the generation." Looking into this, I find that it was spoken when the Jianwen Emperor [Sima Yu 司馬昱 (320–72)] was Prince of Xiang and, having no sons, made a request [of the Perfected]. After this, Lady Li 李夫人 gave birth to the Emperor Filial Martialiity and to the Prince of Guiji.[35]

Anonymous note: Fuhe is likely the private name of Lady Li. At this time she was still a commoner. When the Filial and Martial Emperor died he was thirty-five *sui*, thus he was born in the *renxu* year [362], two years before the *jiazi* year.[36] This means that the various Perfected had already been descending to Yang [Xi] for quite some time [before the events recorded here].

又按中候夫人告云：令種竹〈比〉〔北〕宇。以致繼嗣。　又云。福和者當有二子。盛德命世。尋此是簡文爲相王時。以無兒所請。於是李夫人生孝武及會稽王。（福和應是李夫人私名也。于時猶在卑賤）孝武崩時年三十五。則是壬戌年生。又在甲子前二歲。如此衆眞降楊已久矣。

又按 In the sixth month of the *yichou* year [365], the Certifier of Registers [Mao Gu] instructed the Senior Officer in a text saying "I received your letters of the third month and eighth month of the previous year."[37]

---

32. This heading is added. Tao heads each of the paragraphs below with the phrase "another note" 又按. I leave the phrase untranslated for each paragraph.

33. Lady Central Watchlord, surnamed Wang 王, is one of the Perfected who seldom appears in the pages of the *Declarations*. Tao Hongjing can note only that she is one of two Perfected who report on matters relating to the cavern heavens below Mount Mao (DZ 1016, 10a1–2).

34. Reading 北 for 比 in accord with the Yu Anqi edition. If the latter character were accepted, we would translate "near to the eaves."

35. The Filial and Martial Emperor 孝武帝 was Sima Yao 司馬曜 (r. 372–96) and the Prince of Guiji was his brother, Sima Daozi 司馬道子 (d. 403).

36. Chinese traditionally calculated age (*sui*) from the time of conception, not the date of birth. The year designations belong to the sixty-year cycle. *Renxu* is the fifty-ninth year in the cycle and *jiazi* the first.

37. Part of the deity Middle Lord Mao's reply is given at DZ 1016, 1.4b8–10. But the sentence referenced here occurs in the chapters on the inner topography of Mount Mao (DZ 1016, 11.15b–16a), where it says "I have received your two letters of the first of the third month and the eighth of the eighth month of that former year." On the basis of this passage, I have changed the present text to read "third month and eighth month" rather than "eighth day of the third month" 三月八日.

This ["previous year"] should refer to the *guihai* [363] or the *jiazi* [364] years.

又定錄以乙丑年六月。喻書與長史云：曾得往年三月八日書。此亦應是癸亥甲子年中 也。

又按 [The goddess] Elühua 愕綠華 descended in the third year of the Soaring Peace reign period, the *jiwei* year [359]. This is five years before the *jiazi* year [364]. So, though she did not descend to Lord Yang, Lord Yang knew of it and made a record of it.

又按愕綠華以升平三年降。即是己未歲。在甲子前五年。此降雖非楊君。楊君已知見 而記之也。

又按 In the *yichou* year [365], [the goddess] Consort An said to Lord Yang: "In but another twenty-two years, you, my shining lord, will be riding the clouds and piloting dragons, facing north in audience in Upper Clarity." Thus [Yang Xi] must have departed this life in the *bingxu* year, the eleventh year of the Grand Prime reign period [386]. If so, there must have been quite a few events and words [exchanged] during the twenty-plus-year period [between these two dates], but what survives now is only [the records of] a few years [after 365]. Looking into the beginnings and endings [of the revelations], I realize that not one in a hundred survives.

又按乙丑歲，安妃謂楊君曰：復二十二年、明君將乘雲駕龍北朝上清。則應以太元十一年丙戌去世。如此二十許載。辭事不少。今之所存。略有數年。尋檢首尾，百不遺一。

又按 Before the Perfected began to descend to Yang, they had already ordered Hua Qiao華僑 to transmit their messages and intentions to Senior Officer Xu Mi.[38] But since Hua wildly leaked [the secrets of the Perfected], he was dismissed. As a result Yang [Xi] was ordered to transmit [the revelations]. None of the literary remains of Hua's period of service has circulated in the world.

又按眾眞未降楊之前，已令華僑通傳音意於長史。華既漏妄被黜。故復使楊令授。而華時文迹都不出世。

又按 Although the mystical attainments of the two Xus were excellent and exalted, their physical forms were still hindered by the affairs of the

---

38. What we know of Hua Qiao's Daoism all derives from the pages of the *Declarations*. The information is summarized by Tao later in this chapter, pp. 96–97.

world and so they were not yet able to receive the Perfected. Though most of them contain instructions for the Xus, all of the revelations received were commands received by Yang [Xi] that he would pass on as notes to the Xus. Only the several slips related to Consort An are records for Yang himself.[39] Today, when people see the headings "On such and such a month and day, Lord so-and-so revealed this to Senior Officer Xu [Mi] or Accounts Clerk [Xu Hui], they say that the two Xus received the words and commands personally. This is definitely not the case. And when there are passages written by the two Xus, in all cases they have only written out for themselves a copy of what Yang showed to them.

又按二許雖玄挺高秀而質撓世迹。故未得接眞。今所授之事，多是爲許立辭。悉楊授旨，疏以示許爾。唯安妃數條是楊自所記錄。今人見題目云某日某月某君咬許長史及掾某，皆謂是二許親承音旨。殊不然也。今有二許書者，並是別寫楊所示者耳。

又按 The Accounts Clerk [Xu Hui] himself wrote: "In the third year of the Grand Harmony reign [368], I practiced the Way of X."[40] The two verifications were received in the second year (367–68).[41] After the third year, there are no further statements [from either Xu].[42] Since the Senior Officer's standard calligraphy was not good, those texts he transcribed were few. But, when one affair has now two or three separate copies, all were recopied by the two Xus and contain not a single discrepancy. But

39. These appear in chapters 1 and 2 and contain first-person accounts of Yang Xi's interactions with his proposed celestial mate. For preliminary translations, see Bokenkamp, "*Declarations.*" "Slips" translates 條. These are the slips of paper that Yang Xi used to record the revelations of the Perfected. Tao often mentions the number of "slips" devoted to passages he transcribes. I have tried to use this information to estimate the size of the slips and how many characters they might contain, but have so far failed.

40. This record of Xu Mi's practice appears at DZ 1016, 18.12a5.

41. The Japanese translation team takes 二錄 to refer to the separate transcriptions of the two Xus (SKKY, 676n13). When the term appears later in the postface, Strickmann, who admits his interpretation is "uncertain," takes 錄 as a form of the word "register" 籙 and sets out to find which two registers might be meant (Strickmann, "Maoshan Revelations," 50n107). Instead, the term 受錄 "receive registration" seems to mean something like the Buddhist term 受記 "receive a prediction of future Buddhahood." In the year indicated, Xu Hui and Xu Mi both received promises of appointment in the heavens. (See DZ 1016, 4.13a6–13b.9 for the full predictions, dated 22 January 368.) Following these predictions, the Perfected congratulate them and further intimate just when they will join the Perfected ranks. These predictions are the basis for the death dates Tao Hongjing assigns to them.

42. The term *shu* 疏 has a technical meaning in Daoism. It refers to the statement detailing transgressions, illnesses, and requests that the member wishes the priest to communicate to the deities. (See Kleeman, *Celestial Masters,* 355–56.) Tao seems here to include any written communication that Xu Mi and Xu Hui might have sent to Yang Xi.

those records written in Yang's hand that are entirely lacking copies are clear indication that they were preserved by the Accounts Clerk and so tended to survive until today.[43] We have no way at all of calculating what Yang himself may have preserved. In the six or seven years following Yang's death, we also have no traces of the Senior Officer's writings.

又按掾自記云：泰和三年行某道。二録是二年受。自三年後，無復有疏。長史正書既不工所繕寫蓋少。今一事乃有兩三本，皆是二許重寫。悉無異同。然楊諸書記都無重本，明知唯在掾間者。于今頗存。而楊間自有，杳然莫測。自楊去後六七年中，長史間迹亦悉不顯。

又按 As for the dates that I have been able to determine, records of the *yichou* year [365] are the most numerous. There are only a few slips for the *bingyan* [366] and *dingmao* [367] years. Moreover, it was only in the first chapter that I could approximate temporal order. The dating of [the writings in] the remaining chapters are in disorder, since there was no way to order them accurately.

又按今所詮綜年月，唯乙丑歲事最多。其丙寅丁卯，各數條而已。且第一卷猶可領略次第。其餘卷日月前後參差，不盡得序。

又按 Where they noted the month and day of transmission, in most cases they did not write the year. I have tried to follow the order [of the events recorded on the slips] to put them in temporal order. But when the account of an affair breaks off, I could not necessarily achieve this. Also, if they did not record the year or month or did not note who revealed a passage, there was no way to know and I recorded the text as I had found it, lacking a date.

又按凡所注日月某受，多不書年。今正率其先後，以爲次第。事有斷絶，亦不必皆得。又本無年月，及不注某受者，竝不可知，依先闕之。

• • •

While the following passages are all preceded by the words "another note" 又按 as above, at this point Tao shifts to a discussion of the composition of the revelations and other written fragments that he has put in order. He discusses who received which communications and how, modes

43. To understand why Tao thinks this, see the section on the diffusion of the manuscript corpus later in this chapter. There are a number of passages in Yang's hand for which Tao has access to copies done in the hand of Xu Mi or Xu Hui, but only Xu Mi, as the "good student," would have preserved a number of the more arcane revelations.

of address, calligraphy, and his process for identifying and categorizing the revelations. Tao Hongjing's father for a period made his living as a calligrapher—and one who apparently commanded a high price for his expertise.[44] We thus have every reason to place faith in Tao Hongjing's judgments in these matters. The care he takes to lay out his scholarly process tends to bolster our confidence. At the same time, this is probably the most depressing part of the *Declarations* for the modern scholar to read, for in it Tao details the meticulous editing he performed on the revealed fragments, using color coding and editing marks that are entirely lost to us now. –Trans.

. . .

又按 When a Perfected transmission speaks of the good or evil of others, it was always the case that the Senior Officer made an inquiry through Yang [Xi] and this was their response. In all cases this was kept secret among the Xus. At that time, those others were not necessarily aware of everything [said of them].

又按眞授説餘人好惡者，皆是長史因楊請問。故各有所答，竝密在許間。于時其人未必 悉知。

又按 The matter of the linked lapels and joined phosphors of Yang [Xi] and [Consort] An is explained with brilliant clarity.[45] The poems inspired by the questions of "dependence" or "independence" [of the *Zhuangzi*], with their verbal metaphor and indirect criticism, all refer to the question of whether or not the [Lady Right Blossom] of the Cloudy Grove should descend to marry the Transcendent Watchlord [Xu Mi].[46] The matter is very clear. The Perfected of the Southern [Marchmount, Wei Huacun] is the Master of instruction. [Lady Wang of the Left Palace of] Purple Tenuity is the Craftsperson who brings down the teachings. These

---

44. See Tao Yi's 陶翊 biography of his uncle, the *Huayang yinju xiansheng benqi lu* 華陽隱居先生本起錄 in DZ 1032, 107.3a4–7.

45. This refers to the matter of Yang Xi's spiritual marriage with the Consort An, detailed in the first book of the *Zhen'gao*. (See Bokenkamp, "*Declarations*.") The marriage was to be a union of the glowing bodily gods or "phosphors" 景 of the two participants and will not involve actual physical contact. Nonetheless, Yang uses the language of marriage to describe the union. "Linking lapels" 併衿 seems to be Yang's coinage (DZ 1016, 3.8a7), yet it maps onto the custom of man and wife tying their garments together during the marriage ceremony. Sometimes Yang uses the more common 結裳 or 交裙 ("tying the robes") to describe this custom (DZ 1016, 1.16a10 and 17a9).

46. These poems are translated in chapter 4, in the section "Poems on Dependence and Independence."

two Ladies do not enter into partnerships [with humans]. [Lady Wang] the Central Watchlord and [Lady Li] of the Brilliant Numinosity seem to have a different place as well. But since their involvement is but for a short time, we are never truly clear [about their status]. The remaining male Perfected are brought along in their train or are seen fulfilling official positions. It is the two Lords [Mao] who are the main leaders in this area. When people today read these *Declarations* and events without knowing these facts, they will never comprehend their intent. Thus, I have briefly highlighted the general significance [of these things]. You should keep it all secret.

又按併衿接景陽安，亦灼然顯説。凡所興有待無待諸詩，及辭喻諷旨，皆是雲林應 降嬪儇侯。事義竝亦表著。而南眞自是訓授之師。紫微則下教之匠。竝不關儔結之例。但 中候昭靈亦似別有所在。既事未一時，故不正的的耳。其餘男眞，或陪從所引，或職司所 任。至如二君，最爲領據之主。今人讀此辭事，若不悟斯理者，永不領其旨。故略標大意。宜共密之。

又按 The two Xus needed to practice the scriptures, but since they had not yet been able to meet with the Perfected there was no way for them to see the scriptures. Thus the Perfected of the Southern [Marchmount] first bestowed the scriptures on Yang and had him transmit the scriptures to them. Once he had done this, he became their teacher. This is why the Senior Officer wrote to [Lady] Right Blossom: "The Perfected of the Southern [Marchmount] is compassionate. Last spring she caused the Scripture Master to bestow on me the *Cavern Chamber* [and other scriptures]."[47] Yet the two Xus were sometimes blocked by [their knowledge of] the canons of worldly behavior and were unable to accord him proper ritual respect. Yang, for his part, was also unwilling to place himself [in a higher position]. But, since [this attitude] would violate Perfected Codes, so [the Perfected] announced to him "You have transmitted scriptures and are thus [their] Master. Why are you bashful?"[48] The Perfected of the Southern [Marchmount] is their master in the

---

47. See DZ 1016, 2.22a5–6.

48. DZ 1016, 10.6a6. It is possible that the ordination of the Xus had not been conducted by Yang Xi himself, but by one of the previous Daoist masters they had served. They thus treated him with less respect than the Perfected felt he actually deserved. On the procedures of ordination, see Kleeman, *Celestial Masters*, 282–303.

heavens.[49] Thus, both Yang and the Xus call her their "Master in the Heavens."

又按二許應修經業，既未得接眞，無由見經。故南眞先以授楊，然後使傳。傳則成師。所以長史與右英書云：南眞哀矜。去春使經師見授洞房云云。而二許以世典爲隔，未崇禮敬。楊亦不敢自處。既違眞科。故告云：受經則師。乃恥之耶。然則南眞是玄中之師。故楊及長史皆謂爲玄師。

又按 Those who are ill should announce it to their Master in the Heavens, otherwise they will not be cured.[50] But the Senior Officer, when writing to Lady Right Blossom and the rest of the Perfected, always writes the words "in trembling and fear." This is the same etiquette as that one uses toward a Master, but these [Perfected] are in truth not his Masters.

又云。疾者當啓告於玄師。不爾不差。而長史與右英及衆眞書亦稱惶恐言者。此同於師儀爾。實非師也。

又按 Yang's grass and running style calligraphy have many graphs that are hurriedly done and misshapen or smudged. These were all the result of the times when he received the commands [of the Perfected]. Since he was rushed, he valued abbreviating things. Later he would recall what they had said and make additions or deletions. Those written in precise, formal script are passages that he rewrote in order to show the Senior Officer.

又按楊書中有草行多儳黵者。皆是受旨時書。既忽遽貴略。後更追憶前語，隨復增損之也。有謹正好書者，是更復重起以示長史耳。

又按 The calligraphy of the three Lords, if [the text] has not been traced but is rather hurriedly copied out by hand [by some unknown party], is impossible to distinguish. In each case, I will note this at the end of the passage. If I have not yet been able to see an autograph copy and do not know the copyist, I will note that it was "written out by X."[51]

49. The term literally means "Master from within the Mystery" 玄中之師, and I have previously translated it that way. The "mystery" is a kenning for Heaven, so I have accepted Terry Kleeman's more understandable "master in the heavens." *Xuan* 玄 "mystery, dark obscurity" is a common kenning for "heaven." See Lü Pengzhi, *Tangqian*, 122n1.

50. For this proviso by the Perfected of the Southern Marchmount, see DZ 1016, 7.12a–b.

51. This is the case when Tao Hongjing thinks that the copy is clearly made from a legitimate manuscript originating with Yang or one of the Xus but cannot find a version clearly in their calligraphy. The Chinese word is 某 "a certain person." Tao clearly means to indicate that the copyist was perhaps someone other than Yang or one of the two Xus. I will thus substitute X for this word.

There are, moreover, four or five strange hands [that I can differentiate]. I cannot distinguish whether they were copied at the same time [as the revelations] or by later people. Since there are no names, I cannot attest to their veracity. In all cases, I make a record of this, writing below the slip that it was written in hands A, B, C, or D to distinguish them.

又按三君手書，今既不摹，則混寫無由分別。故各注條下。若有未見眞手，不知是何君書者，注云某書。又有四五異手書。未辨爲同時使寫，爲後人更寫。既無姓名，不證眞僞。今竝撰録，注其條下，以甲乙丙丁各甄別之。

又按 The autograph manuscripts have places where a strange hand has added or deleted things or made insertions and changes. Many of these were done by Counselor Xu [Huangmin 黃民] or his son [Rongdi 榮弟]. In some cases they wanted to make a reputation for themselves; in others to meet the exigencies of their times. In many cases their edits are frivolous and deluded. But Gu [Huan] could not make distinctions and adopted their corrections. Now I fear that if a slip is not a traced copy we will be gradually confused and misled. So, in all cases I have made a note after such graphs. If the correction was made by the hand of one of the true [participants] to their own text, I did not point it out.

又按書字中有異手增損僞改，多是許丞及丞子所爲。或招引名稱；或取會當時，竝多浮妄。而顧皆不能辨，從而取之。今既非摹書，恐漸致亂〈或〉[惑]。竝隨字注銘。若是眞手自治，不復顯別。

The following three entries are of extreme interest in that Tao Hongjing here further describes the calligraphy of Yang Xi and the two Xus, lost to us now. Given the necessity to take dictation from their gods, Yang and other Daoists of his time pioneered new forms of calligraphy. These forms were explained by Daoists as arising naturally from their physical cultivation and expressing outwardly the inner refinement of their qi. While conveying the mysterious qualities of their writing that appeared to him "as if each graph, each stroke, is a shadow hanging in the air as glimpsed from afar," Tao is extremely precise in describing these qi states. These are evocative in ways that make them difficult to translate. For example, the term I have translated "fulsome, energetic" 鬱勃 means something like "shadowy and full, with qi suddenly darting forth." Tao Hongjing, in his commentary to the *Guiguzi*, uses the term to describe the way anger fills one with qi that bursts forth in ways that cannot be controlled.[52]

52. See DZ 1025, 2.21a–b.

"Sharp-pointed forms" translates 鋒勢, literally "lance-shaped qi forces." Unfortunately, the actual forms of some of the graphs that Tao copied have not survived reprintings of the text. -Trans.

又按 As to the calligraphy of the three lords, that of Lord Yang [Xi] is the most excellent. It is neither modern not ancient and can be large or minute. Generally speaking, though Yang's calligraphy takes as a model that of Chi [Yin 郗愔 (313–84)], his control of the brush is equal to that of the two Wangs [Wang Xizhi 王羲之 (303–61) and his son Wang Xianzhi 王獻之 (344–88)].[53] As for why [Yang Xi] was not famous, he was of low status, and his reputation was overshadowed by that of the two Wangs. The calligraphy of the Accounts Clerk [Xu Hui] imitated that of Yang, and the form of his characters is forceful and sharp. His [calligraphy] was particularly well-suited to copying scriptures and writing talismans, as was Yang's. Fulsome, energetic, and with sharp-pointed forms, his writing was not something that could be brought about by human artifice alone. The Senior Officer's seal and grass script was capable, but his standard form was archaic and clumsy. His talismans also are not skillfully executed. As a result of this, he did not copy scriptures. I once met with Zhang Dao'en 張道恩, a man skilled at distinguishing calligraphy, who sighed at the spiritual perspicacity demonstrated by the three Lords' calligraphy.[54] Regarding today the calligraphy of the three Lords, it is as if each graph, each stroke, is a shadow hanging in the air as glimpsed from afar. I believe it is not something that simple knowledge or artistry could reach. Instead, heaven has lent this vision as a mirror, a means to express their enlightenment.

又按三君手迹，楊君書最工。不今不古，能大能細。大較雖祖效郗法。筆力規矩，並於二王。而名不顯者，當以地微。兼爲二王所抑故也。掾書乃是學楊。而字體勁利。偏善寫經畫符，與楊相似。鬱勃鋒勢，迨非人功所逮。長史章草乃能。而正書古拙。符又不巧。故不寫經也。隱居昔見張道恩善別法書。歎其神識。今覩三君跡。一字一畫，便望影懸了。自思非智藝所及。特天假此監，令有以顯悟爾。

又按 The three Lords wrote graphs in ways that varied from the styles of the present. Some examples that all three wrote the same way are

53. On the influence of the calligraphy of the "two Wangs" and their relation to Daoism, see Ledderose, "Some Taoist Elements." Ledderose's translation of the current passage appears on page 258.

54. I have no further information on Zhang Dao'en; nor, it seems, do any of the later works on calligraphy that cite this passage.

龜龍虛華顯服寫辭闕闕.[55] Some examples of graphs that they wrote differently are 飛我靈眞師惡.[56] In addition, the graph "demon" 魔 is written 摩; the word 淨 "pure" is written 盛; and "to fill" 盛 is written 請. This is a general account of character variants, since I cannot record them all. I fear, though, that later persons will copy these texts and of necessity change the graphs into those of the present generations. Thus I highlight a few examples of these changes here that those who receive this might cautiously take note. All of these variants I have completely recorded in the *Secret Instructions on the Ascent to Perfection*.[57]

又按三君手書作字有異今世者。有龜龍虛華顯服寫辭闕闕之例。三君同爾。其楊飛。(掾飛) 楊我。(掾我) 楊靈。(長史靈。掾靈) 楊眞。(長史眞) 楊師。(掾師) 楊惡。(長史惡) 此其自相爲異者。又鬼魔字皆作摩。淨潔皆作盛潔。盛貯皆作請貯。凡大略如此。亦不可備記。恐後人以世手傳寫，必隨世改動。故標示其例，令相承謹按爾。此諸同異，悉已 具載在登眞隱訣中。

又按 Among the characters written by the three Lords are those that do not match any standard character shape. Logically I should just change these for ease of comprehension, but it is important to keep whole the original calligraphic traces of these texts. If I am unable to follow the actual form of the texts and was to secretly make emendations, it would frivolously introduce chaos and would no longer preserve the integrity [of the manuscripts]. So, in all cases, I have written a square outline in red around suspect characters and made a note below them.[58]

又按三君書字有不得體者，於理乃應治易。要宜全其本跡。不可從實，闇改則澆流散亂，不復固眞。今竝各朱郭疑字而注其下。

---

55. This sentence is actually written in the form "Yang 飛, Accounts Clerk 飛." But since our editions of the text correct these graphs to standard forms, there is no sense replicating the actual form of the sentence. I suspect also that the graphs all three wrote differed from standard forms in approximately the same ways, but that distinction is also lost to us.

56. In both of these cases, Tao Hongjing most likely reproduced the variant forms. From the layout of the text, it is certain that he did so at least in the case of those characters that were written differently by the three. In the received editions, however, these graphs have all unfortunately been corrected to the modern forms.

57. Only three of the twenty-four chapters of Tao's *Dengzhen yinjue* 登眞隱訣 (DZ 421) survive. None of these contain lists of character variants. The surviving sections also have the three graphs Tao mentions in their standard forms, showing that this text was corrected as well.

58. In some cases, the boxes survive in received editions, but the red color, alas, does not.

又按 The paper that the three Lords write upon is mostly white letter paper from Jingzhou 荊州. As time has passed, the beginnings and ends of these papers have become torn off or even rotted away. Later people have tried to glue them, but they have not entirely been able to repair the rifts, so in all cases they copied out the characters and discarded those bits that were destroyed. Thus, what is missing is no longer in the true hand [of Yang and the Xus]. Even when others have supplied headings, the event recorded might follow on something said previously. In all such cases, I pieced together the record following the actual chain of events and did not further make divisions.[59]

又按三君多書荊州白牋。歲月積久，或首尾零落；或魚爛缺失。前人糊擒，不能悉相連補。竝先抄取書字。因毀除碎敗，所缺之處，非復眞手。雖他人充題，事由先言，今竝從實綴録，不復分析。

又按 There are also complete scrolls that were written out by the three Lords. For the "Transmitted by the Dao" section, we have only the copy of the two Xus.[60] For the "Record of the Palaces of Fengdu" we have a copy by Yang Xi and the Accounts Clerk Xu Hui. Both of them (*Daoshou* and *Fengdu gongji*) are complete from beginning to end. The affairs recounted also follow in order. As for the rest, we have sections of five sheets, three sheets, one sheet, or even just a fragment. These were each pasted together by later people and were not in the order of the original copies. In all cases I have pulled them apart and made my own selections, linking them together on the basis of date and the events recounted. These fragments are no longer in the order of the previous scrolls.[61]

又按三君書有全卷者，唯道授二許寫。酆都宮記是楊及掾書。竝有首尾完具。事亦相類。其餘或五紙、三紙、一紙、一片，悉後人糊連相隨。非本家次比。今竝挑抚［拔］，取其年月事類相貫。不復依如先卷。

---

59. The phrase that I have translated as "following the actual [chain of events]" 從實, is translated by the Japanese team as "そのまま"; that is, the actual state of the manuscripts (SKKY, 680). But the verb Tao uses, 綴録, does not just mean "to record," but to "compile and record" or even "stitch together." Thus it appears that the "actual" that Tao follows is the events involving the principals participating in the revelations, as he explains subsequently. The importance of this procedure to him is underlined by the fact that he criticizes Gu Huan for not attending to the "conversations" found in the text.

60. The "Transmitted by the Dao" section appears at DZ 1016, 5.1a–17a.

61. By "previous scrolls" 先卷, Tao likely means to refer to the *Traces of the Perfected* of Gu Huan as well as the pasted-up copies of "later persons."

又按 The words and commands of the various Perfected persons all have significance and intent. While sometimes they would be presented in verse, and sometimes in prose injunctions, all of them respond to one another.[62] But in Gu [Huan's] *Traces of the Perfected*, these are separated out by type and each given a section or a scroll. This is done to such an extent that the words [of the Perfected] are extremely disordered and one can no longer understand them. Now I have in all cases followed the basic order of events. Moreover, I have taken into account the relations between the recorded dates, and continuities in the types of paper and ink, in order to interpret them and put these records in order.

又按衆眞辭〈百〉［旨］，皆有義趣。或詩或戒，互相酬配。而顧所撰眞迹，枝分類別，各爲部卷。致語用乖越，不復可領。今竝還依本事，并日月紙墨相承貫者，以爲詮次。

又按 The ten-plus slips that discuss the various methods of the "Treasuring the Spirits in Activity and Repose," the "Bright Hall," the "Incantation for Dreams," and the "Prolegomena on [Eating] *Atractylodes*" are primarily copied from scriptures and have no proper beginning or end.[63] Similar methods like "beams of the sun," "images of the sun," the "Mysterious White," and "ingesting the mists" were not incorporated into the text by Gu [Huan] and thus became separated [from the rest of the *Declarations*].[64] Now, in all cases I have analyzed them and recorded them, in each case like [the previous] examples.

62. As he indicates here, one of Tao's self-appointed tasks was to reconstruct the "conversation" that took place between Yang's Perfected beings and the two Xus.

63. *Treasuring the Spirits in Activity and Repose* 起居寶神 is likely to be equated with the *Scripture for Treasuring the Spirits* 寶神經, spoken by the Perfected of Pure Numinosity (DZ 1016, 9.6a ff.). The longer title of the "Bright Hall" 明堂 is the *Upper Scripture of the Most High on the Mysterious Perfected of the Bright Hall*, (DZ 1016, 9.18a ff.). The "Dream Incantation" 夢祝 is to be found at DZ 1016, 9.16a ff., and the *Prolegomena on the Ingestion of Atractylodes* 服]朮敍 at DZ 1016, 6.1a ff. The 述敍 of the received text is clearly a copyist error for 朮敍.

64. The method for "ingesting the rays of the sun and moon" 服日月芒法 is detailed at DZ 1016, 9.21b8ff.; the method for "ingesting the images of the sun and moon" 服日月象法 at 9.19b1ff.; the "way of retaining the black and the white" 守玄白之道 at 10.2a9 ff.; and the "method for ingesting mists" 服霧之法 at 10.1b6ff. In addition, the word that I am translating as "slips" is *tiao* 條. I suspect that this is a standard-size piece of paper used for writing memorials and the like. The term is used throughout the *Declarations* in phrases like "the previous four slips are in the hand of Yang Xi." If these had a standard size, I have been unable to determine what it is.

又按起居寶神、及明堂、夢祝、朮敘諸法十有餘條，乃多是抄經，而無正首尾。猶如日芒、日象、玄白、服霧之屬，而顧獨不撰用，致令遺逸。今竝詮録，各從其例。

又按 When I have not yet seen an autograph copy, I have no way of calculating whether or not a piece has been passed down from the principals. When what is recorded is internally contradictory and not of the same quality as the rest of the *Declarations* and I am still not willing to precipitously delete it, then in each case I note the reasons for my doubts and list them below the item.

又按有未見眞本，復不測有無流傳。所記舛駁不類者，未敢便頓省除。皆且注所疑之意。各於條下。

又按 With regard to the family background of the Transcendents in the Cavern Palaces or within the various mountains recorded herein, I also wished to carefully annotate information contained in outside sources, to reveal their ancestral roots. But I fear that revealing too much into the sunlit world would violate the regulations of the dark realms. Only when there are discrepancies, doubts, or unclear points do I briefly highlight what is said in different sources. As to the ghost officials of the Palaces of Feng[du], it is permissible and appropriate to speak clearly of these things.[65]

又按所載洞宮及諸山仙人氏族，竝欲以外書詳注，出其根宗。恐大致顯泄，仰忤冥軌。唯有異同疑昧者，略標言之。其酆宮鬼官，乃可隨宜顯説。

又按 The beginning of this book is the descent of the Perfected. After that it continues to relate various incidents. And the first of the Perfected to descend was [Consort An] of the Nine Blossoms. Yet Gu [Huan] placed her in his very last chapter. Moreover, the achievements of the Prior-born Xu Mai's life never approached the stage of Perfection, so there is no justification for predicting that he achieved this level. And yet Gu recorded the *Traditions* [of Xu Mai] written by the General of the Right, Wang [Xizhi 王羲之, 303–61] and his son [Wang Xianzhi 王獻之, 344–86].[66] All

---

65. I suspect that Tao Hongjing maintains this distinction because he regarded some of those in Fengdu as the ordinary dead who have taken up positions in the afterlife. Fengdu also contained the lowest classification of earth-bound Transcendents, the dixia zhu 地下主 "rulers below the earth." For one analysis of these rankings See Zhao Yi, *Liuchao*, 111–17.

66. On this biography, see the Fang Xuanling et al., *Jinshu* entry on Xu Mai (80.2107), which is appended to the biographies of the Langye Wangs. There it is recorded

of this turns truth into falsehood. Now I have placed the "Consort An" incident first and excised the *Traditions of Xu [Mai]*, consigning it to the category of profane books on divine Transcendents. I have only included in the final scrolls the letter that the Prior-born [Xu Mai] wrote after achieving Transcendence and sent to his younger brother.[67]

又按此書所起，以眞降爲先。然後衆事繼述。眞降之顯在乎九華。而顧撰最致末卷。又先生事迹，未近眞階。尚不宜預在此部。而顧遂載王右軍父子書傳，竝於事爲非。今以 安記第一。省除許傳，別充外書神仙之例。唯先生成仙之後與弟書一篇留在下卷。

又按 In his letters, the Senior Officer asked about the matters of the Huayang cavern heavens. The matters pertaining to the Huayang are a response to his letter. If this information is forcibly divided into two sections, the narratives lose coherence. Now, according to content, I have linked them together in order.

又長史書即是問華陽事。華陽事仍是答長史書。強分爲兩部，於事相失。今依旨還爲貫次。

又按 The year and month dates that Gu [Huan] records for the two Xus are particularly contradictory and biased. Now I have carefully determined them through examination of the Perfected announcements. Moreover, I have checked the revelations against the Xu family genealogy. I have made notes on discrepancies in the names of family members at the end of the chapter.

又顧所記二許年月殊自違僻。今謹依眞嗖檢求。又以許家譜參校。注名異同在此卷 後。

又按 When the written traces remaining from the three Lords do not record the verbal transmissions of the Perfected, they copy classics of the world, record their dreams, or write letters to one another. All of these things are inappropriate to mix into the chapters that contain the declarations of the Perfected. But since I value their writings, I have completely copied and recorded them into what is now the sixth chapter.[68] There are several slips that Gu [Huan] left out. I have also recorded these, as with the other examples.

---

that Xizhi "related many numinous and miraculous events which we cannot entirely record here." The *Traditions of Xu Mai* is now lost but seems to have survived through the Song period. (See Shen Yue, *Songshi* 203.5119.)

67. This letter is found at DZ 1016, 18.10a1 ff.

68. These writings are now found in chapters 17 and 18.

又按三君書迹有非疏眞咳，或寫世間典籍，兼自記夢事，及相聞
尺牘。皆不宜雜在眞誥品中。既寶重筆墨，今並撰錄。共爲第六一
卷。顧所遺者復有數條。亦依例載上。

又按 All of the large graphs written in purple that appear within the
announcements of the Perfected are those miscellaneous passages that I
transcribed separately from the scriptures that were written in the hand
of the three Lords that match and serve to verify the annotated passage.
Since I cannot for the time being check all copies of the scriptures, there
is a limit to the examples I can provide. Nonetheless, I cite them here all
the same, for ease in searching out the passages in other copies. Also, all
of the tiny graphs written in red within the first six sections are my
annotations. I have done this to distinguish them from the rest. All the
small characters in black ink are the original texts.[69]

又眞誥中。凡有紫書大字者，皆隱居別抄取三君手書經中雜事各相配
類，共爲證明。諸經既非聊爾可見，便於例致隔。今同出在此，則易
得尋究。又此六篇中有朱書細字者，悉隱居所注，以爲誌別。其墨書
細字猶是本文。

TRANSLATION: ACCOUNT OF THE PERFECTED
SCRIPTURES FROM BEGINNING TO END

· · ·

The following section of Tao's postface is an account not of the
Declarations of the Perfected but of the scriptures that were transmitted to
Yang Xi by the Perfected. Tao attempts a chronological account, beginning
from the time of Yang and the Xus down to his own day. This section was
translated by Michel Strickmann in his path-breaking work on the Shangqing revelations, "The Mao Shan Revelations: Taoism and the Aristocracy," in 1977. The present translation is very much indebted to this previous work. I have, in my notes to this section of the translation, attempted
to outline some of Strickmann's most important findings, but in point of
fact, when his article first appeared, it was itself a revelation. –Trans.

· · ·

Now, when I humbly seek the first appearance in the mortal world of
the Scriptures of the Perfected of Shangqing, I find they began in the

69. All of this careful color-coding is unfortunately lost to us.

second year of the Ascending Tranquility reign period of the Jin Emperor Ai, the first year of the sexagesimal cycle [364]. It was then that Lady Wei of the Southern Marchmount, Primal Lord of the Purple Void and Superior Perfected Directress of Destinies descended and bestowed them upon her disciple Yang [Xi], a retainer in the office of the Minister of Instruction, the Prince of Langye [Sima Yu 司馬昱].[70] She had him transcribe them in clerical script for transmission to Xu [Mi] of Jurong, Senior Officer to the Defensive Army, and his third son [Xu Hui], Accounts Clerk. The two Xus copied them again, put them into practice, and achieved the Dao.

The autograph manuscripts in the hand of these three Lords present in the world today include over ten scriptures and biographies of varying lengths and mostly copied by the Accounts Clerk [Xu Hui] and oral revelations from the Perfected in over forty scrolls, mostly written out by Yang [Xi].

The Prince of Langye is the person who became Jianwen Emperor [of the Jin, Sima Yu]. At the time [of the revelations] he was in the eastern offices and serving as the Minister Prince.

伏尋上清眞經出世之源。始於晉哀帝興寧二年太歲甲子，紫虛元君上眞司命南嶽魏夫人下降，授弟子瑯琊王司徒公府舍人楊某。使作隷字寫出，以傳護軍長史句容許某，并〈弟〉〔第〕三息上計掾某某。二許又更起寫，修行得道。凡三君手書，今見在世者，經傳大小十餘篇，多掾寫；眞唉四十餘卷，多楊書。（瑯琊王即簡文帝在東府爲相王時也。）

The Senior Officer [Xu Mi] and the Accounts Clerk [Xu Hui] set up a residence on the northwestern side of Mount Leiping, just behind the lesser peak of Mount Mao. In this residence, Hui copied scriptures and used them for his practice, secretly transforming himself [and leaving the world] in the fifth year of the Grand Harmony reign period [370]. The Senior Officer departed in death in the first year of the Grand Prime reign [376]. Xu Hui's son, Huangmin 黃民, was seventeen *sui* at the time. He spent several years collecting the scriptures, talismans, and secret registers that they had copied. At this time there were a number of scrolls that were scattered among various relatives and acquaintances. These are the ones that I obtained in Jurong County.

70. We do not know precisely when Yang Xi, at the recommendation of Xu Mi, received his appointment from Sima Yu, but Sima Yu was appointed minister in 366, so it must have been sometime after this.

長史掾立宅在小茅後雷平山　　西北。掾於宅治寫修用。以泰和五年隱
化。長　史以泰元元年又去。掾子黃民時年十七。乃　收集所寫經符祕
籙歷歲。于時亦有數卷散出在諸親通間。今句容所得者是也。

During the third year of the Primal Flourishing reign period [402–404], the capital and surrounding districts were in chaos. Huangmin then carried the scriptures to Shan.[71]

The Senior Officer's father was once the prefect of Shan County. The people were very grateful for his virtue and kindness. The Senior Officer's elder brother also lived in Shan. This is why Huangmin took refuge there.

元興三年，京畿紛亂。黃民乃奉經入剡。（長史父昔爲　剡縣令，甚有
德惠。長史大兄亦又在剡居。是故投憩焉）

Huangmin was supported by the household of Ma Lang 馬朗 of Dongchan.[72]

Ma Lang was also named Wengong 溫公.

爲東闡馬朗家所供養。（朗一名溫公）

Lang and his younger cousin on his father's side, Ma Han 馬罕 joined in providing for all of Huangmin's needs. At that time, all knew that the Prior-born [Xu Mai] had achieved the Dao and his grandfather also had a fine reputation, so all respected Huangmin.[73] The Daoist practice of

71. The Shan County 剡縣 seat was present-day Shengzhou, Zhejiang Province. The "chaos" was the Sun En 孫恩 rebellion, an uprising that depended on a Daoist ideology cobbled together from several sources. (See Espesset, "Sun En.")

72. Strickmann implies that, while Ma Lang and Ma Han are unknown in secular sources, later Daoist texts seem to have a suspicious clarity on their status (See Strickmann, "Mao Shan," 43n78). An undated biography of Xu Huangmin in the ca. 1030 *Seven Lots from the Bookbag of the Clouds* lists Ma Lang and his family as prescient Daoist practitioners (see DZ 1032 4.3b–4a), and the early fourteenth-century monograph on Mount Mao lists Ma Lang and his cousin as the fifth and sixth patriarchs of the Shangqing lineage (DZ 304, 10.9b–11a). The more complete survey of sources made possible by searchable databases only confirms Strickmann's impression. Meng Anpai 孟安排 (fl. 699) records a portion of this information (see DZ 1129, 2.5b), while the ca. 1294 *Comprehensive Mirror of Historical Perfected and Transcendents Who Have Embodied the Dao*, a work that as Verellen notes includes much earlier material (Schipper and Verellen, *Taoist Canon* 2:887–92), includes the rest (see DZ 296, 24.8a–9a). This latter source ends with an abstract of the present account.

73. Biographical information on members of the Xu family appears later in this chapter, together with the genealogy that Tao copies into the text.

Du Daoju 杜道鞠 of Qiantang was rich and flourishing.[74] He repeatedly summoned [Huangmin] to his home. At this time, these people did not yet know to search out and study the scriptures and methods [of Shang-qing]: they only revered him. During the Glory of Duty reign period (405–18), Kong Mo 孔默 of Lu, a man who honored and kept faith with the Dao, became prefect of Jin'an.[75] Then he quit his post and, while returning to the capital, reached Qiantang, where he learned of the presence of Xu, that his forebears had achieved the Dao, and that their scriptures and writings all survived. So he went to pay a visit to Xu, who at first would not see him. Kong advanced on his knees, knocking his head in supplication. This went on for months. He served Xu diligently and his expressions of emotion were intense. Xu eventually had no choice and began to transmit the texts to him. Kong had the clerk of the Jin'an Commandery Wang Xing 王興 transcribe them.[76]

Xing was faithful to and revered the Dao. In addition, he was a capable calligrapher and painter. This is why he was entrusted with the task.

朗同堂弟名罕共相周給。時人咸知許先生得道, 又祖父亦有名稱, 多加宗敬。錢 塘杜道鞠。(即居〈十〉[士]京產之父) 道業富盛。數相招致。于時諸人竝未知尋閱經法, 止稟奉而已。至義 [熙] 中, 魯國孔默崇信道教, 爲晉安太守。罷職還至錢塘。聞有許郎先人得道, 經書具存, 乃 往詣許。許不與相見。孔膝行稽顙。積有旬月, 兼獻奉殷勤, 用情甚至。許不獲已, 始乃傳之。 孔仍令晉安郡吏王興繕寫。(興善有心尚, 又能書畫, 故以委之)

When Kong returned to the capital, he treasured his copies but actually never practiced their contents. During the Primal Commendations reign period (424–52), he became Inciting Notary of Guangzhou. After his death, his two sons, Xixian 熙先 and Xiuxian 休先 who were talented scholars and abundantly intelligent, took the scriptures without trans-

74. Tao notes at this point that Du Daoju was the father of the "retired gentleman" or recluse, Du Jingchan 杜京產 (436–99). On Du and his circle, see Xiao Zixian, *Nan Qishu* 54.942–43 and Li Yanshou, *Nan shi* 75.1881–82. Terry Kleeman suggests that this mention of prosperity hints that Du Daoju had gathered many *daomin* 道民 to his parish (personal communication, 2 November 2018).

75. At this time Jin'an Commandery 晉安郡 was located near present-day Jiujiang, Jiangxi Province. Kong Mo's name is given as Kong Mozhi 孔默之 in Shen Yue's *Songshu* (93.2284), where he is briefly portrayed as a Confucian scholar 儒學 and younger brother of the recluse Kong Chunzhi 孔淳之 (390–448).

76. I have no further information on Wang Xing.

mission and looked through them.[77] They saw that the *Perfected Scripture of the Great Cavern* said that those who chanted it ten thousand times would be able to achieve Transcendence, and they greatly criticized it, saying that it was definitely not so. They held that the Way of Transcendence required elixirs for the transmutation of the body before one could rise up. How could the empty accumulation of chanted sounds deliver feathered garb? There were also a few persons of the [Buddhist] Way who aided him in ridiculing these practices. Someone said that such scriptures should not be preserved and so they burnt all of them at once, leaving not a single one behind.

This was probably because it was the intent of those in the unseen realms not to allow these scriptures to circulate in the outside world. Later Xixian and the rest plotted with Fan Ye 范曄 (398–445) and were executed.[78]

孔還都，唯寶録而已，竟未修用。元嘉中復爲廣州刺史。及亡後，其子熙先休先，才學敏　贍，竊取看覽。見大洞眞經説云。誦之萬遍，則能得仙。大致譏誚，殊謂不然。以爲仙道必須丹藥鍊形乃可超舉。豈有空積聲詠以致羽服。兼有諸道人助毀其法。或謂不宜蓄此。因一時焚蕩。無復子遺。(此當是冥意不欲使流傳於外世故也。後熙〈光〉［先］等復與范曄同謀被誅也。)

Formerly, when Wang Xing was making copies for Kong, he always made another fair copy for himself. Later, he returned to the east to study and practice. When he first crossed the Zhe River, he encountered a wind and [his boat] was overturned in the waves. Only one text, the *Scripture of the Yellow Court*, survived. Xing severely castigated himself [for not having received the scriptures properly]. Then he went to the mountains of Shan, where he began gradually to read and chant the scripture. The mountain spirits burnt his chamber. He then set up an open-air platform to rehearse and intone the scripture. Suddenly there was a rain squall and the paper and ink were soaked through and ruined before he could complete the required number of recitations. Xing was

77. Kong Xixian is best known for his participation in the abortive plot of Liu Yikang 劉義康 (409–51), Prince of Pengcheng, and eventual betrayal of Fan Ye 范曄 (398–445). An account of this event is described in Shen Yue, *Songshu* 69.1820-31. His brother is less well known to history, though he seems to have been a well-respected scholar. The portents section of Xiao Zixian, *Nan Qishu* (18.363) records that in 491 he was consulted on a gleaming bell and went to excavate it.

78. Fan Ye was the author of the *Hou Hanshu*. His transgressions involved his support of the Prince of Pengcheng, and he was executed in 445 at the age of forty-eight.

deeply aware of his transgressions and cut himself off from human society. He wrote out almanacs to exchange for food in order to maintain his existence. His son, Wang Daotai 王道泰 was supervisor to a ferry official and very wealthy.[79] He frequently went to pay respects to his father and to give him presents, including two slaves to serve his needs. But Wang Xing would keep nothing. Finally, he died in the mountains of Shan. With this, both the Perfected Scriptures copied by Kong and those by Wang were destroyed in their turn and did not circulate in the world.

This is likely because Wang Xing did not receive them from a Master, but rather secretly copied and put them into practice illicitly. Thus he came to this end.

王興先爲孔寫，輒復私繕一通。後將還東修學。始濟浙江，便遇風淪漂。唯有黃庭一篇得存。興乃自加切責。仍住剡山，稍就讀誦。山靈即火燒其屋。又於露壇研詠。俄頃驟雨，紙墨霑壞。遍數遂不得畢。興深知罪譴，杜絕人倫。唯書曆日貿粮以續殄命。其子道泰爲晉安船官督。資產豐富。數來拜獻。兼以二奴奉給。興一無留納。而終乎剡山。於是孔王所寫眞經二本前後皆滅。遂不行世。（此當是興先不師受。妄竊寫用。所致如此也。）

And again, there was one Wang Lingqi 王靈期 whose talent and intelligence were refined and extraordinary and who wished to spread the Dao.[80] Seeing that Ge Chaofu 葛巢甫 had fabricated the Lingbao scriptures which had subsequently been transmitted widely, as if the teachings were borne on the wind, Wang became very envious.[81] Thereupon,

79. I have found no further information about Wang Daotai. Strickmann translates his office as "Maritime Bureau" (Strickmann, "Mao Shan," 45) but Jin'an is far from the ocean. I thus postulate that the title 船官 here refers to someone in charge of boat traffic on the Yangzi River.

80. The only reference to Wang Lingqi that I have found outside of Tao Hongjing's account here is in the treatise "Disputing Deceptions" 辯惑論, composed around 480 by the Dharma Master Xuan Guang 玄光法師. In a passage ridiculing Daoist ordinances limiting the amount of alcohol allowed at "kitchen" rites, we read that "Wang Lingqi removed the regulation. As a result the Prior-born [Wang's] Daoist citizens all contributed to him." This led, we are told, to great personal benefit for Wang but also to his movement being labeled deviant. At another spot in the text, Wang is mentioned in an unattributed footnote to the text as a person of Moling County [present-day Nanjing] who first used certain Daoist titles, such as "Prior-born" 先生. (See T. 2102, 52.49a20–28.) While this information is sparse and lacks specificity, it further confirms what Tao writes of Wang Lingqi's efforts to start his own Daoist lineage.

81. On Ge Chaofu (fl. 397), reputed recipient of the Lingbao scriptures that were granted his ancestor Ge Xuan 葛玄 (trad. 164–244), see Bokenkamp, "Ge Chaofu" and "Sources."

he visited Huangmin and begged to receive the higher scriptures. Huang-min would not permit it, but Wang exposed himself to frost and snow, almost taking his life as a demonstration of his determination. Xu Huangmin felt the extent of his sincerity and finally transmitted them to him. Wang was delighted to receive the scriptures and took them back to go through them carefully. Realizing that the ultimate methods could not be widely put into practice and that their essential words were not appropriate to reveal, he stole the gist of them, adding and subtracting bits on his own and embellishing their literary style. On the basis of works mentioned in the *Traditions of [Lord] Wang [Bao]* and *[Lady] Wei [Huacun]*, he expanded the corpus and fabricated his own works to complete their records.[82] In addition, he increased the amount of the faith-offerings necessary for their transmission in order to increase the valuation of his Way. In all, there were over fifty scrolls. Those who chase after the latest fad, hearing of this rich and wide resource, came one after another to offer him reverence and receive the scriptures. Once transmission and copying had become widespread, derivative lineages began to flourish, and the old became mixed with the new so that they were not easily distinguished.[83] If one had not already seen the Perfected Scriptures, it is in fact difficult to prove the distinction.

A fair number of embellished volumes from Wang's hand leaked out and still exist today. When the Prior-born Zhu Sengbiao 朱僧標 was studying with Chu Boyu 褚伯玉, he said:[84] "Those who are brilliant

82. These are two of the higher Perfected who appeared to Yang Xi. Wei Huacun, when alive, had been a Celestial Master Libationer who came south in the early decades of the fourth century. As a deity, she served as Yang Xi's Master. Their biographies, replete with the practices they favored, were themselves revealed works, the compositions of Perfected beings. On the surviving copies of the Traditions of Lady Wei 魏夫人傳, see Robinet, *La révélation*, 2:399–405, and Chang, *Xipu*, 173–224. For the Inner Traditions of Lord Wang, Perfected of Qingxu 清虛真人王君內傳, see Robinet, *La révélation*, 2:369–73.

83. For the flourishing of offshoot lineages, Tao uses a plant metaphor, literally writing "the branches and leaves became lush and intermingled" 枝葉繁雜. Interestingly, the rest of this sentence echoes Lu Xiujing's 陸修靜 (406–77) earlier complaint about the indiscriminate mixing of the Lingbao scriptures with *their* imitations. In his 437 listing of Lingbao scriptures, Lu wrote of the challenge that faced him in distinguishing the true scriptures from the imitations: "There were fifty-five scrolls of new and old scriptures. Students revered them all; few made any distinctions." 新舊五十五卷，學士宗竟，鮮有甄別. See Bokenkamp, "Scriptures New and Old." While "new and old" means something different in Tao's case, he is still concerned with "distinguishing" 甄別 the true from the false.

84. I follow Strickmann, "Mao Shan" 46n93 in correcting 學增 to 曾學. Chu Boyu is a famous recluse whose biography is recorded in Xiao Zixian, *Nan Qishu* 54.926-27. On the prevalence of the seemingly self-contradictory "famous recluses" during this period, see Campany, *Making Transcendents*. Zhu Sengbiao is mentioned as a Daoist of

at expressing themselves naturally rise above the common run of writers. I once set out from the capital in the same ferry as Wang Lingqi. By the time we reached the earthen dam at Dunpo Ridge, he had already composed two scrolls of superior scriptures. It was truly astounding!" But even before Wang Lingqi there were often admixtures [of false materials] in the upper scriptures. In the fourth year of the Resurgent Peace reign period, the *gengzi* year [400], Yang Xi 楊洗 of Hongnong went to Hailing and encountered there over twenty chapters of higher scriptures protected by secret oath, of which a number were not authentic.[85] He said that he had been seeking scriptures for twelve years. This means that he began his activities not long after Lord Yang departed [in death]. From this [we can see that] not all mixtures of [Shangqing materials] with elements of the Lingbao scriptures were the fabrications of Wang Lingqi. It is just that his fabrications were by far the most numerous.

復有王靈期者，才思綺拔，志規敷道。見葛巢甫造構靈寶，風教大行，深所忿嫉。於是詣許丞求受上經。丞不相允。王凍露霜雪，幾至性命。許感其誠到，遂復授之。王得經欣躍，退還尋究。知至法不可宣行；要言難以顯泄，乃竊加損益，盛其藻麗。依王魏諸傳題目，張開造制，以備其錄。并增重詭信崇貴其道。凡五十餘篇。趨競之徒，聞其豐博，互來宗稟。傳寫既廣，枝葉繁雜。新舊渾淆，未易甄別。自非已見眞經，實難證辨。（其點綴手本頗有漏出。即今猶存。又朱先生僧標學增褚公伯玉，語云。天下才情人，故自絶羣。吾與王靈期同船發都。至頓破崗埭竟，便已作得兩卷上經。實自可訝。自靈期已前，上經已往往夾雜。弘農楊洗，隆安〈和〉四年庚子歲，於海陵再遇隱盟上經二十餘篇。有數卷非眞。其云尋經已來一十二年。此則楊君去後，便以動作。故靈寶經中得取以相揉，非都是靈期造製。但所造製者自多耳。）

By now the spread through transmission [of Wang Lingqi's forgeries] within the capital precincts as well as in the several Commanderies of the area east of the Yangzi River was such that there is nearly no one who does not possess a copy. But beyond the area south of the Yangzi River, they are still not numerous.

Redwall Mountain 赤城山, of the Tiantai mountain range in present-day Zhejiang Province, in an entry dated 488. (See Xiao Zixian, *Nan Qishu*, 11.195.)

85. As Strickmann notes as well, in "Mao Shan," 47n94. The text seems flawed at this point. I have deleted the graph 和 rather than adding it to the name of the otherwise unknown Yang Xi. The "secret oath" 隱盟 is a method of scriptural transmission contracted directly with the unseen powers when a human master is unavailable. It is detailed first in the collection of Shangqing materials known as the *Forty-four Prescriptions on Plain Yellow Silk* 上清太上黄素四十四方經 (DZ1369, 4b–5a). On the dating of this text, see Robinet, *La révélation* 2:229–32.

This must be because, while the rites of the Dao should be promulgated, the true wonders of the Perfected cannot be circulated widely. For this reason Wang Lingqi was allowed to fabricate [his scriptures] and circulate them.

今世中相傳流布，京師及江東數郡，略無人不有。但江外尚未多爾。（此當是道法應宣。而眞妙不可廣布。故令王造行此意也）

Once Wang was the only source of these novel marvels, the whole generation began to serve him [as Master]. Consequently, he said falsely that they had been bestowed on him by the Perfected and no longer relied on previous works. Although Xu Huangmin saw Wang's scrolls and book wrappers blossoming forth, the richness of the faith-offerings he collected, the growing abundance of his disciples, and his ever-increasing store of gold and silks, he was still unable to divine why this was so. Subsequently, he began to belittle the books that he possessed and proceeded to Wang's to beg to copy his productions. Thereafter the two separate manuscript traditions were promulgated together and praised in the same tones. This went on until the Xus and Wang were yoked together and the true and false went side by side. "If one rides the current and goes with the wind, even a thousand *li* can be reached." Later, there was one Cai Mai 菜買 who also obtained these [mixed productions], over ten scrolls, from Xu.[86] They contained a good bit of the Perfected texts, but Cai divided them up and transmitted them sheet by sheet so that not even a trace survives.

Cai Mai was a diligent practitioner of the teachings of lower Ways. He did not transmit many of the higher scriptures.

王既獨擅新奇，舉世崇奉。遂託云眞授，非復先本。許見卷裘華廣、詭信豐厚、門徒殷盛、金帛充積、亦復莫測其然。乃鄙閉自有之書而更就王求寫。於是合迹俱宣，同聲相讚。故致許王齊轡，眞僞比蹤。承流向風，千里而至。後又有菜買者，亦從許受得此十數卷，頗兼眞本。分張傳受。其迹不復具存。（菜買善行下道之教。於上經不甚流傳也）

When Ma Lang saw how the number of chapters of scripture that Xu had transmitted to Wang increased, he again desired to receive them. He arranged a faith-offering and set a day when he was to be ordained. Suddenly he dreamt that a jade bowl fell from heaven, dashed on the ground, and shattered. When he awoke, doubts arose: "These scriptures are the

---

86. Cai Mai is otherwise unknown.

treasures of heaven; if brought down to earth, they cannot be used." At this, he ceased in his efforts.

> Although Ma Lang did not practice [the Shangqing scriptures], he was outstanding in treasuring and worshipping the scriptures. This dream was not a mundane one and his interpretation was skilled. He also must have been one who obtained the Dao.

馬朗既見許所傳王經，卷目增多，復欲更受。營理詭信，克日當度。忽夢見有一玉椀從天來下，墜地破碎。覺而發疑云：此經當在天爲寶。下地不復堪用。於是便停。(論馬朗雖不修學。而寶奉精至。夢既不凡。解之又善。亦應是得道人)

In the sixth year of Primal Commendation [429], Xu Huangmin wished to return home to Qiantang.[87] He thus sealed his father's Perfected Scriptures in a chest and placed it in Ma Lang's oratory.[88] He said to Lang: "These scriptures are the traces of my departed forebears; only I should be allowed to remove them from here. Even if a letter [from me] should arrive, be cautious and do not hand them over." Then he divided out over ten scrolls of scriptures, traditions, and miscellaneous writings to take with him to the house of Du [Daoju]. Here he stopped for a number of months. Then he became ill and, fearing that he would not recover, sent someone to fetch the scriptures. But Lang cherished their calligraphy and, moreover, held to the command he had received earlier. He said "When a close friend personally receives instructions, how can he lightly turn over [such treasures]!" As a result, he did not follow the request of the letter. Before long Xu Huangmin died and those texts he had taken with him remained with Du. These are the scriptures and writings that are present today in the world.

元嘉六年，許丞欲移歸錢塘。乃封其先眞經一廚子。且付馬朗淨室之中。語朗云: 此經並是先靈之迹。唯須我自來取。縱有書信，愼勿與之。乃分持經傳及雜書十數卷自隨。來至杜家。停數月。疾患，慮恐不差。遣人取經。朗既惜書兼執先旨。近親受教敕，豈敢輕付。遂不與信。〈我〉[俄] 而許便過世。所齎者因留杜間。即今世上諸經書悉是也。

Xu Huangmin's eldest son Rongdi 榮弟 returned to the family home for the period of mourning. Once he took off the mourning garb, he went to Ma Lang's residence in Shan to seek out the scriptures. But Ma

---

87. Qiantang 錢塘 is roughly modern Hangzhou, Zhejiang Province.
88. A Daoist "oratory" 靜室 (sometimes called jingshe 精舍) was a small structure used for meditation and for sending up petitions to the celestial bureaucracy.

was good at arranging matters to his own advantage and did not give the scriptures to him. Once brought to a halt by his sense of humiliation, Xu Rongdi did not press his case. He took up residence in Shan and again taught and transmitted Wang Lingqi's scriptures, chanting and speaking on them, as well as transcribing authentic scriptures. At the end of each of the scriptures he transcribed, he wrote "In X month of X year, transmitted to Xu Yuanyou 許遠遊 [= Xu Mai] by Perfected X."

He did this because, at this time, most of the profane knew that the Prior-born Xu Mai had ingested drugs, entered the mountains, and achieved the Dao, but they knew nothing of the deeds of Senior Officer Xu and his son.

許丞長子榮弟迎喪還鄉。服闋後上剡，就馬求經。馬善料理，不與其經。許既慙戢，不復苦索。仍停剡住。因又以靈期之經，教授唱言。竝寫眞本。又皆注經後云：某年某月某眞人授許遠遊。（于時世人多知先生服食入山得道，而不究長史父子事迹故也。）

People were at first not aware [of Rongdi's mislabeling]. Over the space of several years, he was only able to obtain two or three scrolls of authentic scriptures from Ma, most of which he leaked to outsiders.

The scriptures obtained by Wang Huilang 王惠朗 and the rest are examples of this.[89]

人亦初無疑悟者。經涉數年中，唯就馬得兩三卷眞經。頗亦宣泄。（今王惠朗諸人所得者是也。）

In the twelfth year of Primal Commendation [435], Rongdi died in Shan and was buried at White Mountain.

When Rongdi was in Shan, he lived a very dissolute life and did not concern himself with studying the scriptures. This is why He [Daojing] 何道敬 was able to search them out and copy them so quickly at Ma's home.

元嘉十二年，仍於剡亡。因葬白山。（榮弟在剡，大縱淫侈。都不以經學爲意。所以何 公在馬家快得尋寫。）

Ma Lang and Ma Han respectfully practiced these scriptural treasures even more so than had their father and lord. They always had two faithful slaves guard the scriptures. Whenever they burned incense, swept, or dusted off the book chest, there would always be spirit lights and

---

89. Wang Huilang is mentioned again, but is otherwise unknown.

numinous qi filling the chamber.[90] It was said that Ma Lang's wife was able to communicate [with spirits]. She said that "many times there were Jade Maidens, clothed in blue, who came and went through the air, shaped just like flying birds." The Ma household subsequently became wealthy, with properties measured in the tens of thousands, and they died of old age when their life mandates were exhausted. Ma Lang's sons Hong 洪 and Zhen 眞 and Ma Han's sons Zhi 智 and the rest still continued to revere the scriptures.[91] Toward the end of their years, though, they came to serve the Buddha and began to abandon the practice of [the Way of Shangqing].

This was all likely brought about due to the fact that the fated cycles mandated that the scriptures should issue forth.

馬朗馬罕敬事經寶有過君父。恆　使有心奴子二人。(一名白首。一名平頭)　常侍直香火，洒掃拂拭。每有神光靈炁見於室宇。朗妻頗能通見云：數有青衣玉女空中去來。狀如飛鳥。馬家遂致富盛，資産巨萬。年老命終，朗子洪、洪弟眞、罕子智等、猶共遵向。末年事佛，乃弛廢之爾。(此當是經運應出所致也。)

He Daojing 何道敬 of Shanyin aspired to single-mindedness and simplicity.[92] He was rather skilled at calligraphy and painting. When young, he had roamed the mountains of Shan and had received the patronage of the Ma family. They entrusted him to perform all the ritual services in the scriptures and writings. He noticed that the calligraphy of the talismans flashed with light and was quite distinct from worldly text. In the eleventh year of Primal Commendation [434], he gradually began to make traced copies of the texts. Since Ma Han resided in a separate dwelling, he also ordered He to make several copies for him. This is why an exact copy of the two verifications remained with Han.[93] Afterward, He replaced many of the authentic copies with his own tracings. He returned to live at Green Platform mountain in Dongshu of the Shan Commandery. There he made a record telling of matters related to the Perfected Scriptures. It was perhaps two or three sheets of paper in length. But by nature He was mean and slow-witted, so he was unable to perfectly practice the Higher Enter-

90. Tao notes that one of these slaves was named "Whitehair" 白首 and the other "Flathead" 平頭. The specificity of this part of Tao's story indicates that he personally checked some of these details.

91. These practitioners are not known beyond the pages of this account.

92. What little is known of He Daojing all derives from this account.

93. On the "two verifications" 二録, see note 41.

prise [of the Shangqing scriptures]. Eventually he lost many [of the texts]. Those scrolls that remained are now with his female disciple, Zhang Yujing 張玉景 of Houtang Mountain in Shifeng.[94]

He commonly practiced [the sexual alchemy of] Peng[zu] and the Plain Woman.[95] He was also rustic and unpolished. When the Recluse Gu [Huan] heard that he had obtained the scriptures, he went to visit him. The first person that he met was He carrying a hoe and coming in from outside. Gu thought he was a slave or servant and asked him if Elder He was at home. He replied "I don't know," and went inside, never meeting with Gu. Gu tarried for several days, begging strenuously in every fashion, but He would still not receive him. People of the time regarded He's [actions] as irredeemably base and held it shameful that he lacked the ability to recognize a person who might understand him.

山陰何道敬，志向專素，頗工書畫。少遊剡山，爲馬家所供侍。經書法事，皆以委之。見此符跡炳煥，異於世文。以元嘉十一年，稍就摹寫。馬罕既在別宅，兼令何爲起數篇。所以二錄合本仍留罕間。何後多換取眞書。出還剡東墅青壇山住。乃記說眞經之事。可有兩三紙。但何性鄙滯，不能精修高業。後多致散失。猶餘數卷今在其女弟子始豐後堂山張玉景間。（何常以彭素爲事。質又野朴。顧居士聞其得經，故往詣尋請。正遇見荷鋤外還。顧謂是奴僕。因問何公在否。何答不知。於是還裏。永不相見。顧留停累日，謂苦備至。遂不接之。時人咸以何鄙恥不除。而失知人之會也。）

Ma Lang was furious that He had taken a portion of the scriptures away and, what is more, leaked their true significance. So he poured molten copper into the lock of the casket and made the members of his household take an oath that they would not open it again. In the seventh year of the Great Brilliance reign period [463], there was a famine in the three Commanderies of Wu, but Shan County had a harvest. The recluse Lou Huiming 樓惠明 had formerly resided in the Shan mountains and now returned, bringing with him the Female Ritual Master

94. Zhang Yujing is not otherwise known.

95. The names 彭素 refer to Peng Zu 彭祖, one of the patrons of sexual arts in the "Ten Questions" and the *Classic of the Unadorned Woman* 素女經, an early manual on sexual vampirism lost in China but preserved in Tamba Yasuyori's *Ishimpō*, compiled circa 983. (On the "Ten Questions" see Vivienne Lo, "Crossing," 21, and for a translation of the *Classic of the Unadorned Woman*, see Douglas Wile, *Art of the Bedchamber*. On the early Celestial Master view of these practices, see Bokenkamp, *Early Daoist Scriptures*, 43–46.) But this charge is likely calumny on Tao's part. I suspect that He Daojing practiced not profane sexual practices, but the "merging qi" 合氣 of the Celestial Masters, an art that Yang Xi and his followers held in equal disdain. (See volume 2 of this work for more.)

Zhong Yishan 鍾義山 of Yanguan and the rest of her family, since there was food in this region.[96] Lou excelled at writing petitions and talismans and understood the five phases as well as how to determine hidden fates. Ma Hong 馬洪 also served him as master and frequented his oratory. There he saw a scripture chest. Now Ma Hong had already seen what He had recorded and, seeing the scriptures, he was very pleased. But the casket was firmly locked and there was no way for him to survey the contents. In the first year of the Luminous Harmony reign period [465] he went out to the capital, where he had Shu Jizhen 夊季眞 of Jiaxing send up a petition [asking that the emperor] command the texts to be confiscated.[97] But, since the emperor was insane, Lou told [Shu and the rest] that the higher scriptures should not be released to the world.[98] [Lou] then made a selection among the texts, taking the Perfected Scriptures, Perfected *Traditions*, and over ten chapters of miscellaneous celestial revelation to leave with Zhong. Taking with him only the Huoluo talismans, twenty-odd slips of Perfected revelation, and the two verifications that had been traced by Gentleman He, he went to the capital.[99] Shu then showed them to the emperor, and they were temporarily displayed in the Flower Grove [garden of the palace] before the emperor entrusted them to the Daoists of his rear halls. Early in the Grand Inauguration reign (465–471), Shu requested that they be removed to his private retreat.[100]

96. I follow Strickmann in correcting 女師 to 法師. Zhong Yishan is elsewhere so identified and was an acquaintance of Tao Hongjing. (See DZ 300, 8b1 and DZ 1032, 107.8a9.) Lou Huiming is provided with a brief biography in Xiao Zixian, *Nan Qishu* (54.946) and, from a lost version of the *Qishu*, *Taiping yulan* (505.3a). Both record that Lou Huiming resided as a Daoist on Golden Flower Mountain 金華山, that upon leaving the mountain, the emperor attempted to install him in the capital, and that the Qi emperor built a temple for him on Jiang Mountain 蔣山 (near present-day Nanjing) around 485. Yanguan 鹽官 village is in present-day Haining of Zhejiang Province.

97. Nothing is known of Shu Jizhen beyond the events recounted here.

98. The emperor 劉子業 (449–66) is here referred to by his reign title. Cruel and delusional, he ruled for a little more than one and a half years before being assassinated by his ministers in 466. (See Shen Yue, *Songshu* 7.141ff.)

99. The Huoluo Talismans 豁落符 were so widely copied and altered in later Daoism that it is difficult to know what form they might have had at this time. The full name of the talismans seems to have been Huoluo Seven Primes 豁落七元符. The "seven primes" are the deities of the seven visible stars of the Big Dipper. According to the *Declarations*, the talismans could be used to quell demons and defend against envoys from the realms of the dead. (See DZ 1016, 10.3a and Robinet, *La révélation*, 2:430, discussing DZ 392.)

100. Reading 廨 for 解. On the use of this term, which originally meant "postal station / roadhouse," to denote an individual religious establishment, see Pettit, "Learning" 42n81.

何既分將經去，又泄説其意。馬朗忿恨，乃洋銅澆廚籥。約敕家人，不得復開。大明七年，三吳飢饉。 剡縣得熟。樓居士惠明者，先以在剡，乃復攜女［法］師鹽官鍾義山眷屬數人，就食此境。樓既善於章符。五行宿命亦皆開解。馬洪又復宗事，出入堂靜。備覘經廚。先已見何所記，意甚貪樂。而有鑰嚴固，觀覽無方。景和元年，乃出都，令嘉興㕥季眞啓敕封取。景和既猖狂。樓謂上經不可出世。乃料簡取眞經眞傳及雜唉十餘篇，乃留置鍾間。唯以谿落符及眞唉二十許小篇，并何公所摹二錄等將至都。㕥即以呈景和。於華林暫開。仍以付後堂道士。〈秦〉［泰］始初，㕥乃啓將出私解。

When Lu Xiujing 陸修靜 (406–77) came to the capital from the south and established the Abbey for Veneration of the Void 崇虛館, he took [the scriptures] to his establishment.[101] When he died, the scriptures were returned [with his body] to Mount Lu.[102] Xu Shubiao 徐叔標 [Lu's disciple] later took them down to the capital [again]. When Xu died they came to his nephew Xu Guiwen 徐瓌文.[103]

Among the documents were Perfected revelations written out by the three Lords. Some later person had glued the sheets together, forming twenty-four chapters. In the third year of the Establishing Prime reign [481], [the emperor] ordered Dong Zhongmin 董仲民 to go to Mount Lu to establish merit [for the emperor].[104] Dong wished to find a spiritual oddity. Xu thus divided one chapter of Yang's writings into two and gave it to Dong, who returned with it to the High Thearch [of the Qi dynasty, Xiao Daocheng 蕭道成, r. 479–482]. The High Thearch then entrusted it to his Library Clerk, [in charge of the Confucian] five classics, Dai Qing 戴慶.[105] When Dai Qing went away from the court, he kept the manuscripts with him. After the death of Xu [Shubiao], [Lu Xiujing's] disciple Li Guozhi 李果之 also took one chapter and the Huoluo talismans and

101. Lu was summoned to the capital in 467 by Liu Yu 劉彧 (r. 465–72) and was presented with an estate in the northern outskirts of the capital. This became his Abbey for the Veneration of the Void. For a translation of the earliest biography of Lu, collector and codifier of the Lingbao scriptures, see Bumbacher, *Fragments*, 204–19 and for his work on the canon, see Bokenkamp, "Lu Xiujing."

102. Mount Lu 廬山 is in the northern part of present-day Jiangxi Province. It was the center of Lu Xiujing's activities before he went to the capital.

103. Neither Xu Shubiao nor Xu Guiwen are further known.

104. Dong Zhongmin does not have a biography in the received histories, but he does figure as the Clerk 主書 sent by the emperor to Redwall Mountain 赤城山 to verify the miracle reported by the Daoist Zhu Sengbiao in the entry dated 488 that we mentioned previously. (See Xiao Zixian, *Nan Qishu*, 11.195.) Since Redwall Mountain is part of the Tiantai Mountain range, Dong must have been adept at finding portents there.

105. I have no further information on Dai Qing.

went away with them.[106] Only twenty-one chapters of the original work remained, and it was entirely returned and placed in storage in the Loft for Illumining [the Numinous].[107]

陸修靜南下，立崇虛館，又取在館。陸亡，隨還廬山。徐叔標後將下都。及徐亡，仍在陸兄子瓛文間。（此中有三君所書眞受。後人糊連裝撿，分爲二十四篇。建元三年，敕董仲民往廬山營功德。董欲求神異。徐因分楊書一篇爲兩篇與董。還上高帝。高帝以付五經典書戴慶。戴慶出外，仍將自隨。徐因亡後，弟子李果之又取一篇及豁〔落〕以去。所餘惟二十一篇。悉以還封昭臺也。）

When Lou [Huiming] returned from the capital, he went again to reside in Shan. There he went to pay a call on Zhong [Yishan] to request the Perfected Scriptures that he had formerly left with him. Zhong would not return them. Lou thus began to copy them and, after a long time, had obtained a number of chapters in this fashion. Since he had an inimical relationship with Ma Hong, he then returned to the Long Mountains of Dongyang.[108] Ma later came to steal the scriptures, but he mistakenly took other scriptures instead. Still, while the scriptures were with Lou, there seem to have been some losses. Today, one or two chapters should still survive there.

These two scrolls have already been returned and secreted in the Loft for Illumining [the Numinous].[109]

樓從都還，仍住 剡。就鍾求先所留眞經。鍾不以還之。乃就起寫。久久方得數篇。既與馬洪爲恨，移歸東陽長山。馬後遂來潛取而誤得他經。樓中時似復有所零落。今猶應一兩篇在。（其二卷已還封昭臺。）

When Kong Zao 孔璪 was still in obscurity [before 466], Recluse Du Jingchan 杜京産 took the scriptures and writings and went to live in Daxu, in Nanshu of Shan.[110] He began to read and consider them with

106. Beyond the fact that he was one of the primary disciples of Lu Xiujing, nothing is known of Li Guozhi. (See DZ 1032, 5.7a and DZ 296, 24.19b.)

107. The text has 昭臺 "illumining loft." There is some confusion over the full name of this building. Strickmann cites a passage in the *Declarations* that refers to it as the Loft for Illumining the Numinous 昭靈臺 (DZ 1016, 13.18a9), but Liu Dabin 劉大彬 (fl. 1317–1328) collected material that names it the Loft for Illumining the Perfected 昭真臺 (DZ 304, 8.5a6–9). Whatever the correct name of the building, it was the structure in which Tao Hongjing stored his scriptures.

108. Dongyang is located in the center of present-day Zhejiang Province.

109. This is an indication that at least a portion of Tao's interlinear notes were added at a later time.

110. This method of dating is strange, to say the least, but Strickmann is likely correct ("Mao Shan," 54n122). Kong Ji 孔覬 and his sons rebelled against the throne in 466 on

Gu Huan 顧歡, Qi Jingxuan 戚景玄, Zhu Sengbiao, and a few others.[111]
Gu had already copied the scriptures in the possession of Lou [Huiming] and was fairly competent in recognizing the Perfected writings. So he made distinctions and selected [as authentic] four or five scrolls of scripture and traditions and seven or eight chapters of Perfected revelation. These are still in the Du household.

Of these scriptures, two scrolls of Perfected revelation have already been returned to the Loft for Illumining [the Numinous]. At the end of the Great Illumination reign of the Song (457–464), Dai Faxing's 戴法興 elder brother Dai Yanxing 戴延興 became prefect of Shan.[112] He was also fond of the Dao. Together with all those who excelled in the mysteries on Heaven's Eye Mountain 天目山 in Wuxing, they were able to obtain and copy a number of the Du family scriptures. Lou [Huiming's] younger cousins Daoji 道濟 and Fazhen 法眞, together with Zhong Xing's 鍾興 daughter Fuguang 傅光, obtained and copied scriptures held by Lou and Zhong.[113] These people also all had dealings with one another. As a result, although they each traced each talisman, there would be many mistakes and elisions, and they imaginatively elaborated them and chose the best copy on the basis of its elegance. In no case did they pay attention to the regularities or the force of the brushstrokes. Further, many of the scriptures they copied were frivolous and deluded. Coming to the *gengwu* year [490], when I entered the Dongyang circuit, those who had come late to the Study had gradually come to make copies of excellent quality. Among the accomplished were Pan Wensheng 潘文盛 of Shanyin, Du Gaoshi 杜高士 of Qiangtang, Jiang Hongsu

---

the advice of an obscure functionary from the Bureau of Waterways and possible relation, Kong Zao. (See Shen Yue, *Songshu* 84.2156; Li Yanshou, *Nan shi* 27.736.) Thus this seems a polite way of pointing to the beginning of the end for the Liu-Song dynasty. Du Jingchan is a member of the Qiantang Du family, the great grandson of Du Zigong 杜子恭 and the son of Du Daoju, as mentioned previously. Biographical information on him is to be found in Xiao Zixian, *Nan Qishu* (54.942–43) and Li Fang, *Taiping yulan* (505.2a–b).

111. For Gu Huan, whose *Traces of the Perfected* was such a challenge to Tao Hongjing's own work, see Xiao Zixian, *Nan Qishu* (54.928–35) and Li Fang, *Taiping yulan* (505.3b–4a). Qi Jingxuan is unknown beyond these pages.

112. The biographies of the Dai brothers are found in Shen Yue, *Songshu* 94.2302–6 and Li Yanshou, *Nan shi* 77.1914–17. There is no further information concerning his patronage of Daoism.

113. With regard to Zhong Xing and his daughter, Strickmann has the following to add: "It is stated below (20.1b) that since the death of Zhong Yishan, such autograph texts as Tao had not been able to obtain from him doubtless remained in the possession of his niece and a disciple. The niece was in all likelihood the Zhong Fuguang mentioned here, and Zhong Xing would thus have been the brother of Zhong Yishan. We have already seen that Zhong came to Shan accompanied by several members of his family (19.14b)" ("Mao Shan," 55n126).

蔣弘素 of Yixing, and Xu Lingzhen 許靈眞 of Jurong.[114] People of the
present know enough to trace the calligraphy of the two Wangs, but
have never thought to trace the Perfected Scriptures.[115] In truth, this
began with me. Nor is it always necessary to fill in an outline. One
can draw it with a single stroke. In this way, the force and direction
[of your stroke] will in nowise be different than that of the original.
As for talismans, no matter whether they are large or small, they all
should be outlined and then filled in.

孔璪賤時，杜居士京産將諸經書。往剡南墅大墟住。始與顧歡、戚景
玄、朱僧標等數人共相料視。顧先已寫在樓閒經。粗識眞書。於是分
別選出。凡有經傳四五卷，眞唉七八篇，今猶在杜家。（其經二〈
眞〉［篇］並眞唉。已還封昭臺。宋大明末，有戴法興兄延興作剡縣
亦好道。及吳興天目山諸玄秀，並頗得寫杜經。樓從弟道濟及法眞，
鍾興女傳光，並得寫樓鍾閒經，亦互相通涉。雖各摹符而殊多麤略。
唯加意潤色，滑澤取好。了無復規矩鋒勢。寫經又多浮謬。至庚午
歲，隱居入東陽道。諸晚學者，漸效爲精。山陰潘文盛，錢塘杜高
士，義興蔣弘素，句容許靈眞，並是能者。時人今知摹二王法書而永
不悟摹眞經。經正起隱居手爾。亦不必皆須郭塡，但一筆就畫，勢力
殆不異眞。至於符無大小。故宜皆應郭塡也。）

In the fourth year of the Grand Inception reign [468],[116] [Ma Han] died
in Shan and [Zhong Yishan] moved to Mount Tiao in Shining. [Ma
Han's son] Ma Zhi 馬智 was convinced by monks late in life and changed
his allegiance to the Buddha dharma.[117] He sent several tens of scrolls of
Daoist scriptures to Zhong. These were all texts that He had copied for
his father, as well as assorted scriptures written by Wang Lingqi. Only
four or five chapters and six of seven chapters of Perfected revelations
were original copies and not related to those acquired by Lou [Huiming].

114. Wensheng is the byname of Pan Hong 潘洪, one of Tao Hongjing's most notable
disciples and an aide in his search for the scriptures. (See Bumbacher, *Fragments*, 233–34
and DZ 1050, 2.6a.) Ironically, Du Gaoshi may be the Du-surnamed disciple of Tao
Hongjing whose "Rhapsody on Painting and Calligraphy" is sharply criticized by Yan
Zhitui 顏之推 (531–91) as the work of someone who, "not very literate" 未甚識字,
"relies for fame on his venerated master" 託名貴師. (See Yan Zhitui, "Zayi," *Yanshi
jiaxun*, 42.) Jiang Hongsu was the second son of Jiang Fuchu 蔣負芻 (fl. 480), who built
several Daoist belvederes on Mount Mao that preceded Tao Hongjing's. Hongsu apparently took charge of them for his father. (See Bumbacher, *Fragments*, 238, 439.) Xu
Lingzhen, a sixth-generation descendant of Xu Mi, will be discussed later with other
members of the Xu family.

115. The "two Wangs" are the renowned calligraphers Wang Xizhi 王羲之 (303–61)
and his son Wang Xianzhi 王獻之 (344–88).

116. A phrase seems to be missing at this point. We can supply the name Ma Han
based on context.

117. Ma Zhi is otherwise unknown.

Of these scriptures, two scrolls, all revelations of the Perfected, have
been returned and stored in the Loft for Illumining [the Numinous].
The remainder of the lost scriptures was after Zhong's death likely
placed in possession of [Zhong's] niece and Qi Jingxuan 戚景玄.

〈秦〉［泰］始四年，終於剡。移還始寧昭山。馬智晚爲衆僧所説，
改事佛法。悉以道經數十卷送與鍾。皆是何公先爲其父寫者，亦有王
靈期雜經。唯四五篇并眞哎六七篇是眞手。不關樓所得者。（其經二
卷。此眞哎等悉已還封昭臺。鍾亡後。所餘亡應在兄女
及戚景玄處。）

Previously there was one Chen Lei 陳雷 who was a person of Dongyang
and a retainer of the Senior Officer [Xu]. He was respectful and had
faith, so the Senior Officer allowed him to look after some of the scriptures and writings, finally instructing him and transmitting them to him.
Chen also replaced [some of the originals] with his copies. He also
obtained the *Diagram of the Seven Primal Stars* 七元星圖 that the Senior
Officer had himself paced.[118] After the Senior Officer passed, he took
these things with him and returned to Dongyang. In the thirteenth year
of the Glory of Duty reign [417], he compounded an elixir with two
nephews of the prefect of Rencheng Wei Xin 魏欣. After the elixir was
completed, the three ingested it in turn and had marvelous spiritual
results. They entrusted themselves to temporary death, hid away through
transformation, and departed.[119] Lei had a grandson, named X, who was
styled Changle 長樂. At present he lives north of the Heng River bridge
in Yongkang. The Jing Mountain Daoist Fan Xian 樊仙 frequently went
there to obtain those scriptures that [Chen Lei] had copied.[120] But the
star chart for pacing is still with Changle, who employs it.

昔有陳雷者東陽人，是許長史門附。謹敬有心。長史常使典看經書，頗
加訓授。其亦換有 所寫。兼得長史自步七元星圖。長史去後，因還東
陽。義熙十三年，與東陽太守任城魏欣 之兄子二人共合丹。丹成，三
人前後服。服皆有神異。託迹暫死，化遁而去。雷有孫名某，號爲長

---

118. As mentioned above in footnote 22, the "seven primes" 七元 are the deities of
the visible stars of the Northern Dipper. While the chart Tao mentions here doubtless
came from the Perfected of Yang Xi, methods for pacing up the stars of the Dipper pre-
cede Shangqing Daoism. (See Robinet, *La révélation*, 2:59–65.)

119. In other words, they performed some version of "release by means of a corpse."
In fact "hiding away through transformation" 化遁 is described in the *Declarations* as the
highest form of release by means of a corpse 化遁，上尸解也. (See DZ 1016, 12.10b and
Campany, *To Live as Long*, 52–60, for a concise description of these techniques and
practitioners.)

120. Transcendent Fan 樊仙 is probably the female Daoist 樊妙羅 mentioned later.

樂。今居永康橫江橋北。菁山道士樊仙亦頗就得所寫經書。但步圖猶在
其處。今所服用，即是其本。

The scriptures and writings, their locations, and the numbers of chapters
that I have mentioned to this point are included in a separate index.[121] As
for those items for which only a single page survives or those of one or
two chapters, I now reveal their titles and numbers of scrolls as follows:

A copy of the *Five Talismans of Lingbao*, one scroll.[122] This was originally in the possession of Ge Can 葛粲 of Jurong. During the Grand
Inception reign (465–71), Ge showed it to Prior-born Lu [Xiujing]. Lu
had already circulated and discussed the *Perfected Texts Written in
Red*, the *Five Man-Bird Talismans*, and more, and they had achieved
wide circulation.[123] He did not wish to reveal this divergent text and
thus purchased it with silk goods from Ge and kept it in the strictest
secrecy. Gu [Huan] heard about it and strenuously begged to be allowed
to view it, but [Lu] would not allow him a glimpse. Lu transmitted it
only to Sun Youyue 孫遊嶽 (399–489) of Dongyang and to his female
disciple Mei Lingwen 梅令文.[124] When Lu perished, they took it with
them back to Mount Lu. Xu Shubiao later took it out with him [to the
capital]. When Xu died, it was with Xu Guiwen.[125]

I have already stored it in the Loft for Illumining [the Numinous].

自此前凡諸經書在處者。其篇數並別有目錄。若止零牒一兩篇者。今
復顯題卷目如後。楊書靈寶五符一卷，本在句容葛粲間。泰始某年，

---

121. This work unfortunately does not survive.

122. The *Five Talismans of Lingbao* 靈寶五符經 is a scripture that likely originated in
third-century Wu. The copy mentioned here was received by Yang Xi in 350 from Liu Pu,
the living son of Wei Huacun. (See DZ 1016, 20.12a.) On the history and contents of the
Five Talismans, see Raz, "Creation of Tradition"; on the copy that Lu Xiujing included in
his catalog of original Lingbao scriptures, see Bokenkamp, "Sources."

123. The *Perfected Texts Written in Red* 眞文赤書 refers to the first of the Lingbao
scriptures in Lu Xiujing's catalog, DZ 22. The *Five Man-Bird Talismans* 人鳥五符 are
more difficult to identify. I originally thought that the word might refer to another manuscript version of the Five Talismans of Lingbao (see Bokenkamp, "Sources" 454–57).
Another possibility, though it breaks the four-four rhythm of the text, might be to read
"Man-Bird and Five Talismans." The Five Talismans would refer to the third-century
Lingbao text, while the "Man-Bird" might refer to the text in the canon now called *Chart
for a Mystical Overview of Man-Bird Mountain* 玄覽人鳥山圖 DZ 434. But this latter
text is not known to have been part of Lu's scriptures.

124. Mei Lingwen seems not known beyond this passage.

125. The text has 陸瓊文. I believe this is an error for Xu Guiwen, the nephew of Xu
Shubiao mentioned previously.

葛以示陸先生。陸既敷述眞文赤書人鳥五符等教授。施行已廣，不欲
復顯出奇迹。因以絹物與葛請取。甚加隱閉。顧公聞而苦求一看。遂
不令見。唯以傳東陽孫遊嶽及女弟子梅令文。陸亡。亦隨還廬山。徐
叔標後將出。徐亡。乃在陸瓊文間。（已還封昭臺。）

The Traditions of Lord Wang, written by Yang [Xi] in one scroll.[126] This
was originally possessed by Ge Yongzhen 葛永眞 of Jurong. Finally, it
came into the possession Ge Jingxian 葛景仙 of Mount Mao after having belonged in the interim to Wang Wenqing 王文清.[127]

I have already retrieved this text and stored it in the Loft for
Illumining [the Numinous].

楊書王君傳一卷。本在句容葛永眞間。中又在王文清家。後屬茅山道
士葛景仙。（已還封昭臺）

The Flying Paces Scripture in one scroll copied by Xu Hui.[128] Originally
this copy was in the household of Yan Qiu 嚴虯 of Jurong.[129] In the
seventh year of the Great Illumination reign [463], there was a famine
and food was scarce. Wang Wenqing, of the same village, went to Yan
with money and food to exchange for the text. After that, it was in the
Wang household.

I have retrieved this text and stored it in the Loft for Illumining [the
Numinous].

掾書飛步經一卷。本在句容嚴虯家。大明七年，饑荒少粮。其里王文
清。以錢食與嚴。求得之。因在王家。（已還封昭臺。）

*Talismans of the Duke of the Western Marchmount for Interdicting
Mountain [demons]* copied by Xu Hui and the *Talismans of the Central*

126. The full title of this work seems to have been the *Inner Traditions of Wang
[Bao], Perfected of Pure Vacuity* 清虛真人王[褒]君內傳. It is a revealed work said to have
been composed by Wang's disciple, Wei Huacun herself. On surviving editions of this text,
see Robinet, *La révélation*, 2:369–73.

127. While the two Ge's are otherwise unknown, Tao notes that Wang Wenqing was
commanded by the Prince of Changsha to build a temple, called Honoring the Prime 崇元
館, on Mount Mao sometime between 473 and 477. (See DZ 1016, 11.15b and DZ 304,
17.3a–b.)

128. The *Flying Paces Scripture* 飛步經 is likely the text titled Scripture of Flying
Paces along the Celestial Mainstays of the Seven Primes 飛步七元天綱之經, mentioned
elsewhere in the *Declarations* (DZ 1016, 5.3a). It is a method for pacing across the stars
of the Dipper, thereby gaining control of space and time. (See Robinet, *La révélation*,
2:59–65 and Andersen, "Practice.")

129. Yan Qiu is otherwise unknown.

Yellow [God] for controlling Tigers and Leopards in the hand of Yang Xi, two short scrolls.[130] Originally Wu Tanba 吳曇拔 of Shangyu obtained a calabash full of miscellaneous Daoist writings from Xu Huangmin.[131] These two scrolls were then given to the Prior-born Chu Boyu 褚伯玉. At this time Boyu lived in Nanhuo and was roaming through its various mountains. He always carried these talismans with him. Once he died, he left them with his disciple Zhu Sengbiao 朱僧標. Afterward, the fifth grandson of Chu's fifth younger brother, Chu Zhongyan 褚仲儼, got them from Zhu.

I have already retrieved these talismans and stored them in the Loft for Illumining [the Numinous]. Wu Tanba, a person of Jumi in Shangyu, was fairly talented.[132] At first he was a Daoist master. Xu Huangmin gave him a calabash full of writings, all vital practices and miscellaneous oral instructions from the three Lords. Later, though, Wu served the Buddha, left home [as a monk], and gave the writings to anyone who asked until he had no more. Later, he gave up on the Buddha and returned to lay life. He took to reclusive roaming and passed away.[133] I have not been able to determine the whereabouts of the various writings and oral instructions that he once owned.

掾書西嶽公禁山符，楊書中黃制虎豹符。凡二短卷，本上虞吳曇拔所得許丞一瓠蘆雜道書。吳以此二卷與褚先生伯玉。伯玉居南霍。遊行諸山，恆帶自隨。褚亡，留在弟子朱僧標間。後褚〈弟〉[第] 五弟之孫名仲儼又就朱取之。(已還封昭臺。吳曇拔者上虞且麋人。頗有才致。初為道士。許丞以一瓠蘆書，皆三君小小要用雜訣以與之。其後事佛出家。悉分散乞人都盡。後又罷佛還俗。遂留宕而終。諸書〈決〉[訣] 並未測所在。)

130. The *Talismans of the Duke of the Western Marchmount for Interdicting Mountain [demons]* 西嶽公禁山符 contains talismans and methods for protecting one's person when traveling in the mountains or elsewhere beyond the bounds of civilization. It is a pre-Shangqing text attributed to Chijiangzi 赤將子, a person of the [mythical] Yellow Emperor's times. (See DZ 1138, 84.8a, and DZ 1185, 17.21a ff., where copies of the talismans are reproduced.) The *Talismans of the Central Yellow [God] for Controlling Tigers and Leopards* 中黃制虎豹符 was received by Yang Xi from his Perfected informants in 349. (See DZ 1016, 20.12a.) Elsewhere in the *Declarations*, the talismans are associated with Luan Ba 欒巴 and Lady Fan 樊夫人, both associated with the control of tigers in tales collected in the *Traditions of Divine Transcendents* (see Campany, *To Live as Long*, 147–48 and 252–55.)

131. In his "Treatise on Contending over the Correct" 辯證論, the Buddhist Falin 法琳 (572–640) remarks hyperbolically that before the Qi dynasty (479–502), all Daoist scriptures were stored in gourds. (See T. 2110, 52.535a, and, on the symbolism of the gourd, Stein, *World in Miniature*, 58–76.)

132. Shangyu was a prefecture that includes modern Shaoxing, Zhejiang Province. I have no information on Jumi.

133. I follow the suggestion of Lü Pengzhi (personal communication, 23 January 2020) that *liudang* 留宕 is a graphic variant of the homophonous 流宕, "unrestrained roaming."

The Five Spirits and Twenty-four Spirits of the Great Immaculate, together with the *Secret Method for Return to the Origin,* copied out by Xu Hui in one scroll.[134] Also, the *Songs of Yin and Yang of the Eight Immaculates,* copied by Xu Hui in one scroll.[135] These texts were acquired by chance by Zhang Lingmin 章靈民 of Dongyang when he first went out to the capital.[136] At that time Zhang did not yet recognize authentic writings and just said that they were only common Daoist scriptures. When he returned to Dongyang, he showed them to Gu [Huan]. Gu did not speak to him about them, he just kept them for himself. Gu divided the *Return to the Origin* into two scrolls. Zhang later came to understand [his mistake] and came to beg for their return. Today they are with Zhang. As for the single scroll of *Songs of Yin and Yang,* Zhang had already given that to Sun Youyue.

I have already retrieved these texts and stored them in the Loft for Illumining [the Numinous]. Zhang said, "At that time I also had a number of scrolls, including the *Winding Immaculate,* the *Golden Perfected,* and the *Gold Flower.*[137] These scrolls were rotted, full of

134. These are three distinct methods often appearing side by side in several Shang-qing writings. The five vital governing spirits 五神 of the body are Grand Unity 太一, Nonpareil 無英, White Prime 白元, Director of Destiny 司命, and Peach Vigor 桃康. (See Robinet, *Taoist Meditation,* 100–101 and Bokenkamp, *Early Daoist Scriptures,* 384–85.) The twenty-four spirits, called the "eight phosphors of the three primes" 三元八景 in their perfected state, are eight in each of the three regions of the body, centering on the forehead, the heart, and an area below the navel. Knowing their names and how to convene them is a method preparatory to other Shangqing practices. "Returning to the Origin" 廻元 is a method of erasing one's transgressions from the books of life with the aid of the stars of the Dipper. (For these latter methods, see Robinet, *La révélation,* 2:67–81.)

135. The *Songs of Yin and Yang of the Eight Immaculates* 八素陰陽歌 are songs praising and activating the Eight Immaculates, feminine deities who stand as counterpart to the Eight Phosphors. Sometimes the Eight Immaculates are presented as chariots of cloud, metonymic for the deities who ride in them. (See Robinet, *La révélation,* 2:51–57.) A version of these fifteen songs, nine *yang* and six *yin,* can be found at DZ 1138, 20.4b–8b. See also Schipper, *L'Empereur,* 54–58.

136. There is no further information on Zhang Lingmin.

137. The *Winding Immaculate* 曲素 seems to be a shortened form of the title Decisive Lyrics of the Winding Immaculate, which the *Declarations* elsewhere describes as a text that can be used to command the demons of the unholy Six Heavens. (See DZ 1016, 5.3b, and DZ 1032, 8.21a–b; for information on the current version of this text, see Robinet, *La révélation,* 2:187–90.) The *Golden Perfected* 金眞 most likely refers to the Jade Beams of the Golden Perfected 金眞玉光, mentioned in the *Declarations* (DZ 1016, 5.4b). On DZ 1378, the surviving version that contained this text, see Robinet, *La révélation,* 2:45–49. The *Gold Flower* 金華 seems to have been an authentic early Shangqing scripture, but all that survives now are late recensions. Robinet holds that surviving versions date to the seventh century at the earliest and DZ 253, the most likely candidate, seems later than that. (See Robinet, *La révélation,* 2:264 and 282–83.)

holes, and torn, and I did not yet recognize that they were autograph manuscripts. I did not know how to paste them together or copy them precisely, so I merely copied out their wording and buried the texts themselves."

掾書太素五神二十四神。并廻元隱道經一卷。及八素陰陽歌一卷。竝東陽章靈民先出都，遇得之。章于時未識眞書。唯言是道家常經而已。歸東陽以示顧。顧不即向道，仍留之。分廻元爲二卷。章後既知，方就求得。今在章間。其二景歌一卷。章已與孫公。（已還封昭臺。章云：于時又有曲素金眞〈舍〉［金］華等數卷，魚爛穿壞。既未悟其眞手。不知擒錄，惟寫取文字而已。經本悉埋藏之也）

A copy of the *Annals*, written on yellow silk by Xu Hui to carry on his person, one short scroll.[138] Originally Xu Huangmin gave this text to his disciple Su Daohui 蘇道會. Daohui gave it He Faren 何法仁 of Shangwu, who transmitted it to Zhu Sengbiao.[139] Sengbiao presented it to the Ritual Master Zhong Yishan 鍾義山. The recluse Lou Huiming 樓惠明 saw it and requested it. It is probably still in his possession.

掾書所佩列紀黃素書一短卷。本許丞以與弟子蘇道會。道會以授上虞何法仁。法仁以傳朱僧標。僧標以奉鍾法師。樓居士見而求取。今猶應在樓間。

Passages from the *Scripture of the Yellow Court* copied from the *Traditions of Lady Wei* and several sheets of Perfected revelation, copied out by Xu Hui.[140] These were first in the possession of Wang Huilang 王惠

138. The *Annals of the Sage Lord of the Dao of the Latter Heavens* 後聖道君列紀 tells of the impending arrival of Li Hong 李弘, the deity who will descend from the heavens to separate the electi, or "seed people" 重民, from the wicked at the end of the present world age. At some point, this text was joined together with others under the title, *Purple Texts Inscribed by the Spirits* 靈書紫文. See the translation and study in Bokenkamp, *Early Daoist Scriptures*, 295–99 and 339–62. As the Lord himself promises in this text: "By wearing my *Annals* at your sash, you may pass unscathed through calamity and pestilence, flood, fire, and warfare. None of the myriad sprites of the mountains and forests or the multiple forms of perversity and disaster will dare stand against you. When others see you, they will be filled with joy. This is because the writing is attended by Jade Lads that might protect your person. If evil persons malevolently drive you off or curse you, I will send the holy spirits of the mountains and streams to take their lives" (Bokenkamp, *Early Daoist Scriptures*, 352).

139. We have no further information on either Su or He.

140. The *Scripture of the Yellow Court* 黃庭經 is a book in seven-character verse on the gods of the body and actualizations for nurturing them. The "outer" book is actually the oldest, dating back to the third century, while the "inner" book is a revision associated with Wei Huacun. (See Robinet, "*Huangting jing*.") The *Traditions of Lady Wei* 魏夫人傳 was said to have been composed by Fan Miao 范邈 and included the *Scripture of the Yellow Court*. The version that appears here might be that mentioned by Xu Hui in a dream, dated 366. (See Chang Ch'ao-jan, *Xipu*, 173–77.)

朗 in the Shan mountains. After he died, they likely went to his female disciple and his fellow student Zhang Lingmin 章靈民.

捃抄魏傳中黃庭經。并復眞授數紙。先在剡山王惠朗間。王亡後，今應是其女弟子及同學章靈民處。

In Yongxing there is a family named Xie 解 that, through supporting Xu Huangmin long ago, acquired a few small bits of miscellaneous writings. Later, the female Daoist of Jing Mountain, Fan Miaoluo 樊妙羅, was destined to obtain their single scroll in Yang's hand relating the matter of the Palaces of Fengdu.[141] When she died, it remained with her female disciple Shen Ou 沈偶. Shen gave it to Kong Zong 孔總 of Mount Siming.[142]

> I have already retrieved this text and stored it in the Loft for Illumining [the Numinous].

永興有一姓解家者，昔亦經供養許郎，又得小小雜書。後菁山女道士樊妙羅，因緣得其楊書酆宮事一卷。樊亡，在其女弟子沈偶間。沈又以與四明山孔總。（已還封昭臺。）

The remainder of the texts in the possession of the Xie family have now vanished without a trace. I have also heard that several families in Shanyin and Qiantang have ancient writings that I suspect may have missing texts or be intermingled with original manuscripts. But until now I have not had the opportunity to search them out and verify them. I hope that some studious person with an outstanding allotment might strenuously seek them out.[143] Were such a person to view these texts, he or she would at a glance be able to distinguish gems from dross.

> Moreover, when the younger son of Lady Wei, [Liu] Xia 劉遐 was prefect of Guiji, he took along the Lady's writing box and ritual robes, together with some scriptures and writings for his own worship. Later, he left these in Shanyin. Today they are still there. I have not yet been able to seek them out.

解家所餘，今絕蹤迹。又聞山陰及錢塘數家皆有古經。恐脫雜眞書。從來遂未獲尋檢，想好學挺分之子，可殷勤求之，脫有所得見，使一覩則

---

141. The account of the underworld palaces of Fengdu 酆都宮 and the bureaucracy that staffed them is preserved in the *Declarations* (DZ 1016, 15–16).

142. Kong Zong seems not to have been a very inspiring figure, but he was able to compose poetry to match the reed-organ stylings of his slave. (See Bumbacher, *Fragments*, 331 and Li Yanshou, *Nan shi*, 75.1881–82.)

143. The term 挺分 literally "outstanding allotment," implies celestial selection.

瓊礫辨矣。（又魏夫人小息〈還〉［退］爲會稽時，攜夫人〈中〉［巾］箱
法衣，并有經書，自隨供養。後仍留山陰。于今尚在。未獲尋求之。）

. . .

TRANSLATION: GENEALOGY OF THE
PERFECTED FOREBEARS

Tao Hongjing's account of the persons involved in the revelations is the best
account we have of their lives. He begins with Xu Mi's sixth generation ancestor. This is curious in that, according to Daoist belief, it was the seventh-
generation ancestor whose fate was most closely connected to one's own.
When we finally come to a record of Xu Mi's seventh-generation ancestor, we
find that there is a discrepancy between the name found in the *Declarations*
and that of the family records. While in some cases this would elicit an
attempt at explanation from Tao, here he simply notes the fact and does not
inquire further. –Trans.

. . .

As this account is written today it is appropriate to call them
"Perfected Forebears."

眞冑世譜。（此是今日伸述。故可稱眞冑。）

*Senior Officer Xu's sixth-generation forebear was named Guang 光
and had the byname Shaozhang少張. He was the fifth son of the Minister over the Multitudes, Xu Jing 許敬. At the time of the Numinous
Thearch [of the Han, Liu Hong 劉宏, r. 168–189], his elder brother Xun
訓 and Xun's son Xiang 相 belonged to a faction that attached itself to
the palace eunuchs and had therefore become well known and rich.[144]
Xu Guang worried that trouble was imminent so, in the second year of
the Central Peace reign period (185) he crossed the Yangzi River and
took residence in Jiyang Village, county seat of Jurong in Danyang. In
the early years of the Wu Kingdom (222–80), he was granted the rank
of Chamberlain of Shining and Meritorious Achievement. The present

---

144. Fan Ye's *Hou Hanshu* (68.2234–35) contains a brief biography of Xu Jing's
nephew, Xu Shao 許劭. This account provides the information that Xu Jing, together with
his son and grandson, served as the "Three Ministers," the inner cabinet of the emperor.
On several occasions, they invited Shao to join their clique. Shao refused. It is likely that
the existence of this clique is the "trouble" 患 that Xu Guang feared.

"Grave of Xu the Shining and Meritorious" is his. At the time of Xu Zhao 許肇, the family still lived in Pingyu of Runan.[145]

[Gu] Huan mentions "Zi'a 子阿 of Jurong County." This is wrong.

謹按許長史六世祖名光字少張，即司徒許敬之第五子也。靈帝時，兄訓及訓子相，並儻附閹人貴盛。光懼患及，以中平二年乙丑歲來渡江，居丹陽之句容縣都鄉吉楊里。後值　吳初，事爲光祿勳。今許光祿墓是也。則肇時猶居汝南平輿。（顧云。句容子阿。謬矣。）

The *Declarations of the Perfected* says that the seventh-generation ancestor of the Senior Officer was Xu Zhao 許肇, with the byname Zia 子阿.[146] Now, examining the family genealogy, we find that his seventh-generation ancestor was Jing 敬, with the byname Hongqing 鴻卿. Xu Jing was Chamberlain of the Shining and Meritorious during the time of the Pacific Thearch of the Latter Han [Liu Hu 劉祜, r. 106–125]. In the first year of the Eternally Established reign (126) of the Compliant Thearch [Liu Bao 劉保, r. 126–144], he was named Minister over the Multitudes.[147] This name is different from that in the *Declarations of the Perfected*. I do not know the reason for the discrepancy. There was a great famine in the second and third year of Beginning of Eternity reign of the Pacific Thearch [108–109].[148] Rice was two thousand cash per peck and people ate one another. The four hundred eight persons that Xu Mi's seventh-generation ancestor saved must have been during this time. Ying Shao's 應邵 (153–196) *Ceremonials of Han Officialdom* records a memorial from Cui Yuan 崔瑗 that said: "when Xu Jing was nearly one hundred years of age, he still occupied the position of Minister."[149] In this fashion Jing's hidden merit not only flowed down to his descendants, but his manifest merit also was known throughout the generations. This is why his years were long and his body remained healthy.[150] His own rank

---

145. The Xu clan's native place was Pingyu 平輿 in Runan 汝南, the southeastern region of modern-day Henan Province.

146. See DZ 1016, 4.11a and 12.3a. This is a matter of some moment, since one's fate was held to be particularly tied to the deeds of the seventh-generation ancestor. But Tao says no more than that the Perfected were mistaken.

147. Xu Jing's promotion is recorded in Fan, *Hou Hanshu* (6.254), as is his removal from the office three years later (6.257).

148. DZ 296, 21.13b–14a, has only the second year (108).

149. This work no longer survives and I have been unable to locate the cited reference in the reconstituted work. Xu Jing is, however, mentioned at *Hou Hanshu*, 6.254 and 6.257.

150. This also implies that no one wanted or dared to injure him.

reached that of one of the Three Ministers.[151] His son Xun 訓 and grandson Xiang 相 were both members of the Three Ministers. Further, after Xu Guang crossed the Yangzi, the descendants carried on the tradition for generations to the point of becoming divine Transcendents.

The Minister over the Multitudes of the Kingdom of Shu, Xu Jing 許靖, with the byname 文休 was a sixth-generation ancestor of the Senior Officer.[152] The Han Dynasty Official Recruit Xu Shao 許劭, with the byname Zijiang 子將, is a fifth-generation ancestor.[153] The Chancellor Xu Yan 許晏, with the byname Xiaoran 孝然, is a fourth-generation ancestor.[154] All of these men descend from [Xu Mi's] eleventh-generation ancestor, the Inciting Notary of Jiaozhou, who served under the Brilliant and Marshal Thearch (r. 25–29 CE). The Notary's son was named Shengqing 聖卿. The clan name Xu came from the Jiang clan 姜氏 of the time of the Blazing Thearch. Then the Martial King of the Zhou enfeoffed Xu Shu 許叔 in the region of Xu, which corresponds to present-day Xuchang of Yuzhou. In the fifteenth year of the Respectful King of the Zhou [trad. 505 BCE], this kingdom was destroyed by the Kingdom of Zheng. At that time, the family went into exile in Changyi of Shanyang and took their old kingdom name as a surname. It was at the time of the [Inciting Notary] of Jiaozhou that they moved to Pingyu in Runan.

眞誥云。長史七世祖肇字子阿，有振惠之功。今檢譜，七世祖名敬字鴻卿。後漢安帝時爲 光祿。順帝永建元年拜司徒。名字與眞誥不同。未詳所以舛異。安帝永初二年三年大饑。 斗米二千文，人相食。若所救活四百八人，必應在此時也。應邵漢官儀載崔瑗表云：許敬年且百歲，猶居相位。如此非唯陰德遠流後胤。敬〈目〉[自] 陽功著世。[155] 所以年永身安，位至台鼎。子訓孫相，並爲三公。光來過江，奕世丕承，遂至神仙。 （蜀司徒許靖，字文休，是長史六世族祖。漢徵士許劭，字子將，是五世族祖。丞相許晏，字孝然，四世族祖。並同承十一世祖。光

151. The term "step and tripod" 台鼎 is metonymic for the Three Ministers 三公, offices at the apex of court administration: Minister of Instruction 司徒, Minister of Works 司空, and Grand Marshal 太尉. The term comes from a line in Cai Yong's 蔡邕 (133–92) "Memorial Stele for Grand Marshal Li of Runan" 《太尉汝南李公碑》: Heaven suspends [the Constellation] three steps, earth establishes the five Marchmounts. These gave birth to our Worthy, appropriate to be one leg of the tripod." 天垂三台，地建五岳，降生我哲，應鼎之足。 See Yiwen leiju, 46.820.
152. Xu Jing has a biography in Chen Shou, Sanguo zhi, 38.963–69.
153. An "Official Recruit" 徵士 is someone nominated by local officials and called to the capital to possibly take office. Xu Shao's biography is to be found at Fan Ye, Hou Hanshu, 68.2234–35.
154. Xu Yan served Sun Quan 孫權 (182–252), emperor of the Wu Kingdom, and was decapitated in 233 on a diplomatic mission to the Wei Kingdom. (See Chen Shou, Sanguo zhi, 3.101 and 47.1138–39.)
155. Replacing 交 with 敬 after DZ 295, 21.13b.

武時許交州，後交相子名聖卿。許姓本出炎帝時姜氏。至周武王封許
叔於許。今豫州許昌也。至周敬王十五年，爲鄭所滅。徙居山陽昌
邑。因國爲姓。至交州乃移於汝南平輿也）

Jing's father was named Fu 甹 and he was a Clerk in a Duke's Offices.

敬父名甹。公府掾。

Jing's fifth son was named Guang 光 with the byname Shaozhang 少張.
He crossed the Yangzi and, at the beginning of the Wu Kingdom, was
appointed Chamberlain of Shining and Meritorious Achievement.

His principal wife was of the Dai 戴 clan. They are buried together in
Ancheng Village of Jurong. The tomb is the first [Xu tomb south of
the Yangzi]. The people of the county call it the "Grave of Xu the
Shining and Meritorious." Even today the tumulus and the stele
inscriptions are clearly defined. The tomb faces the *jia* direction
[East].

敬第五子名光，字少張。尚書郎鉅鹿太守少府卿。過江，值吳初，爲
光祿勳。（妻戴氏。同葬今句容安成里。墓爲刱造之始。縣人傳呼云
許光祿墓。今墳碑顯然。竝甲向。）

Guang's second son was named Que 闕, with the byname Jiyou 季優.
He was learned and talented. The Wu kingdom named him Squire of
the Imperial Secretariat and Commandant of Changshui.[156]

His wife was of the Dai 戴 clan. They are buried together.

光第二子名闕，字季優。有才學。吳尚書郎。長水校尉。（妻戴氏。
同葬墓次。）

Guang's third son was named Xiu with the byname Wenlie. He roamed
freely in the purity of the Dao, maintaining loftiness and purity. The
District appointed him to the position of aide-de-camp, but he did not
take the post.

His first wife was of the Hua 華 family of Jinling. Later he married a
woman of the Ge 葛 family of the same county. She was the daughter
of the Palace Attendant Ge Xiang 葛相, and they are buried together.

闕第三子名休，字文烈。優遊道素。高尚其氣。州辟別駕。不就。（前
妻晉陵華氏。後妻同縣葛氏。侍中葛相女。同葬墓次。）

156. This rank was established during the Han dynasty, but by this time was discon-
nected from the place-name Changshui.

Xiu's eldest son, Shang 尚 with the byname Yuanfu 元甫, was renowned
for his talent and learning. In the third year of the Phoenix reign period
of the Wu Kingdom [274], he was appointed Squire of the Palace Secretariat. He died at fifty years of age.

His wife was of the Tao 陶 clan of the same commandery. She was
the daughter of Tao Jun 陶濬, the Regional Inspector of Jingzhou.
They are buried together.

休長子名尚，字元甫。有才學令聞。吳鳳凰三年，爲中書郎。年五十
亡。（妻同郡陶氏。即荊州刺史陶濬女。同葬墓次。）

Shang's second son, Fu 副 with the byname Zhongxian仲先, was the
child of a secondary wife. This was the Senior Officer's father. He was
honest, affable, and known for virtue throughout the District and even
the Commandery. The Primal Thearch of the Jin [Sima Rui 司馬睿, r.
317–22] appointed him military advisor in Andong and, concurrently,
military advisor for the Northern Campaign and Grand Warden of Xia-
pei. Later he was made General of Ningshuo and, together with Kong
Tan 孔坦 (286–336), conquered [the rebel] Shen Chong 沈充 (d. 324).[157]
He was enfeoffed as Marquis of Xicheng County and took office as
Magistrate of Shan. He was stylish and often roamed with Xie Yi 謝奕
(d. 358) and his younger brother [Xie An 謝安, 320–85].[158] When the Su
Jun 蘇峻 (d. 328) rebellion broke out [in 327], he took his clan to Shan.
When the uprising had been quelled [the next year], he was appointed
Defender of Chariots. He died at the age of seventy-seven *sui*.

Fu's first wife was Hua Zhuan 華轉, the younger sister of Hua Qi 華
琦, the Palace Aide to the Censor. His second wife was Ying Laizi 應
來子, daughter of Ying Yanhui 應彥徽, Grand Warden of Jinling.
They are buried in a large tumulus south of the county seat.

尚第二子名副，字仲先。庶生。即長史之父也。淳和美懿。州郡所
稱。爲晉元帝安東參軍。又 征北參軍。帶下邳太守。後爲寧朔將軍。
與孔坦討沈充。封西城縣侯。出爲剡令。有風化。與謝奕兄弟周旋。
值蘇峻亂，又攜親族往剡。事平，還拜奉車都尉。年七十七亡。（前
妻晉陵華氏名轉。御史中丞華琦妹也。後妻應氏名來子。竟陵太守應
彥徽女。同葬縣北大墓也。）

157. Shen Chong participated in the rebellion of Wang Dun 王敦 (266–324), and
Kong Dan was instrumental in defeating him. See Fang Xuanling, *Jinshu* 78.2055–56.
158. On these important officials, see Mather, *New Account*, 526–27.

Fu had eight sons. The first was Xu Fen 奮, with the alternate name Shou 守 and the byname Xiaofang 孝方. He was born of a secondary wife. He had both military and civil talents. He was given as stepson to his paternal uncle Xu Chao and served as the military advisor to He Cidao 何次道 (= He Chong, 242–346).[159] Later, he was slandered by his younger stepbrother Yiwu 夷吾, and the Robust Thearch [Sima Yue 司馬岳, r. 342–44] had him executed. He was thirty-six *sui*.

His wife was surnamed Wang. They are buried together in a large
tumulus north of the county seat. He had a great grandson named
Huizhi 薈之 who reached the rank of Grand Minister.

副有八男。第一奮，一名守，字孝方。庶生。有文武才望。出繼权父朝。爲何次道參軍。後爲所後弟夷吾所譖。康帝誅之。年三十六。(妻王氏。〈墓〉[同] 葬縣北大墓。有曾孫薈之。位至三府。)

Fu's second son was named Zhao, with the byname Xingming. He was a child of Fu's principal wife, and so he inherited his father's rank. He was open, generous, and considered extremely capable by those of his generation. He also served He Cidao as military advisor. He held the posts of Attendant Censor of Nantai and Grand Warden of Huailing. He died at the age of seventy-one *sui*.

His wife was surnamed You 游. She is buried separately east of the
county seat in Heliu village.

第二炤，字行明。正生。承嫡襲封。通濟有當世局度。亦爲何次道參軍。南臺侍御史。淮陵太守。年七十一亡。(妻游氏。別葬縣東合留村。)

His third son, named Qun 群 with the byname Taihe 太和, was also a child of Fu's principal wife. He was intelligent and talented. He served Yu Tan 虞譚 as military advisor and died at the age of forty-four *sui*.

His wife was a member of the Liyang Shao 邵 clan. They are buried
together in the great tumulus north of the county seat.

第三群，字太和。正生。明爽有才幹。爲虞譚參軍。年四十四亡。(妻歷陽邵氏。同葬縣北大墓。)

His fourth son was Xu Mai 邁, the Prior-born.

第四邁。即先生也。

159. On He Chong, see Mather, *New Account*, 522.

Fu's fifth son was the Senior Officer, who was also born of the principal wife. His biography is recorded below.

第五某。即長史也。並同正生。別記在後。

Fu's sixth son was Maoxuan 茂玄. Born of a secondary wife, he died young.

His mother was surnamed Chen 陳.

第六茂玄。庶生。早亡。（母姓陳也。）

Fu's seventh son was Que 礭, with the byname Yixuan 義玄 and the youthful name Sibo 嗣伯. He was the son of a secondary wife.

His mother was surnamed 朱Zhu.

第七礭，字義玄，小名嗣伯。庶生。（母姓朱也。）

Que was given as stepson to his paternal uncle, Xu Jie 捷.[160] As a person, he was resolute, expansive, and delighted in learning. His first post was to serve Huan Wen 桓溫 (312–73) as retainer in Yangzhou.[161] He served Xie An as Military Advisor of the Guards and performed meritorious service under Xie Xuan 謝玄 (343–88) in the attack on Fu Jian 符堅 (338–85).[162] He was then enfeoffed as Watchlord of Fengdu and granted the titles Gentleman of the Granaries Section and Riders Section of the Imperial Secretariat, Cavalry Commandant, and Attendant-in-Ordinary for General Duties. Later, he was wind-struck and could not speak.[163] He died in the second year of the Resurgent Peace reign [398] at the age of seventy.

His wife was of the Ji 紀 clan of Xuancheng and is buried together with him in the large tumulus north of the county seat.

出後伯父捷。梗概有大度。好學。出爲桓溫楊州從事。謝安衞軍參軍。隨謝玄討符堅有功。封都鄉侯。尚書蒼部駕部郎。正員郎。通直常侍。後患風不能言。隆安二年亡。年七十。（妻宣城紀氏。同葬縣北大墓。）

160. Lü Pengzhi (personal communication, 28 January 2020) suggests that 出後 should be read 出繼, to give as stepson to a relative so as to continue the lineage.

161. For a brief biography of Huan Wen, the general who ruled from behind the throne, see Mather, *New Account*, 536–37.

162. Xie Xuan was the nephew of Xie An and served as general under Huan Wen. Fu Jian was the emperor of the Northern Qin dynasty who reigned from 358 to 385, when he was defeated by Xie Xuan at the head of Jin forces. For brief biographies, see Mather, *New Account*, 527 and 520.

163. The term "troubled by the wind" 患風 likely describes a stroke.

Fu's eighth son was Lingbao 靈寶. He was born of a secondary wife and died young.

He was also the son of the wife surnamed Chen 陳.

第八靈寶。庶生。早亡。（母亦姓陳。）

Fu had four daughters.

The eldest, born of his principal wife, was named Qiang 姜 and died young. The second, also a daughter of the principal wife, was named Ehuang 娥皇. She married Huang Yan 黃演, the prefect of her native prefecture, Jiankang.[164] The third daughter, Xiurong 修容, was born of a secondary wife surnamed Zhang 張. She married the prefect of An'gu, Hong Sheng 弘升 of the Jinling Hongs. The fourth daughter, Huirong 暉容, was Que's twin. She married Ji Quan 紀詮 of Jurong.

副有四女。（長女名姜。正生。早亡。第二女名娥皇。正生。出適同郡建康令黃演。第三女名修容。庶生。母姓張。出適安固　令晉陵弘升。第四女名暉容。與礭同生。出適同郡紀詮也）

Fu's younger brother was named Chao 朝, with the byname Yangxian 楊先. He was fierce and known for his martial valor. He was, successively, Grand Warden of Xiangyang, Xinye, Nanyang, and Xunyang. Later, together with Gan Zhuo 甘卓 (d. 322) he plotted to attack Wang Dun 王敦 (266–324).[165] The matter was discovered, Zhuo died, and Chao committed suicide. He was fifty-three *sui*.

His body was returned to be buried in the large tumulus north of the county seat. His wife was the daughter of Ge Ti 葛悌, who was the elder sister of "He Who Embraces Simplicity" [Ge Hong 葛洪, ca. 283–343].[166] At first they raised Fen 奮 as their child, but later they gave birth to Yiwu 夷吾 and Gaozi 高子. Both died young. They had no progeny.

副弟名朝，字楊先。勇猛以氣俠聞。歷爲襄陽新野南陽潯陽太守。後與甘卓謀討王敦。事　覺卓死。朝自裁。年五十三。（還葬縣北大墓。妻葛悌女。抱朴姊也。　初養奮。後自生夷吾高子。竝又（幼）亡。無後。）

164. For a foretaste of the fate of this couple, which will appear in a later volume of this translation, see Bokenkamp, *Ancestors and Anxiety*, 130–57.

165. General Gan Zhuo's biography is to be found in Fang Xuanling, *Jinshu*, 70.1862–66. For a brief biography of Wang Dun, another powerful opportunist, see Mather, *New Account*, 596.

166. Ge Ti is mentioned as Hong's father in Fang Xuanling, *Jinshu*, 72.1911.

The Prior-born was named Mai 邁 and had the byname Shuxuan 叔玄. His youth name was Ying 映. Pure and vacuous, he embosomed the Dao and took distant lodging beyond the generations of humanity. So he changed his name to Yuanyou ["roaming afar"]. He had cordial relations with General of the Right Wang [Xizhi] and his sons [Xianzhi and Huizhi]. Ziyou [Wang Huizhi] even accorded him the threefold respect [due a father, a teacher, and a ruler].[167] According to his hand copy on his reception of the "Talisman of the Six *Jia* Yin and Yang," he was twenty-three *sui* in the first year of the Eternally Robust reign [322] and so was born in the *xingyou* year, the first of the Eternally Vigorous reign [300].[168] The family genealogy says that traces of him vanished at West Mountain of Lin'an in the autumn of the fourth year of the Eternally Harmonious reign period [348], when he was forty-eight. This would mean that he was born in the first year of the Eternally Stable reign period [301], but he was forty-nine *sui* when he disappeared.

先生名邁，字叔玄，小名映。清虛懷道。遐棲世外。故自改名遠遊。與王右軍父子周旋。子猷乃修在三之敬。按手書授六甲陰陽符云。永昌元年，年二十三歲，則是永康元年庚申歲生也。而譜云：永和四年秋。絕迹於臨安西山。年四十八。此則永寧元年辛酉生。爲少一年。今以自記爲正。絕迹時年四十九矣。

Xu Mai married the daughter of Sun Hong 孫宏, byname Yanda 彥達, of Wu Commandery. [Sun Yanda] was the grandson of Cavalry General Sun Xiu 孫秀 (fl. ca. 300 CE).[169] When [Mai] parted from his wife, there were no children to return to the lineage. As for the Prior-born's achieving the Dao, this is fully described in the second chapter [of the *Zhen'gao*] when the Certifier of Registers [Mao Gu] instructs by means of the story of the tests undergone by Xu Mai.

娶吳郡孫宏，字彥達，女。即驃騎秀之孫。既離好。無子歸宗。先生得道。事迹在第二卷中，定錄所喻被試事，已具載焉。

---

167. The phrase "threefold" is based on a passage in the *Guoyu* 國語: "The livelihood of the people arises from three positions; they should be served in the same way—fathers give birth to them; Masters instruct them; Rulers provide food for them 民生於三，事之如一.' 父生之，師教之，君食之。 (*Guoyu*, Jinyu, 7.1b, SKQS ed.)

168. On Xu Mai's reception of the "Talisman of Six Jia" from the Libationer Li Dong 李東, see Lü Pengzhi, *Tangqian*, 100.

169. Sun Xiu, a Celestial Master follower, was an official in the Western Jin (Mather, "Chinese Letters," 605).

The Senior Officer was named Mi 謐, with the byname Sixuan 思玄 and the alternate name Mu 穆. He was born of the principal wife and became well known while still young. Scholarly, elegant, and pure, he had wide learning and possessed of literary talent. The emperor [posthumously styled] the Frugal and Cultured [Sima Yu 司馬昱, r. 371–72] deigned to take him under his protection for a lengthy period of time. Xu Mi had friendships with a number of worthies of the time. When he was young, he served the Commandery as Senior Recorder and Merit Officer. When Wang Dao 王導 (276–339) and Cai Mo 蔡謨 (281–356) were in Linchuan, they wanted to appoint him as retainer, but he would not take the post. He was selected to fill the post of Erudite in the Imperial College and became prefect of Yuyao, Squire of the Imperial Secretariat, Commandery Rectifier, Senior Officer Protector of the Army, Palace Steward, and Cavalier Attendant-in-Ordinary. Even though he outwardly mixed in the affairs of the world, he practiced the study of Perfection within. He secretly transmitted teachings and records and reverently practiced the higher Way. As a result of his remarkable allotment, he became a Shangqing Perfected with a rank equal to that of Marquis or Earl, a Chamberlain Overseer, charged with aiding in the rule of Transcendents and to aid the Sage in leading the people.[170]

長史名謐，字思玄，一名穆。正生。少知名。儒雅清素。博學有才章。簡文皇帝久垂俗表之顧。與時賢多所儔結。少仕郡主簿功曹史。王導蔡謨臨川辟從事不赴。選補太學博士。出爲餘姚令。入爲尚書郎。郡中正。護軍長史。給事中。散騎常侍。雖外混俗務而內修眞學。密授教記，遵行上道。挺分所得，乃爲上清眞人。爵登侯伯，位編卿司。治仙佐治，助聖牧民。

I note that in the second year of Grand Harmony, when the year was in *dingmao* [367], the Director of Destinies announced that [Xu Mi] should depart in the *bingzi* year [376]. At that time, [Xu] was seventy-one *sui*, which means that he was born in the *yichou* year, the second year of the Eternally Flourishing reign [305], and departed in the first year of the Grand Prime reign period [376]. And yet the family genealogy says that he died in the first year of the Filial and Martial Thearch's [Sima Yao 司马曜, r. 372–96; so 373) Tranquil Vigor reign at seventy-one *sui*. This would mean that he was born in the *guihai* year, second

---

170. The "Sage" is not specified, but is likely to be the messianic Li Hong, the sage of the latter age.

year of Grand Peace [303], but this is two years too early. I take the Perfected's announcement to be correct.

Gu Huan says that Xu departed in the first year of the Tranquil Vigor period at the age of seventy-two, this is also incorrect.

按泰和二年丁卯歲，司命所告云：丙子年當去。時年七十二。此則永興二年乙丑生。太元元年去也。而譜云：孝武寧康元年去世，年七十一。此爲泰安二年癸亥生。爲多二年。今以眞爲 正。（顧云。寧康元年。七十二。又非也。）

[Xu Mi] married the daughter of Tao Wei 陶威 of the same commandery. Her name was Kedou 科斗. She died during the Ascending Tranquility reign (363–65) and then entered the Palace of Mutation and Promotion to receive instruction.[171]

She is buried together with him in the old grave two li northwest of the county seat.

妻同郡陶威女。名科斗。興寧中亡。即入易遷宮受學。（同葬縣西北二里舊墓。）

The Senior Officer had three sons and one daughter. His eldest son was named Quan 𡿭, with the youth name Kui 揆. He was born of a secondary wife and served as the Commandery Merit Officer. He married a woman of the Liu 劉 clan. Their youngest son, named Fengyou 鳳遊 was the Commandery Senior Recorder. Fengyou's son was Daofu 道伏 with the byname Mingzhi 明之. Mingzhi's youngest son was Jingtai 靜泰, with the byname Yuanbao 元寶, and he served as the prefect of Haiping County. He resided for a long time on Mount Yu's Well in Guiji and reverentially inherited the ritual practices of his family. He received and transmitted [Shangqing] scriptures, but only made tracings.[172] Jingtai married a woman of the Ge family of the same commandery. They had only one son who they named Lingzhen ["holy Perfected"]. He was born in the *xuwu* year [478] and still resides in Guiji. Lingzhen venerates and upholds the Daoist enterprise and is skilled at talismans and calligraphy. The Senior Officer has only this single sixth-generation male descendant.[173]

171. The Palace of Mutation and Promotion 易遷宮 is the underworld study center for women.

172. This probably implies that he did not practice the contents of the scriptures (Lü Pengzhi, personal communication, 28 January 2020).

173. Calculating this is important to Tao Hongjing, since the seventh-generation ancestor was believed to have a special relationship with a person. Lingzhen's son could

長史三男一女。長男名䣄，小名揆。庶生。郡〈公〉[功]曹。妻劉
氏。少子名鳳遊。郡主簿。鳳遊子道伏，字明之。明之少子靜泰，字
元寶。爲海平縣令。久居會稽禹井山。頗遵承家法。傳受經書。皆摹
而已。靜泰妻同郡葛氏。唯有一子名靈眞。戊午生。今猶在會稽。亦
敦尚道業。善能符書。自長史後。唯有此六世孫一人而已。

The Senior Officer's second son was named Lian 聯, with the byname
Yuanhui 元暉 and the youth name Huya 虎牙 [tiger tooth]. He was
born of [Xu Mi's] principal wife and was honest and trusting. He served
as the Senior Recorder and Merit Officer for the Commandery and was
made Protector of the Army by Xie An. He was again made Merit
Officer and then was appointed successively as prefect of Yongkang,
chamberlain for the Palace Garrison, and Grand Warden of Jinkang,
but he did not take the posts. He did however serve as Commander in
Support of the Kingdom. In the third year of the Primal Flourishing
reign of the Pacific Thearch [of the Jin, Sima Dezong 司馬德宗, r. 396–
419; so 404], he died at home at the age of sixty-eight *sui*. This means
that he was born in the *dingyou* year, the third year of the Accomplished
Thearch's [Sima Yan 司馬衍, r. 325–42] Concordant Vigor reign [337].

Gu [Huan] says that he was born in the third year of the Concordant
Harmony reign [328]. This is another huge mistake!

中男名聯，字元暉，少名虎牙。正生。敦厚信向。郡主簿功曹。謝安
爲護軍。又引爲功曹。除永　康令。衞尉丞。晉康太守。不之官。又爲
輔國司馬。安帝元興三年，於家去世。年六十八。則成　帝咸康三年丁
酉歲生也。（顧云。咸和三年生。亦大謬。）

[Xu Lian] married a granddaughter of Hua Qi 華琦 of Jinling named
Zirong 子容.

They are buried together in Xin'an Village on the border of
Jiang-Sheng.

妻晉陵華琦孫。名子容。（同葬江乘界新安里中。）

Their child is named Chisun 赤孫, with the byname Xuanzhen 玄眞. He
is earnest, composed, and reclusive. He served as Senior Recorder

---

thus have proven to be the new Xu Mi. But as Strickmann notes ("Mao Shan," 56n131),
he apparently disappointed his mentor. In 516, Tao, in assessing who among those on
Mount Mao might be destined for Transcendence, wrote that Lingzhen had "family involvements and was not able to fully involve himself in the Study" 有家累亦未得涉學.
(See DZ 302, 3.8b4.)

and Merit Officer for the Commandery. He died at the age of seventy-four *sui*.

There were four sons and grandsons who all died young. They have no descendants alive today.

子赤孫，字玄眞。篤實和隱。郡主簿功曹。年七十四亡。有四子及孫
並早亡。今無後也。

The Senior Officer's youngest son is named Hui 翽, with the byname Daoxiang 道翔 and the youth name Yufu 玉斧 [jade axe]. Even as a youth, he was of outstanding merit and truly exceptional. The Senior Officer regarded him as special and valued him. In the commandery, he was made Accounts Clerk and Senior Recorder, but he did not take these posts. Of high aspirations and purity, he regarded the labors of the dusty world as chaff and husks. He dwelt below Leiping Mountain, where he practiced zealously.[174] He was ever determined to roam the cavern chambers early and did not wish to remain long among humans. As a result he visited the northern cavern, where he announced his end. Then he resided in the Square Source Hall at a cavern of Square Corner Mountain. He also frequented the Square Terrace of [Mount?] Siping. Thus, the Declarations of the Perfected say "even when a person of the hidden world is in the human world, there is joy in residing there." Also, a letter that Lord Yang sent to the Senior Officer asked "I do not know whether or not the hidden person of Square Corner Mountain has already set up that residence for himself at the door to the Palace of Mutation and Promotion?[175] Sixteen years after his death, Xu Hui was to cross over to the [Palaces of the] Eastern Flower, where he would receive documentation as a Transcendent Duke of Shangqing, Higher Minister at the Thearch's Levee.[176] The family genealogy says that he died at thirty *sui*, but does not record the year of his departure. According to the two verifications, he was to die in the *dingmao* year, the second year of the Grand Harmony reign [367] at the age of twenty-seven.

174. This means that he lived at the hermitage Xu Mi established on Mount Mao. See Pettit, "Learning from Mao Shan," 20ff.

175. See DZ 1016, 17.18a. Tao explains that Xu Hui wished to practice near to the residence of his recently deceased mother, Tao Kedou, who had moved on to this underworld study center.

176. For this prediction, see DZ 1016, 18.3b. This is the otherworldly residence of Director of Destinies Mao Ying.

That means that he was born in the *xingmao* year, the seventh year of Concordant Vigor [341].[177]

Gu Huan states that Xu Hui was born in the sixth year of the Concordant Harmony reign and also wrote that the Minister of Multitudes [Sima Yu] made him clerk. This is all false.

小男名翽，字道翔，小名玉斧。正生。幼有珪璋標挺。長史器異之。郡舉上計掾主簿。竝不赴。清秀瑩潔。糠粃塵務。居雷平山下。修業勤精，恆願早遊洞室。不欲久停人世，遂詣北洞告終。即居方隅山洞　方原館中。常去來四平方臺。故眞誥云：幽人在世時，心常樂居焉。又楊君與長史書亦云：　不審方隅山中幽人，爲己設坐於易遷戶中未。亡後十六年，當度往東華，受書爲上清仙公上相帝晨。譜云：年三十，而不記去歲。按二錄，泰和二年丁卯，時年二十七。則是咸寧七年辛卯生也。（顧云：咸和六年生。又云：司徒辟掾。皆爲非實。）

After the third year of Grand Harmony [368] we have no further traces of Xu Hui. According to the genealogy, he left the world at thirty *sui* in the *gengwu* year [370].

Also, the *Declarations of the Perfected* say that he employed the "night-time liberation method" of Queller of the South, Zhang [Lu 張魯, the third Celestial Master]. But I do not know what method of liberation Zhang used. According to the traditions passed on by aged persons [of the neighborhood], the Recorder [Xu Mi] offered incense and worshipped at a stone altar north of the northern cavern, then lay down and did not arise. The next day they looked at his body and it was if he were still alive. This altar still exists in unaltered shape. Thus, Xu Hui sought a method of concealment and transformation to leave early the dust of the world. The event is recorded in the second chapter.[178]

自泰和三年已後，無復蹤迹。依譜年三十。即是庚午年去世。（又眞誥云：從張鎭南之夜解，而未審張解之法。耆老傳云：掾乃在北洞北石壇上燒香禮拜，因伏而不起。明旦視形如生。此壇今猶存歷然。則是故求隱化。早絶世塵也。事別在第二卷中。）

Xu Hui's wife was the daughter of the prefect of Jiankang, Huang Yan 黄演. She was the child of his aunt Ehuang 娥皇, named Jingyi 敬儀. She

177. The *xingmao* year (331) was actually the sixth year of the Concordant Harmony reign, as Gu Huan claimed. There was a Concordant Tranquility reign during the Jin, but the seventh year of that reign would correspond to 281, had it lasted that long. I have corrected to what Tao seems to have meant, the *xingchou* year and the seventh year of Concordant Vigor.

178. See DZ 1016, 4.14a.

gave birth to Huangmin 黃民 and then was sent back to her home. Later, they divorced. Then she married the prefect of Yuanling Dai Shizhi 戴耆之.

妻建康令黃演女。即姑娥皇之子。名敬儀。生黃民。乃遣還家。後離絕。又出適宛陵令戴耆之。

The Senior Officer had one daughter, born to a secondary wife, named Suxun. She married Guang 廣, the son of Commandant of Surpassing Cavalry Huaying 華瑛, both of them Jinling Huas.

長史一女名素薰。庶生。出適越騎校尉晉陵華瑛子，名廣。

Xu Hui's son was named Huangmin 黃民, with the byname Xuanwen 玄文. He was born in the *xinyou* year, the fifth year of Ascendant Peace [361]. At that time, Xu Hui was twenty-one. Huangmin served as Commandery Senior Recorder. By means of official examination, he was found filial and incorruptible and served as aide to the National Treasury, military advisor on the Southern Man, and prefect of Linju. He died in the sixth year of the Song dynasty Primal Commendation reign [429], at the age of sixty-nine. His wife was the daughter of Ge Wan'an 葛萬安, prefect of Xiyang.

Ge Wan'an was the grandson of Baopuzi [Ge Hong's] second elder brother.

掾子黃〈名〉［民］，字玄文。升平五年辛酉生。時掾年二十一。仕郡主簿。察孝廉，司農丞。南蠻參軍。臨沮令。宋元嘉六年亡。年六十九。妻西陽令葛萬安女。（萬安是抱朴子第二兄孫也。）

Huangmin's eldest son was Rongdi 榮弟, with the alternate name Yuzhi 預之. He died in the twelfth year of Primal Commendation [435]. I do not know his age at death. He had a daughter named Daoyu 道育. She was born in the *dingyou* year, the first year of Resurgent Peace [397] and died on Mount Rendai of Shan in the *jiawu* year, the first year of the Song Filial Establishment reign [454].

She was called Grand Mistress Xu. Her corpse was laid in a stone chamber and she was not encoffined. Her body constantly emitted a fragrant odor.

黃民長子榮〈第〉［弟］，一名預之。宋元嘉十二年亡。不知年幾。有女名道育。隆安元年丁酉生。宋孝建〈元〉元年甲午歲。於剡任埭山亡。（世謂之許大娘。臥尸石壙。不殯。常有芳香之氣。）

Huangmin's youngest son was named Qing 慶. He also died on Mount Rendai of Shan, but in the *jiyou* year, fifth year of Grand Inception

[469]. I do not know his age at death. He had a daughter named Shener 神兒, with the variant name Qionghui 瓊輝. She was born in the *jisi* year, the sixth of Primal Commendation [429] and died in the *bingyin* year, the fourth of the Qi dynasty Eternal Brightess reign [486].

People called Shen'er the Lesser Mistress Xu. Many of the Daoists of Dongguan knew of her.

黃民小子名慶。宋泰始五年己酉歲，亦於剡任埭山亡。不知年幾。有女名神兒，一名瓊輝。元嘉六年己巳生。齊永明四年丙寅歲亡。（世謂許小娘。東關道士多有識者。）

To this point, I have listed the descendants of the Senior Officer. Today only Xu Quan's great-great-grandson Xu Lingzhen survives.

右所承長史後如此。今唯有揆玄孫靈眞而已。

Lord Yang was named Xi and was born in the ninth month of the gengyin year, the fifth year of the Concordant Harmony reign of the Accomplished Thearch [Sima Yan 司馬衍, r. 325–42; 330]. He was a person of Wu who came to reside in Jurong County. When the Perfected began descending to him, he still had a mother and younger brother. As a person, Lord Yang was pure, of fine physique and face, and excelled at calligraphy and painting. When he was young, he delighted in study and, it seems, was familiar with the [Confucian] scriptures and the histories. By nature, he was profound, virtuous, and withdrawn. From youth, he had the perspicacity to communicate with the numinous powers. Though there was a vast difference between his age and that of the Senior Officer, they early on established a relationship through the gods. The Senior Officer even recommended Yang to the Prince of Xiang [Sima Yu] who employed him as a personal retainer in his offices. After [Sima Yu] ascended to the emperorship, we see no further traces of him [in the *Declarations*].

Gu said that he was a teacher to Sima Yu and reported that some said he was an Erudite, but Yang was ten years younger than Sima Yu, so I suspect that this is inaccurate.

楊君名羲。成帝咸和五年庚寅歲九月生。本似是吳人。來居句容。眞降時，猶有母及弟。君爲人潔白，美姿容，善言笑，工書畫。少好學讀書。該涉經史。性淵懿沈厚。幼有通靈之鑒。與先生長史年竝懸殊。而早結神明之交。長史薦之相王。用爲公府舍人自隨。簡文登極後。不復見有迹出。（顧云：是簡文師，或云博士。楊乃小簡文十歲，皆恐非實也。）

According to the *Declarations of the Perfected*, Yang was to depart in the *bingxu* year, the eleventh of Grand Prime [386]. They also stated: "If you cannot bear the winds and fires [of the mortal world], you may practice the method of liberation by means of sword, and thereby master the art of announcing your end."[179] Because of this, I fear he may have departed early to take a Perfected post and not necessarily in the *bingxu* year. [His departure] may have been when the [Perfected Consort] Nine Blossoms pronounced that Yang should assist Eastern Flower as Director of Destinies, with ultimate charge of all the spirits and ghosts of Wu and Yue.[180] Yang first received the *Talismans of the Central Yellow [God] for Controlling Tigers and Leopards* in the *jiyou* year, the fifth year of Eternal Harmony [349]. In the *gengxu* year, the sixth year [350], he went to Lady Wei [Huacun's] eldest son Liu Pu and received from him the *Five Talismans of Lingbao*. At that time, he was twenty-one *sui*. In the *yichou* year, the third year of Ascending Tranquility [365], the Perfected descended [to Yang] to orally bestow [scriptures]. At this time, he was thirty-six. The place where the Perfected descended to him was not fixed. Sometimes it was in the capital, sometimes it was in the home oratory, sometimes it was in the mountain hermitage. The "mountain hermitage" seems to have been Senior Officer Xu's official offices on Mount Leiping. Yang constantly went there to visit Xu Hui. He did not live alone on the mountain.

按眞誥云：應以太元十一年丙戌去。又云。〈苦〉[若] 不〈奈〉[耐] 風火，可修劔解之道，作告終之術。如此恐以早逝。不必丙戌也。得眞職任。略如九華所言，當輔佐東華，爲司命之任，董司吳越神靈人鬼。一皆關攝之。楊先以永和五年己酉歲，受中黃制虎豹符。六年庚戌，又就魏夫人長子劉璞，受靈寶五符。時年二十一。興寧三年乙丑歲，衆眞降嗳。年三十六。眞降之所，無正定處，或在京都，或在家舍，或在山館。山館猶是雷平山許長史廨。楊恆數來就掾。非自山居也。

The previous relates in general all that pertains to Lord Yang [Xi]. I await the release of a [Perfected] biography to record more about him.

右楊君事。大略如此。須傳出更記。

• • •

179. See DZ 1016, 2.10a.

180. DZ 1016, 2.8a. Tao is here paraphrasing a longer speech in which the Perfected Consort relates how she will rule beside him. Eastern Flower is one of the palace complexes of Fangzhu and the residence of the Younger Lord Mao, Protector of Destinies, Mao Zhong. See DZ 1016, 3.15a and 4.14b.

At this point I have deleted a dozen entries on specific items of terminology and intimate family names used by the Xus that Tao identified. These are invaluable bits of information, but best introduced into the text when the cited passage occurs. I pick up the text again at page 20.13a9. —Trans.

. . .

"Those who ascend will be three."

This refers to Xu Mai, Xu Mi, and Xu Hui.

"Those who pass out of the world [without dying] will be five."[181]

This refers to Xu Lian, Xu Huangmin, Xu Rongdi, Grand Mistress Xu Daoyu, and the Lesser Mistress Xu Shen'er. With regard to Xu Lian, they said "Subsequently you will achieve not dying and cross over in safety the *renchen* year [392]."[182] Thus, he is certainly among the number who will pass from the world. There are no such clear records for the remaining four, but Huangmin transmitted and reverenced the scriptures, and when Daoyu passed away there were miraculous signs, so I think that they would be included. The remaining two could also be among later generations of descendants. If it should be someone in the seventh generation, then the son of Lingzhen is the one to inherit this blessing.[183] Although Xu Mi's wife [Tao Kedou], the daughter of Tao Wei, entered the Palace of Mutation and Promotion, I believe this was because she received the blessing of the Tao family line. It does not necessarily place her among the five of the Xu family mentioned here.

登升者三人。（先生長史掾也。） 度世者五人。（虎牙，黃民，榮弟，大娘，小娘。尋虎牙云：遂得不死，過度壬辰。必是 度世之限。其餘無迹顯出。黃民傳奉經業。道育亡，有異徵。恐或預例。其二人亦可更在後世子孫。若必以七世爲限，則靈眞之子寔鍾斯慶。長史婦陶威女，雖入易遷。恐此自承陶家福 耳。不必關許氏五人之數也。）

The revelations also mention Li Dong 李東. He was the Libationer ordinarily employed by the Xu family. The Prior-born Xu Mai regarded him as Master. His home was at Qu'a.[184] He was the Supervisor

181. Both of these predictions are attributed to Xu Mai as reported by the Middle Lord Mao. They are to be found at DZ 1016, 4.11b5–6.

182. DZ 1016, 2.14a3. This prophecy was given by Lady Right Blossom.

183. On the seventh-generation descendant of Xu Mi, the son of Lingzhen, see note 173.

184. Qu'a 曲阿 was a county seat corresponding roughly to present-day Danyang City of Jiangsu Province. It was also the name of the village in Jurong County where the Xu family settled. See DZ 304, 20.8a.

of Deities, Libationer of the Left of the Celestial Master, Jiyang Parish.[185]

有云李東者。許家常所使祭酒。先生亦師之。　家在曲阿。東受天師吉陽治左領神祭酒。

Hua Qiao was a member of the eminent family from Jinling.[186] For generations they had worshipped profane spirits. Qiao himself at first was able to communicate with the spirits and the dead. He often dreamt that he banqueted and drank with them. Each time he would always sleep soundly without waking. When he did awaken he would vomit wildly in his drunkenness. The profane gods often had him nominate talented people.[187] This happened several tens of times. If he delayed or opposed them, he would be found guilty and punished. Qiao was alternatively angered and distressed at this. So he entered the Dao and put a stop to his service to the dead. Gradually the Perfected and Transcendents came to roam with him, at first only in dreams but, as the years passed, increasingly appearing physically to him in the middle of the night. Pei Qingling and Zhou Ziyang both appeared to him, causing him to pass their intentions and instructions on to Xu Mi. But by nature Qiao was quick to judgment. He often leaked secret pronouncements and was chastised for it.[188] So Lord Yang Xi came to replace him. Qiao later became county magistrate of Jiangsheng江乘 and took his family there to live.[189] The Hua family of Jiangsheng of today are his descendants.

185. On the Celestial Master rank of "Supervisor of Deities" 領神職, see Kleeman, *Celestial Masters*, 334. In the same work, Kleeman also presents evidence that Jiyang was one of the "roving parishes" (p. 339). Jiyang is just northeast of present-day Ji'an 吉安, Jiangxi Province.

186. Jinling 晉陵 was the name of a commandery with the seat southeast of modern Zhenjiang city in Jiangsu Province.

187. Strickmann, with his usual lively prose, gives the most likely explanation for this sentence as follows: "The specters discovered in him a fine judge of talent, and made increasing use of his perspicacity in selecting their own officials. That is, they compelled him to select living men of administrative promise for immediate employment in the realms of the dead" (unpublished ms., 117; for the published version, see *Le Taoïsme*, 153).

188. Hua Qiao's leaking of secrets was reported by the Younger Lord Mao. See DZ 1016, 7.6a2–3.

189. Jiangsheng County seat was in the district today known as Xixia 栖霞区 of modern Nanjing.

The Hua family was connected to the Xus in marriage. That is why when Xu Mi wrote to Lord Pei, he importuned [Hua Qiao] to transmit it to the Lord.[190] But, as the Protector of Destinies [the Younger Lord Mao] announced, as recorded in the previous chapter, Hua Qiao was found guilty.[191] The biography, *Traditions of Zhou Ziyang*, was written by Hua Qiao. This biography is related to the *Declarations of the Perfected*.[192]

華僑者晉陵冠族。世事俗祷。僑初頗通神鬼。常夢共同饗醊。每爾，輒靜寐不覺。醒則醉吐狼藉。俗神恆使其舉才用人，前後十數。若有稽違，便坐之爲譴。僑忿患，遂入道。於鬼事得息，漸漸眞仙來游。始亦止是夢。積年乃夜半形見。裴清靈周紫陽至。皆使通傳旨意於長史。而僑性輕躁，多漏説冥旨。被責。仍以楊君代之。僑後爲江〈城〉[乘] 縣令。家因居焉。今江乘諸華。皆其苗裔也。（華與許氏有婚親。故長史書與裴君，殷勤相請也。若如前篇中有保命所告，則僑被罪也。今世中周紫陽傳。即是僑所造。故與眞誥爲相連也。）

190. This letter is recorded at DZ 1016, 12.1a–2a.

191. The Younger Lord Mao's report includes the fact that Hua Qiao "father and son were investigated by the Water Office." See DZ 1016, 7.6a2–3.

192. The biography deals with the life and practices of Zhou Yishan 周義山, the Perfected of Perfect Yang. For an account, see Robinet, "Ziyang Zhenren"; for a translation, Porkert, *Biographie*, and Miller, *Way of Highest Clarity*.

CHAPTER TWO

The "Poems of Elühua"

The very first entry in the *Declarations of the Perfected* is not a revelation to Yang Xi, but to another man with the homophonous, and related, surname Yang 羊. According to Tao Hongjing, whose reconstruction of events we are following, this Yang's given name was Quan 權, and his byname was Daoyu 道輿. All that we know of his political career is that Yang Quan served as Gentleman at the Palace Gate in the court of Jianwen of the Jin (r. 371–72).[1] He was a son of Yang Chen 忱, byname Changru 長如, and a forebear of the more famous Yang Xin 羊欣 (370–442).[2] The revelations to him are dated precisely and said to have begun on 15 December 359.

The goddess who appeared to Yang Quan bestowed upon him some teachings and, what is more important, three poems. She claimed to have originally been surnamed Yang 羊 herself, perhaps in a previous life. She gave her current name as Elühua 愕緑華 (var. 蕚綠華), an exotic, foreign-sounding name which matches the strange gifts she gave Yang Quan—asbestos cloth and two helical bracelets, one of gold and

---

1. Wang Jiakui has suggested that Yang and the Xus were using divine knowledge to earn the favor of this member of the imperial family (*Tao Hongjing*, 146–50).

2. Yang Xin's biography is to be found in Shen Yue, *Songshu* 62.1661–62. The Jianwen emperor of the Jin, Sima Yu 司馬昱 (320–72) and his circle seem to have a close relationship with the Xu family.

one of jade. She proposed to join Yang Quan in a union that looks almost like the marriages that the goddess Consort An would propose to Yang Xi and the Lady of Right Blossom to Xu Mi. This helps to confirm that, while his revelations were the most complete to survive, Yang Xi was clearly not the only literate medium of the early medieval period. He was not even the only medium courting divine females in the circle around Sima Yu 司馬昱 (320–72), the eventual Jianwen emperor.[3]

Finally, Elühua gave Yang Quan a drug for *shijie* 尸解, release from the world by means of a simulated corpse. This would allow Quan to escape the mortal world altogether, leading colleagues below and the celestial record keepers above to believe that he had died.[4] Since Tao Hongjing and the histories all say that he later in 371 or 372 served in office, it seems that Quan did not use the drug immediately, if at all.

The Yang 羊 family had several pursuits that might have allied them to Yang Xi and the Xus. First, they were hereditary Daoists. Second, their ranks included several members who were adept at calligraphy, especially the "running style" 行書 favored by Daoists, who had to jot down quickly the words of their deities.[5] Third, they all seem to have had some connection with Sima Yu, then only a promising member of the royal family. It is likely that Wang Jiakui is correct in his assertion that Xu Mi was using the revelations passed to him by Yang to raise his official and social status.[6] If so, this is the circle of initiates among which the revelations first moved. We will discover further families in the following sections.

3. The introduction to the next chapter on the revelations for Sima Yu will highlight some of these mediums. For more, particularly those who reported on the status of the dead, see Bokenkamp, *Ancestors and Anxiety*.

4. *Shijie* 尸解 refers to methods intended to confound the official records of death kept by men and the spirits through replacing the practitioner's body with a substitute "corpse." Of course, the method requires sneaking away, as Yang Quan does in this tale. See Campany, *To Live as Long*, 52–60.

5. Yang Chen is mentioned, together with Tao Hongjing, already by Yu Jianwu 庾肩吾 (487–551) in his *Shupin* 書品, 7b (SKQS edition). The *Yunji qiqian* biography of Tao Hongjing notes that his father excelled at calligraphy, especially the style practiced by Yang Chen's descendant Yang Xin, and commanded a high price for his services (See DZ 1032, 106.3a). Yang Xin, in fact, composed one of the earliest theoretical works on calligraphy. (See Ledderose, "Some Taoist Elements," 251–53, among others.)

6. See Wang Jiakui, *Tao Hongjing*, 146–60. Michel Strickmann was the first to propose that Xu and other southerners were using the Shangqing revelations as a status marker. (See Strickmann, "Mao-shan Revelations," 11–12.) In some later works, this insight was expanded by others to make the revealed material a sort of "ideological weapon." This is perhaps overstating the point.

As it appears in the *Declarations*, the account of Elühua that Tao Hongjing discovered in Yang Xi's hand had been inexpertly altered. The name of Yang Quan had been scratched out of the paper manuscript. Yet enough of the surname and one missed instance of the character "Quan" were enough for Tao Hongjing to determine the true recipient of Elühua's attentions. Tao explains his discovery carefully if briefly in the notes to this chapter.

Two collections that cite the *Declarations* provide further textual alternatives. The *Sandong qunxian lu* 三洞群仙錄 of Chen Baoguang 陳葆光 (fl. 1154) contains the following passage that it ascribes to the *Declarations*:

> [Elühua] said to [Yang] Quan: "Without thoughts, without concerns, without greed, without seeking, without pursuits, without deliberate action—I have practiced that which humans cannot practice; learned that which humans cannot learn. Unperturbed and placid, I only strive to work on internal practices. This is why I have practiced already for nine hundred years!"[7]

> 乃謂權曰: 無思、無慮、無貪、無求、無事、無爲。行人所不能行，學人所不能學。恬淡苦勤內行。故我行之已九百年矣。

The *Yunji qiqian* contains an even fuller version of the passage:

> [Elühua] thereupon said to [Yang] Quan: "You should be cautious and not reveal that I have descended to you. If you reveal it, we will both be guilty of a crime." Then she said, "The masters who study the Dao view brocades and embroideries as tattered cloth; emoluments and titles as if they were passing guests; and gold and jades as if they were tile shards.[8] Without thoughts, without concerns, without pursuits, without deliberate action—I have practiced that which humans cannot practice; learned that which humans cannot learn;[9] labored at that which humans cannot work on; and achieved that which humans cannot achieve. Why? People of the world act on what they like and desire; I practice single-minded integrity. People of the world learn common pursuits; I learn to be tranquil and unmoving. People of the world work at fame and profit; I work on internal practices. People of the world reach old age and death; I achieve long life. This is why I have lived to the age of nine hundred years!" She bestowed drugs for release by means of a [substitute] corpse on Quan, who then hid his shadow, transformed his physical shape, and departed.

---

7. DZ 1248, 9.14b. The same work gives an abbreviated account, again referencing the *Declarations* at 18.4b5–10.

8. The *Daode jing*, no. 45, contains the line "Music and fine food make the passing guest stop over" 樂與餌，過客止。

9. This phrase is drawn from the Heshang Gong commentary to the Laozi, which compares the Sage to the common person. The cadence of the surrounding passages of the commentary is also similar to this. (See DZ 682, 4.5a1.)

Today he resides in the mountains to the east of the Xiang River.[10] When Elühua first descended, she presented Yang Quan with poems that said. . . .[11]

謂權曰：慎無泄我下降之事。泄之則彼此獲罪。因曰: 修道之士，視錦綉如弊帛，視爵位如過客，視金玉如瓦礫。無思無慮， 無事無爲。行人所不能行, 學人所不能學, 勤人所不能勤, 得人所不能得。何者? 世人行嗜欲，我行介獨；世人學俗務，我學恬漠；世人勤聲利，我勤内行；世人得老死，我得長生。故我今已九百歳矣。授權尸解藥， 亦隱影化形而去。今在湘東山中。緑華初降贈詩曰：

Since the *Declarations* mentions that Elühua was nine hundred years old, this prose section may well have been part of the original revelation. The *Sandong qunxian lu* cites the *Declarations* as source, but the *Yunji qiqian* does not. However, both sources cite the rest of the narrative largely as we have it in the *Declarations* and give the poems precisely as in the *Declarations*, with only the few variants noted here. It is therefore likely that the above passage was originally included in Tao Hongjing's *Declarations*. We shall encounter further passages that seem to have dropped from the received editions of the *Declarations*, as well as passages that have clearly been misplaced. In this case, it seems likely that later editors may have seen the prose teachings of Elühua as somewhat uninteresting and simply cut them, placing the poems first. On the other hand, Tao Hongjing does mention that there was a one-inch gap in the copies he gathered, so it is also possible that the above passage derives from a different manuscript tradition that did not pass through Tao's hands.

More significant, perhaps, is the question of why Yang Quan's name was cut out of the manuscript. All three slips containing this narrative and the poems are in Yang Xi's cursive calligraphy, but that does not necessarily mean that he made the alterations himself. The manuscripts passed through many hands before reaching Tao Hongjing. One clue may be that, unlike the Perfected who appeared to Yang Xi and who offered their hand to Yang and the Xus, Elühua was not a Perfected being. She was a mere Transcendent. More shamefully, Elühua was a banished Transcendent. She had not come down to earth attracted by the excellence of her prospective mate, Yang Quan. Instead, she had been driven from one of the Transcendent isles in the Eastern Sea when it was discovered that she had

10. Xiangdong 湘東 means "area east of the Xiang River," including the eastern part of modern day Hubei Province and the western reaches of Jiangxi.

11. DZ 1032, 97.3b–4a. This longer passage incorporates several of Tao Hongjing's notes as part of the text, so it is clearly drawn from the *Declarations* as a source. The *Taiping guangji* 太平廣記 contains the same extra passage and does give the source as the *Declarations* (SKQS edition, 57.9a–b).

committed a crime in a previous life. She had, on behalf of a female Master (or perhaps the wife of a male Master) poisoned a pregnant woman. We learn no more about this crime, but it does make Elühua very much less attractive than the Perfected women who will appear to Yang.

Further, the matter of leaking celestial secrets comes up in the Elühua story, as it will with respect to the Hua family Daoists we will encounter in the passages on Tao Kedou, Xu Mi's wife.[12] Yang Quan was enjoined not to leak Elühua's revelations and yet Yang Xi had a copy, so the secret is out now. For both of these reasons, Yang Xi or later redactors might have had cause to cross out the name. Finally, though, since Tao Hongjing does not speculate, the reasons for the attempted erasure of Yang Quan's name are likely not recoverable today.

For our purposes, the revelation of Elühua serves as it did for generations of readers of the *Declarations*. It introduces the more complex revelations that are to follow. My translation of the "Poems of Elühua" places the narrative first, as in the versions just quoted.[13]

ELÜHUA TRANSLATION

愕緑華詩。 The Poems of Elühua[14]

Elǚhua said that she came from the southern mountains, but it is not known which particular mountain. She was twenty or so and wore green above and below. Her complexion was exquisite. On the night of the tenth day of the eleventh month in the third year of Ascendant Peace reign era [15 December 359] she descended to [Yang Quan].[15] After this, she came frequently, once arriving six times in a single month. She said that her original surname was [Yang].[16] She bestowed a poem on [Yang].[17] She also gave him an asbestos cloth and two helical bracelets,

---

12. These will appear in volume 2.

13. The title in the *Yunji qiqian* is given as "Three Poems Presented to Yang Quan by E Lühua, with introduction" 萼緑華贈羊權詩三首并序 (DZ 1032, 97.3b). Thus it is clear that the poems were regarded as the most important part of the revelation.

14. This is the original title. I have moved the poems below the prose text.

15. Tao Hongjing notes: "Two characters are missing. These should be Yang Quan 羊權."

16. Tao Hongjing notes at this point: "Another character has been cut out. It should be the graph Yang 楊."

17. Tao Hongjing notes here that "The final character should be Yang. A later person has scratched out the graph and replaced it with the character *this*." Thus the line would read "She presented this single poem."

one of gold and one of jade. The bracelets were large and of extraordinarily fine workmanship.

愕綠華者，¹⁸　自云是南山人。不知是何山也。女子年可二十。上下青
衣。顏色絕整。以升平三年十一月十日夜。降〔厶厶〕。（剪缺此兩
字。即應是羊權字。）自此往來，一月之中，輒六過來耳。云本姓〔
厶〕。（又剪除此一字。應是楊字。）贈〔此〕（此一字本是權字。
後人黶作此字。）詩一篇。并致火澣布手巾一枚，金玉條脫各一枚。
條脫乃太而異精好。

The divine woman said to <Quan>:¹⁹ "You should be cautious and not reveal my existence. If you reveal me, we will both be guilty of a crime." [Quan] asked about her and she said she was a woman who had achieved the Dao at Mount Jiuyi named Luo Yu 羅郁.²⁰ In a previous life she poisoned a pregnant woman for her female Master.²¹ Because she had not expiated this former transgression, the Mystical Isles banished her to descend to the world of stench and impurity, there to make up for the transgression.²² She gave <Quan> drugs for release by means of a simulated corpse.²³ Today he is in the mountains of the eastern Xiang region.²⁴

At this point in the text there is a space one inch in width.

神女語〔見〕：（此本是草作權字。後人黶作見字。而乙上之）君慎勿
泄我。泄我則彼此獲罪。訪問此人，云是九嶷山中得道女羅郁也。宿命
時，曾爲師母毒殺乳婦。玄州以先罪未滅，故令謫降於臭濁以償其過。
與〔權〕（此權亦草作。故似前體而不被黶耳。）尸解藥。今在湘東
山。（本懸此中一寸）

This woman is already nine hundred years old.

此女已九百歲矣。

• • •

18. Both DZ 1032 and 1248 give the name as 萼綠華.

19. Tao notes at this point: "The final graph was originally the character Quan 權 written in grass style calligraphy. A later person scratched it out and replaced it with the graph *jian* 見.

20. Mount Jiuyi is approximately fifty kilometers south of the county seat of Ning-yuan County in modern Hunan Province.

21. The term she uses for "previous life" originates in Buddhist translation and literally means "time of lodging destiny."

22. "Mystical Isles" 玄州 is the abode of Transcendents floating in the Eastern Seas off the coast of China. The term is here metonymic for the officials who reside there.

23. Tao Hongjing notes here that "This Quan 權 was also written in grass-style calligraphy like the previous example, but it had not been scratched out."

24. East of the Xiang River, that is, in present-day Jiangxi Province.

The following poems are typical of the style of Perfected verse that we will encounter throughout the *Declarations*. They begin with a description of a fantastic cosmic scene, the parts of which stand metaphorically for the people who will be the true subject of the poem. These descriptions are replete with coinages that, while giving a sense of the landscape they purport to describe, in fact defy analysis. Their purpose is to create an aura of mystery. For example, two coinages appear in the opening couplets of the first poem. They are both binomials, compounds composed of two words that are rhymed or joined by assonance (like "wishy-washy") Binomials are common in classical Chinese and present a particularly knotty translation challenge. One cannot determine the meaning of a binomial by the characters that make it up, but lacking sufficient alternate examples, such a procedure is almost unavoidable.[25] "Faintly caged" is my attempt to render the alliterative binomial 寥籠 /lew-luwng/.[26] The only other early example, I have found, from Dai Kui's 戴逵 (326–96) "In Praise of Mountains" 山贊 also uses the term to describe an empty space in the mountains: "Faintly caged, the vacant sourcemounts" 寥籠虛岫.[27] The term I translate "dense and murmuring" is 蔚蕭 /jwi-sew/. The only further example I have found of this binomial is Pan Ni's 潘尼 (ca. 250–ca. 311) "Rhapsody on the Mulberry Tree" 桑樹賦, which contains the couplet "Dense and murmuring, the grove extends in the four directions. Distant and overflowing, the trees stand brave and straight" 蔚蕭森以四射，邈洪傭而端直.[28] My annotations below will not include further examples such as these, but I will cite classical allusions when they appear. Further, attentive readers will notice the way in which the parallel couplets describing Yang Quan's fine qualities alternate between portraying him as having the abilities of a scholar-official and, on the other hand, the retiring nature of a Transcendent. –Trans.

. . .

[The poems read:]

The spirit-filled Marchmount parts the empyrean as it rises,
Its flying peaks shadowy presences across a thousand furlongs.
Thus faintly caged, the numinous valley is void,

25. See Knechtges, *Wenxuan* 2:2–13, for a precise description of the problems involved.
26. Reconstructed pronunciations follow Baxter, *Etymological Dictionary*. These will be enclosed in forward slashes, /like so/.
27. YWLJ, 7.127.
28. YWLJ, 88.35a.

Its rose-gemmed groves dense and murmuring.
Student [Yang Quan] shows the utmost in beauty and talent,
From his capping ceremony on, pure tones have flowed [praising
    him].[29]
He invests his emotions in the crux of Zhuangzi's meeting with
    Huizi[30]
And excels over the ranks arrayed before governmental gates.[31]
Though now casting luster within vermilion gates,[32]
He harbors within the desire to surge beyond the common run.

神嶽排霄起。飛峯鬱千尋。寥篁靈谷虛。瓊林蔚蕭森。〈X〉（此一字被
墨濃黶。不復可識。正中抽一脚出下。似是羊字。其人名權。）生標
美秀。弱冠流清音。棲情莊慧津。超形象魏林。揚彩朱門中。內有邁
俗心。[33]

29. Tao Hongjing notes: "The surname was blotted out with black ink and unrecognizable. But a single stroke extending from the middle protrudes below. It thus seems to be the character Yang 羊. Yang's given name was Quan 權." Yang Quan was the grandfather of Yang Xin 羊欣 (370–442). (See Shen Yue, *Songshu*, 62.1661.) The capping ceremony took place at the age of twenty.

30. Following DZ 1032, 97.4a, which reads 莊惠 "Zhuangzi and Huizi" rather than 莊慧. Hui Shi [Huizi] 惠施 was a fourth-century BCE sophist whose discussion on some fishes with Zhuangzi is cited in the collection of the latter called *Zhuangzi*. Burton Watson translates this famous exchange as follows: "Zhuangzi and Huizi were strolling along the dam of the Hao River when Zhuangzi said, 'See how the minnows come out and dart around where they please! That's what fish really enjoy!' Huizi said, 'You're not a fish—how do you know what fish enjoy?' Zhuangzi said, 'You're not I, so how do you know I don't know what fish enjoy?' Huizi said, 'I'm not you, so I certainly don't know what you know. On the other hand, you're certainly not a fish—so that still proves you don't know what fish enjoy!' Zhuangzi said, 'Let's go back to your original question, please. You asked me how I know what fish enjoy—so you already knew I knew it when you asked the question. I know it by standing here beside the Hao'" (Watson, *Complete Works*, 188–89). The clever response is untranslatable in that the interrogative phrase 安知 can mean both "how did you know?" and "where did you know?" The reference implies that Yang Quan has a natural affinity with the world that defies mundane definition.

31. According to a gloss by Zheng Xuan 鄭玄 (127–200) to the *Zhouli*, the *xiangwei* 象魏 mentioned here were gate towers outside of the Zhou imperial palace where laws and other government documents were displayed. See *Zhouli zhushu* 周禮注疏, Tianguan 天官, 2. 23b–24a (SKQS edition) and Wu Hung, *Monumentality*, 277. The point of this couplet is that while Yang Quan has taken himself out of public life and has an unspoken affinity with the carefree fish as did Zhuangzi, he yet possesses the qualities of a high official.

32. The "vermilion gates" 朱門 are metonymic for wealthy, powerful families. (See Guo Pu 郭璞 [276–324], "Transcendent Roaming" 遊仙 no. 1, *Wenxuan* 21.460.) "Casts luster" 揚彩 follows Knechtges, *Wenxuan* 2.37.

33. DZ 1032 has 內外 for 內有.

Now I am of the same clan as my lord—
Our heredity extends from the same deep font.
But our vast clan was divided by later deeds
And today we come from different branches.
Now orchid fragrance and golden endurance mark a fine match[34]
And we have a full complement of the three beneficial things.[35]

我與夫子族。源胄同淵池。宏宗分上業。於今各異枝。蘭金因好著。三
益方覺彌。

Having sought in stillness, you delight in this meeting;
Our fine pairing will extend the blessing of our years.[36]
Who says that probing into the Hidden is difficult?
You have found it within the square inch of your heart.
Letting your thoughts soar beyond their worldly cage,[37]
You will join the gentlemen of the mountain precipices.
But do not arise on empty pinions[38]
That fly up when struck by urgent winds.[39]
Although transformational change begins with the self,
It is best not to imitate the ram stuck in the hedge.[40]

34. The term *orchid and gold* derives from a saying attributed to Confucius in the "Appended Words" of the *Changes*. "When two people are of like mind, their sharpness can cut through metal; when they speak in accord, it is as fragrant as orchids." See the *Zhouyi zhushu* 周易注疏, 系辭上, 11.25b (SKQS edition).

35. According to the Analects, Confucius said "There are three beneficial friendships . . . friendship with the upright, friendship with the honest, and friendship with the learned." See the *Lunyu zhushu* 論語注疏, "Jishi" 季氏篇, 16.9a (SKQS edition).

36. The term 齡祀 "age and sacrifice" appears to be a *hapax legomenon*. I am uncertain what it signifies. The Japanese translation team paraphrases "I hope that our bond will last for a very long time." (See SKKY, 2.)

37. As examples of this use of a birdcage to symbolize the confined world of office holding, the Japanese team cites Xu Ling's 徐陵 (507–83) "Letter to Li Na" 與麗邢書 and the more famous 歸園田居 of Tao Yuanming 陶淵明 (365–427). Both are later than the *Declarations*, which uses the word twice more. (See DZ 1016, 2.12b and 17.1a. and SKKY 5n22) I have found no earlier uses of the metaphor.

38. The image of "mounting pinions," but in this case applied to actual birds rather than feathered Transcendents, is found in the "Rhapsody on Residing in the Mountains" 山居賦 by Xie Lingyun 謝靈運 (385–433): "I observe the dip and rise of the mounting pinions" 覩騰翰之頡頏." (See Shen Yue, *Songshu*, 67.1770.)

39. This might be an allusion to the criticism of Liezi found in the *Zhuangzi*, where we read that he was able to fly on the wind, but that this was not true freedom, since there was still something on which he relied. See p. 129 in chapter 4.

40. The *Book of Changes* contains the following line: "The ram buts against the hedge and gets its horns tangled . . . it is able neither to retreat or advance." See Yijing zhushu 周易注疏 Dazhuang 大壯, SSJZS 1:48c. "Ram" 羊 is Yang Quan's surname.

It is not just the morning flowers to which you aspire,
In that way, the years will come to an end for you.[41]

靜尋欣斯會。雅綜彌齡祀。誰云幽鑒難。得之方寸裏。翹想篤樊外。
俱爲山巖士。無令騰虛翰。中隨驚風起。遷化雖由人。蕃羊未易擬。
所期豈朝華。歲暮於吾子。

The three items are written in the hand of Yang Xi.[42] Looking into
this story, it appears that Elühua descended to Yang Quan 羊權,
whose byname was Daoyu 道輿. He was the younger son of Yang
Chen 忱. Later Quan became Gentleman at the Palace Gate in the
court of Jianwen of the Jin (r. 371–72).[43] That is to say, he was the
forebear of Yang Xin 羊欣 (370–442). Thus, Xin also practiced the
Dao and Daoist dietetics.[44] That this text was written out in Yang
Xi's own hand is likely because [he and Yang Quan] were of the
same surname. It might also be the case that Yang Xi asked Yang
Quan and, when told about the matter, wrote out a summary. I note
that the third year of the Ascendant Peace reign period was a *yiwei*
year, six years before the *yichou* year [365]. At this time the various
Perfected had not yet descended to Yang Xi.

(尋此應是降羊權。權字道輿。忱之少子。後爲晉簡文黄門郎。即羊欣
祖，故欣亦修道服食也。此乃爲楊君所書者，當以其同姓。亦可楊權
相問。因答其事而疏説之耳。按升平三年是巳未歲在乙丑前六年。衆
眞竝未降事。)

右三條楊君草書於紙上。

41. This is a difficult couplet. I take the "morning flower" 朝華 image to play off the
"evening of life" 歲暮 image. The sense would then be something like "why are you wor-
rying about regaining youth when, at your age, you should be thinking of end-of-life
issues like heaven?"

42. I have moved this note below the poems. As the original manuscripts that Tao
Hongjing is reading no longer survive, we must follow his judgement on these matters.
The word I translate as "items" or "passages" is *tiao* 條, which likely referred to a slip of
paper of a certain size. I have no evidence as to its dimensions.

43. The Jianwen emperor of the Jin, Sima Yu 司馬昱 (320–72) and his circle seem to
have a close relationship with the Xu family, as is evidenced in the previous entry. Wang
Jiakui has suggested that Yang and the Xus were using divine knowledge to earn the favor
of this member of the imperial family. See Wang Jiakui, *Tao Hongjing*, 146–60.

44. According to Yang Xin's biography in the *Songshu*, when he was ill, he only
drank talisman water and he sent up petitions in his own hand. He thus seems to have
followed Celestial Master practice. (See Shen Yue, *Songshu* 宋書 62.1662.)

CHAPTER THREE

The Sons of Sima Yu

INTRODUCTION

The following fragments of text constitute the earliest evidence we have of Yang Xi's work. They record the predictions and advice that Yang Xi received from his Perfected visitors regarding the male progeny of Sima Yu 司馬昱 (320–72), the man who eventually became the Jianwen [Straightfoward and Cultured] Thearch of the Jin 晉簡文帝. The Perfected provide a method for promoting the birth of male offspring and, further, predict correctly that Sima Yu will engender two males who will rise high in the realm. Prophecies such as this one raise issues for us modern observers. Chinese histories are full of what can only be regarded as *ex eventu* prophecies. Since Tao Hongjing marks this particular event as the earliest recorded appearance of Yang Xi's Perfected beings, the matter of whether or not the prediction was actually made after the fact becomes a matter of some interest.[1] The first to be born of the two imperial males predicted was Sima Yao 司馬曜 (362–96), so the Perfected had been descending to Yang, Tao reasons, at least two years earlier than the earliest dated manuscript he possesses. Was Tao overly credulous?

We cannot hope to solve a sixteen-hundred-year-old mystery. Still, some modern scholars have cast doubt on Tao's dating, so the matter

---

1. On Tao Hongjing's treatment of this incident in his postface, see pp. XX–XX in chapter 1.

deserves exploration.[2] And we can certainly develop a hypothesis. Along the way, we will have an initial glimpse of Yang Xi's methods in presenting his revelations as he did.

We begin with a source that is not included in the Daoist canon but is mentioned by Tao's modern critics. This is one of the dynastic histories, the *Book of the Jin* 晉書, compiled by an editorial board under Fang Xuanling 房玄齡 (579–648) in the seventh century. Because it draws heavily on anecdotal materials, the *Book of the Jin* is regarded as one of the less reliable sources.[3] Still, insofar as it repeats popular anecdotes from the Jin period, the work will serve us well. The following anecdote demonstrates that Sima Yu's concern over finding a healthy male heir was well known. The following appears in the biography of his eventual Empress:[4]

Empress Dowager Li was named Lingrong 陵容. Her origins were common. When Sima Yu was Prince of Guiji, she had three sons. All died young. . . . Afterwards, the Palace Consorts were all unable to bear children for ten years. Sima Yu ordered the fortune-teller Hu Qian 扈謙 to divine by yarrow stalk about it.[5] [Hu] said: "In the rear quarters there is a woman who will raise two imperial sons. One will in the end bring glory to the Jin house." At this time there was Honored Person Xu, the concubine who had given birth to the future Princess of Xin'an. She was favored by Sima Yu for her virtue and beauty. Sima Yu kept waiting for her to become pregnant, but over a year she was still without a child. Sima Yu met the Daoist Xu Mai 許邁, whom all the courtiers and persons of consequence said had achieved the Dao.[6] Sima Yu, with seeming indifference, asked him about the matter. Mai replied, "I am just one who loves the mountains and waters and have no Daoist arts. How can I pass judgement on a matter such as this? But I can say that your majesty's virtues are full and your good fortune is deep. This is appropriate for a posterity that will bring honor on successive generations. You should listen to Hu Qian's words." Sima Yu agreed. He increased his selection of women from the rear quarters but was still without a son. He then summoned a person good at physiognomizing people and showed him all of his most favored concubines.[7] The person said "none of these." Then

2. For an alternative view of what might have happened, see Wang Jiakui, *Tao Hongjing*, 146–49.

3. See Mather, *New Account*, xiii.

4. In translating the following anecdote, I have used given names to replace the posthumous titles of the principal persons used in the history. Where the title proves important, I have included it parenthetically or added "the future" X.

5. Hu Qian is mentioned in the *Jinshu* several times for his abilities as a diviner, but I have found no further information about him.

6. On Xu Mai, Xu Mi's older brother, see the family biographies, p. XX in chapter 1.

7. "Physiognomizing" 相人 was the art of determining a person's character and fortune through reading the lineaments of their facial features.

Sima showed the physiognomer all of the serving women and maids. At that time, the future Empress was just a palace servant, working in the weaving quarters. She was tall and of dark complexion, so all of the palace people called her "Kunlun."[8] Once she arrived, the physiognomer exclaimed in surprise: "That's the person!" Sima Yu, calculating for the future, summoned her to his bedchamber. The future empress dreamt several times of two dragons pillowing their heads on her knees and of the sun and moon entering into her bosom. She thought this was auspicious and told her associates, so that Sima Yu heard of it and was amazed. Subsequently, she gave birth to Sima Yao 司馬曜[the future Emperor Xiaowu of the Jin, r. 372–96] and to Sima Daozi 司馬道子 [the future Prince of Guiji, 363–402].

孝武文李太后諱陵容，本出微賤。始簡文帝爲會稽王，有三子，俱夭 ... 其後諸姬絕孕將十年。帝令卜者扈謙筮之，曰：「後房中有一女，當育二貴男，其一終盛晉室。」時徐貴人生新安公主，以德美見寵。帝常冀之有娠，而彌年無子。會有道士許邁者，朝臣時望多稱其得道。帝從容問焉，答曰：「邁是好山水人，本無道術，斯事豈所能判！但殿下德厚慶深，宜隆奕世之緒，當從扈謙之言，以存廣接之道。」帝然之，更加採納。又數年無子，乃令善相者召諸愛妾而示之。皆云非其人，又悉以諸婢媵示焉。時后爲宮人，在織坊中，形長而色黑，宮人皆謂之昆侖。既至，相者驚云：「此其人也。」帝以大計，召之侍寢。后數夢兩龍枕膝，日月入懷。意以爲吉祥，向儕類說之。帝聞而異焉。遂生孝武帝及會稽文孝王、鄱陽長公主。[9]

To modern observers, this story will seem to feature male dominance. A spoiled Prince, in his search for a male heir, manipulates the lives of many women, until, finally, he has to reconcile himself to the fact that the woman who can produce children for him is not as good looking as he had wished. And it is quite true that, if women did not give birth, they would not feature prominently in Chinese histories at all. In the context of fourth-century China, however, the reason for preserving a tale like this one in the standard histories was not just interest in blind lust or dynastic succession. Tales of prophecy are ubiquitous in Chinese historical writings. In one way or another, they underscore the participation of an anthropomorphized Heaven in governance. They usually fall into two types. In both types, the prophecy is held to be correct. Heaven does not err, but humans do. The stories either aim to illustrate this directly, as in this case detailing how the celestial message is finally received, or they illustrate the difficulties of understanding Heaven's will through presenting an ironically incorrect interpretation by erring

8. *Kunlun* 昆侖 was a name for island peoples off the coast of southeastern China and Vietnam. They are likely related to modern Malay peoples.
9. Fang Xuanling et al., *Jinshu*, 32:981.

humans. There is a hint of that latter type in this story, insofar as the prince doubts Hu Qian's reading of the yarrow stalks, becomes impatient over time, and finally has to be reminded. But the primary message of the story is that higher powers can provide insight into the future. The unseen powers are shown once again to be particularly concerned with imperial progeny.

This tale helps us assess the prophecy found in the *Declarations*. The very frequency of Sima Yu's attempts to seek divine aid regarding the birth of a son lends an air of believability to Yang Xi's account. There must have been many diviners seeking to win the approval of the imperial house in this case, especially since, given the size of Sima Yu's harem and the prior birth of children, the outcome must have seemed easy to predict. The appearance of Xu Mi's elder brother Xu Mai provides a possible means by which Xu Mi might have introduced his own seer to Sima Yu. While he does not mention the account we have surveyed, this is in fact how Tao Hongjing reads the relationship between Sima Yu and Xu Mi. The fact that Sima Yu had impatiently tried several different diviners would indeed have made it likely that he would eventually consult Yang Xi. Further, the fact that the future empress dreamt of paired things meant that she was determined to produce two appropriate offspring, so, all things considered, it might not have actually been so daring to "predict" that she would indeed accomplish what she set out to do. Finally, the names eventually given the two children seem to point to the prophecies Yang Xi received from his Perfected. Daozi, "child of the Dao," is suggestive, though not explicit, but Yao's name shows up twice in the instructions the Perfected give on how to engender an heir. First, Sima Yu's psychophysical health is described as having rendered his five qi "fructified and glistening" *ciyao* 滋曜—a clear reference to his sexual potency that he is likely to have remembered. And the bamboo he is enjoined to plant to hasten pregnancy is said by another deity to attract the "essences" of the Big Dipper, which is described as a "circling coruscation" *xuanyao* 旋曜 for the way it seems to point in different directions throughout the year.

Of course none of this can prove that the tale recorded in the *Declarations* is *not ex eventu* prophecy. In a literate society conditioned to deploying prophecy for all sorts of mundane ends, rich and convincing details are too easy to furnish after the fact. Still, as in much regarding these records, I tend to believe Tao Hongjing and will treat the event as presented by him.

More important than the truth value of this record is what we today stand to learn from it. Looking closely at Yang's practice, we can see some of the features that may have distinguished him from other Daoist mediums. First, Yang channels not one, but a society of spiritual beings. This feature would, at the very least, distinguish the Daoist medium from those representing popular gods who, likely in the past as in the present, tended to be possessed by a single deity. Second, though it is nearly impossible to present in translation, each of these Perfected speak in their own distinctive voices. They present divergent opinions on any matter and, while they do not often disagree, they do provide a variety of responses to human dilemmas and offer different levels of encouragement or censure. This allows Yang to act at once as the nurturing father and the critical teacher. Third, since Yang's Perfected include both males and females, he is able to enact gender roles in a way that would be unavailable to other mediums. As we will see eventually, he is even able to take on the voice of Xu Mi's departed wife in a convincing way.

In this short series, we will encounter only three voices. The first is that of Lady Wang the Central Watchlord 中候王夫人, the official title of Guanxiang 觀香, the younger sister of the well-known Transcendent Wang Ziqiao, who ascended to the position of Hereditary Consort of the Purple Clarity Palace 紫清宮内傳妃 in the Eastern Seas.[10] Despite this exciting pedigree, Lady Wang the Central Watchlord shows up only a few times in the *Declarations*. This illustrates another advantage of channeling a number of divine beings. If one proves unpopular or makes an incorrect prediction, he or she can be silently dropped from the roster. Neither Tao Hongjing nor we have any information as to why Lady Wang Guanxiang appears so infrequently.[11] The second voice is that of Lady Wang of the Left Palace of Purple Tenuity 紫微左宮王夫人, Wang Qing'e 王青娥 (byname Yuyin 鬱音), twenty-fourth daughter of the great ancient goddess, the Queen Mother of the West.[12] Wang Qing'e often presents her proclamations in highly allusive poetic form, as in this case. Despite the fact that she has never been human, she often cites the classical *Book of Poetry* 詩經. The third voice comes from Lady Right Blossom of the Palace of the Cloudy Grove 雲林宮右英夫人, Wang Meilan 王媚蘭 (byname Shenlin 申林), thirteenth daughter of the Queen Mother of the West. She provides a bit of comforting, almost motherly, advice following up on what must have been some disconcerting news

10. DZ 1016, 3.2a8–b3.

11. Tao explains that she only appears for a short time and is thus difficult to place. See his comments in his postface. This comment seems to insinuate that she was being prepared as a Perfected mate for some new recruit to the practices of Shangqing.

12. See Cahill, *Transcendence and Divine Passion*.

of stellar movements and their effect on the royal family. We will see her in this role often in the revelations that follow. Most importantly, though, she is the goddess who will be promised in spiritual marriage to Xu Mi.[13]

This series of pronouncements is, in essence, prophecy, predicting that Sima Yu will have offspring if only he heeds the advice of the Perfected. Worldwide, good prophecies are difficult to decipher. Both in pursuit of deniability and to allow for the widest chance that they would come true, prophetic messages are constructed to be mystically allusive. But given that the symbolism employed is culture specific, prophecies are difficult of interpretation in different ways. Take a key line from the first part of these revelations. It follows upon allusions to propitious celestial omens that betoken good things both for the kingdom and for Sima Yu. I translated this line as "This is why, through mystic moisture, there is fetal sprouting which subsequently flows into the root."

With regard to such gnomic utterances, we should remember that the images that comprise it were meant to be vaguely allusive even to their intended recipients, so no interpretation is unreservedly correct. Put another way, prophets require deniability if they are to stay in business. Even allowing for that, the multiple signification of terms in Daoist physio-spiritual practice makes the task of interpretation nearly impossible. In our example, "fetus" 胎 can, of course, refer to the actual physical object, but the term is also used in descriptions of meditation to describe the growth of the Transcendent embryo within.[14] The "root" 根 can refer to the penis or vagina and equally to the embryonic qi that grows to fruition within the body.[15] What I have translated as "moisture" 潤 can also mean "grace" since in an agricultural society such as China's rain was often seen as due to the grace of the gods. Thus this line might be interpreted to mean that Consort Li is already pregnant, that Sima Yu will impregnate her in the future, or that his Daoist practice will bear fruit while his consort remains barren. The final conclusion must be: unbounded allusiveness is always a desirable feature of such predictions.

The series ends with an absolutely undecipherable bit of prophecy 讖. The Perfected present it in a complicated palindrome form called *zong huiwen* 綜迴文, in which the characters are not only read from the end

13. For this development, see chapter 1, p. X, and chapter 4, pp. XX–XX.
14. See Bokenkamp, *Early Daoist Scriptures*, 284–85.
15. Bokenkamp, *Early Daoist Scriptures*, 45–46 and 314–15.

forward but also sentences are woven within the block of text.[16] Fortunately, this is the only example in the *Declarations*, another indication of the importance Yang Xi accorded this communication with the royal house. Tao Hongjing, while claiming that the text is extremely difficult, has "broken" the code. His rearrangement of the graphs, though it might once have communicated something to Sima Yu, is even so almost entirely unintelligible to us today. My translation is meant only to indicate the outer limits of gnomic communication that could be achieved. We find represented in this short series of pronouncements, then, a range of divine communication that extends from the prosaic ("Fuhe will bear two sons") to the enigmatic and scarcely comprehensible.

The text begins by referring obliquely to the prince in the most flattering terms as "such a one . . . 者" or the "artisan of virtue 德匠."

. . .

TRANSLATION: THE SONS OF SIMA YU
(dz 1016, 8.9b6–8.12a8)

[The following was] announced to the Gentleman on the twenty-third day of the sixth month by Lady Central Watchlord.[17]

One who through observing things easily adjusts their inclinations, who inwardly follows the bright numina, who gives his inborn nature and fate over to the High Perfected and entrusts his body and qi to the management of the spirits—such a one may overcome the boundaries of time and space and, turning back his autumnal age, maintain Perfection. Now this artisan of virtue has concentrated his spirits and maintained trustworthiness, purifying his mind through secrecy and stillness, and has complied perfectly through wide-ranging respectfulness, thereby solidifying the aid of heaven. However, his progeny are not numerous and will, perhaps, wither away over time. This will make it as if the numinous passes were to become disordered, as if the submerged trigger

16. I know of only one person who has even attempted to work out and translate one of these linguistically dense and impossibly allusive poems. (See Kroll, "Palindrome Poem."). With Tao Hongjing's help, we might do it, but it would require four chapters of this length.

17. This translation covers DZ 1016, 8.9b6–8.12a8. Tao Hongjing notes that it is on four slips of paper in the calligraphy of Yang Xi and that he has copies of the first three slips in Xu Hui's hand. Also, on the very last appearance in this series of revelations, Tao Hongjing notes that "all references to the Gentleman 公 refer to the [future] Jianwen emperor [Sima Yu]."

were not yet secure.[18] At present, [his] five qi are fructified and glistening, bringing a constant gleam to the residences of Literary Glory.[19] The three stars have flowered, and each glows within the ambit of Jade Cog and Transverse.[20] This is why, through mystic moisture, there is fetal sprouting which subsequently flows into the root.

I note that the *Text on the Inner Aspirations of the Ninefold*[21] states: "Bamboo is the highest essence of the northern trigger and receives the qi of the asterism Celestial Coach.[22] This is why it is round, empty, and

18. The "numinous passes" 靈關 exist on both the macrocosmic and microcosmic levels. In the otherworld, various passes are given this name. (See, for instance, DZ 1016, 16.9a, where Tao Hongjing comments on a numinous pass in Fengdu.) According to the Tang period Wucheng zi 務成子, the term in the *Inner Phosphor Scripture of the Yellow Court* 黃庭內景經 (possibly revealed to Yang Xi), refers to any of the vital passes within the body. (See DZ 1032, 12.11b–12a.) Whatever the referent here, the loss of order implied is the same. The term "submerged trigger" 潛機 refers to the hidden motive forces of society and governance, grasped only by sages. (See, for instance, Lu Yun's 陸雲 [262–303] dirge for his relative Lu Xi 陸喜, in Yan Kejun, *Quan Shanggu* 104.7b.)

19. This is the only reference to "five qi" in the *Declarations*. It likely refers to the five elements and, through metonymy, to the parts of the body associated with them. "Literary Glory" 文昌 is the name of a personified constellation in Ursa Major, the Big Dipper. Its seven stars were also regarded as offices that stood as interrelated counterparts to earthly officers. (See Kleeman, *God's Own Tale*, 46–51; Schafer, *Pacing the Void*, 121–23.) The image here is that the imperial way represented by the prince has received celestial approbation.

20. The "three stars" 三星 allude to a line in the "Chou mou" 綢繆 ode of the *Shijing*, which begins "Tied around is the bundled wood; the three stars are in heaven." The Mao commentary takes this ode to be critical of the Jin 晉 kingdom (of the same name as the kingdom that Sima Yu served), highlighting the fact that, due to its disorder, marriages did not take place at the correct time. But the first lines point to the proper time to marry, when the "three stars" appear in the east. Zheng Xuan (127–200) argues that the "three stars" are those of the heart constellation. (See SSJZS 1.364a; for the constellation, see Schafer, *Pacing the Void*, 76–77.) Jade Cog and Transverse 璇衡 are two stars of the Dipper, the first in the bowl and the second in the handle, that stand often for the constellation as a whole. This is also the name given for an ancient instrument, possibly a jade sighting tube. (See Needham and Lu, *Science and Civilisation*, 3:332–39.) Here, I think, the term should refer to the Dipper that figuratively encompasses the "three stars" by pointing at them.

21. There is no further record of such a text. The "ninefold" 九合 may refer to the vertical nine heavens.

22. The Japanese translators state that the "northern trigger" 北機 is the Dipper (SKKY, 290). Perhaps they say this because the Dipper always points to the "northern culmen" 北極 (see Schafer, *Pacing the Void*, 44–46). *Xuanxuan* 玄軒 is here named an asterism 宿, but it is apparently not one known to mundane Chinese astronomy. The term appears in He Yan's 何晏 (d. 249) "Rhapsody on the Hall of Great Blessings" 景福殿賦 where it seems to denote dark-railed balconies. Knechtges translates "Black balconies rise one after another, their lustrous designs bright and brilliant." (See Knechtges, *Wenxuan*, 2:293, lines 228–29). But *xuan* 玄 "dark, mystic" is often glossed as "heaven" and *xuan* 軒 was a type of royal coach with high railings. I suspect that the translation "celestial coach" gets closer to what Yang may have had in mind.

fresh within, a redoubled yin containing pure white. In addition, bamboo all possess straight roots and broadcast their seeds.²³ Their interconnections are extremely numerous and varied."²⁴ The gentleman should try planting bamboo just beyond the northern portico of the inner quarters and have the beauteous one roam freely beneath it. If you do so, then Heaven will move the deities of the [northern] Trigger to bring you great progeny, to protect and fulfill the pregnancies, and to ensure those born have a long life.²⁵ Once the subtle becomes manifest and begins to flourish, it will be ever protected, advantageous, and correct.²⁶ These are the secret regulations of those within the mysterious realms. If you accord with them, you will receive extremely positive verification.

Filial Martiality [Sima Yao 司马曜, r. 372–96] was born in the *renxu* year [362], so this should have been revealed in the *xingyou* year [361].²⁷ Below it says that "The position of the Upper Minister moves, later it will ascend to the apex."²⁸ The [fulfillment of this prophecy] occurred in the latter *wuwei* year [370 and 371].²⁹ This is quite a gap of time.

23. Bamboo are semelparous, all flowering at the same time at intervals of 30–120 years, depending on the location and species. But the mass production of seeds is what is at issue here.

24. Since this text does not exist, it is impossible to determine precisely where the citation from it ends. The Japanese translation team ends the citation after the first sentence, allowing Lady Wang to continue rhapsodizing on the bamboo on her own (SKKY, 290). I choose to think that the citation ends when she addresses Sima Yu directly.

25. The term "triggering deities" or "deity" 機神 appears only once in the *Declarations*, but sporadically in nearly contemporary texts. Ge Hong 葛洪 (283–343) mentions the term several times in contexts that suggest the god is in charge of perception. (See Ge Hong, *Baopuzi waipian*, 1:477 and 2:126.) But there is also an undated passage on the stars in DZ 1032 (24.2a–b) that gives the role of the sixth star of the Dipper as "fate triggering spirit" 命機神. Once again, it is difficult to know whether we have to do here with a god of the macrocosm or the microcosm.

26. The last two terms "advantageous and correct" are common language in the Book of Changes.

27. "Filial Martiality" 孝武 is the imperial temple name posthumously given to Sima Yao. He reigned as emperor of the Jin from 372 to 396.

28. The "Upper Minister" 上相 is a star in our Virgo but located among the four stars of the Eastern Barrier 東蕃, part of the bulwark around the important southern stellar residence of the Thearch known as Grand Tenuity 太微. (See Schafer, *Pacing the Void*, 52.) Chinese portent astronomy held that movement of this star meant that a member of the higher bureaucracy was plotting to become emperor. (See Fang Xuanling et al., *Jinshu*, 11.291–92.)

29. These are the dates of Sima Yu's tenure as emperor.

夫觀物適任，³⁰ 內順明靈，託性命於高眞，委形氣於神攝者，亦剋疆
以永遐，迴秋齡以保眞。今德匠既凝神杖信，澄心密靜，圓順廣敬，
固天祐焉。然胤嗣不多，或時彫落。將猶靈關失緯，潛機未鎭耳。當
今五氣滋曜，常朗文昌之房。三星結華，每煥璇衡之內。是以玄潤胎
萌，遂其流根矣。我案九合內志文曰：竹者爲北機上精，受氣於玄軒
之宿也。所以圓虛內鮮，重陰含素。亦皆植根敷實，結繁衆多矣。公
試可種竹於內北宇之外。使美者游其下焉。爾乃天感機神，大致繼
嗣。孕既保全，誕亦壽考。微著之興，常守利貞。此玄人之祕規，行
之者甚驗。³¹

六月二十三日。中候夫人告公。（孝武壬戌生。³² 此應是辛酉年。而
後又云。上相座動。後以臨登極。乃是後午未年。此爲大懸。）

[The following poem] was composed by Lady Purple Tenuity.

The numinous plant will be protected in the dark direction,
Looking up to incite the essences of circling coruscation.[33]
Multitudinous, flourishing, densely sprouting—[34]
He of multiple virtues will certainly be fecund.

靈草廳玄方。仰感旋曜精。〔洗洗〕（似草作言邊。³⁵ 應詵詵字。即
毛詩螽斯羽洗洗兮宜爾子孫之義也。）
繁茂萌。重德必克昌。³⁶
紫微夫人作。

That same night, [Lady] Central Watchlord revealed [the following]:

30. I am following the Yu edition in correcting 天 to 夫.

31. This portion of the text is cited in the *Guang bowu zhi* 廣博物志, 43.33b (SKQS edition).

32. Correcting 王 to 壬 on the basis of sense. which gives her name as 陵容.

33. The Japanese translation team holds that "circling corruscation" 旋耀 refers to a god of the northern Dipper. (See SKKY, 291.) This is plausible, but they give no evidence.

34. After the first graphs of this line, which appear as 洗洗, Tao notes: "These seem to be grass-style forms of the speech radical. The characters should read 詵詵 'multitudinous.' The meaning is the same as the lines 'The wings of the locusts are multitudinous; it is right that your sons and grandsons be multitudinous' from the "Zhongsi" 螽斯 ode no. 5 of the Shijing." (For this poem, see Karlgren, *Book of Odes*, 4.)

35. Following the Yu edition in correcting 竹 to 言.

36. After Du Guangting's listing of this poem as one of a series of seven in his *Yongcheng jixian lu* (DZ 783, 3.10b2–4), the poem appears in the same way in DZ 980, 22b and DZ 1032, 97.16a. DZ 980 and 1032 give the first graph of the poem as "cloud" 雲 rather than "numinous" 靈.

Fuhe will bear two sons. They will be replete in virtue and will command the generation.[37]

Fuhe 福和 seems to be the youthful name of Lady Li before she was ennobled. The present *Jinshu* gives her name as Junrong 俊容.[38] Her two sons were Filial Martiality and his younger brother, Sima Daozi 司馬道子 [364–403]. The previous three slips were written out by Yang Xi and also copied by the Accounts Clerk Xu Hui.

福和者當有二子。盛德命世。（福和似是李夫人賤時小名也。今晉書名俊容。二子即孝武并弟道子也）

同夜中候告。（右三條楊書。又掾寫）

Since the architect of virtue has consolidated his powers, the mystic plan will come from heaven. It is not yet proper to inquire as to safety or peril. The Gentleman has fully poured forth [his thoughts]. The reason we have not yet responded is that future affairs are difficult to discuss. Recently the qi of Heaven has been rushing about tumultuously. The yin glow has changed repeatedly, while Grand White dissolves between the two chronograms, then transgresses, bursting out below the Purple Chambers.[39] These are evil portents for the Prince and sorrow for the child of heaven [his father, the emperor]. The position of the Upper Minister moves.[40] Now I have provisionally completed a prediction that I show to you secretly.

This prediction was copied out by Accounts Clerk Xu Hui on the same sheet of paper on which he himself had made a note of Daoist practices.[41] I have found that the plaited palindrome arranged by the Perfected is extremely difficult to understand. Now I have rearranged it to pull out the meaning and decode it on a separate sheet. When this was received from the Perfected, they only spoke the lyrics and Lord Yang Xi then deciphered it himself. It speaks of the affairs of the Jin period and has been clearly verified.

37. This is the one line that seems to argue against Wang Jiakui's reconstruction of the events connected to these prophecies. The sentence seems to read "Fuhe *will* [in the future] give birth to two sons who . . ."

38. This is not the *Book of Jin* mentioned above, which gives her name as 陵容.

39. "Yin glow" 陰景 likely here refers to the moon. Grand White 太白 is Venus and the "two chronograms" 二辰 are the sun and the moon. "Purple Chambers" 紫房 stands for the circumpolar constellation, the Palace of Purple Tenuity 紫微宮.

40. This line does not end as Tao's previous note says that it should.

41. At DZ 1016, 10.2b, there is, for instance, a record of the method for retaining the black and the white 守玄白之道 that was copied out by Xu Mi. This may be the sheet that Tao mentions here.

德匠既凝，玄範自天，安危之事，未宜問也。公傾注甚至，所以未相
酬者，豫事難論耳。頃天氣激逸，陰景屢變。太白解體於二辰之中，
愆勃於紫房之下。王者惡焉，天子有憂。上相座動。今聊作讖，密以
相示。（右此及讖有掾寫。⁴²在掾自記修事後共紙。尋眞綜迴文令難
解耳。今拘連相取。又別疏出之。其授之時，維當道其辭。楊君後自
更錯義。皆是說晉代之事，竝有明徵也。）

. . .

I have omitted the original palindrome and translate only Tao Hongjing's
reconstruction. It is dense enough to give the reader some idea of the
level of mystification found in such texts. Under such conditions, the
translation I provide can only be hypothetical. –Trans.

. . .

When one's essences, qi, and spirits are wondrous, one might make a
　triad with the two mechanisms.[43]

What one might be cautious in transmitting to a mortal, the sage
　ones put into practice.
Sealing heaven, controlling earth, there is nothing inappropriate.
If you are able to treasure it in secrecy, Heaven will know of it.
My Way is essential and wondrous, how could it deceive you?
Since you possess wondrous inner spirits, you set measures before
　warfare breaks out.
If fire appears even briefly across the three and five, Heaven pro-
　vides it with auspiciousness.[44]
Outstanding ages in alternation, calculated through cyclical fate.
If the brilliant artisan preserves his virtue, he should be cautious not
　to contemplate it.
To drive off evil and eradicate the recalcitrant, one urgently seeks a
　Master.

42. Following the Yu edition in correcting 有 to 右.
43. The "two mechanisms" 二儀—variously glossed as heaven and earth, sun and
moon, yang and yin—are best seen as the fundamental principles underlying existence
itself. When the world cycle ends, the two merge into undifferentiation. Thus to "make a
triad" 參 with the two is to live to the end of the world age.
44. The three and the five are, respectively, vertical and horizontal and represent a
variety of interlocking categories: heaven-man-earth and the five phases, for example.

A technique worth ten thousand in gold—the rising of the dragon.
Outstanding fates end with three—a loss of one's sons.[45]
Do not calculate its origins, Liu Xiang knows.[46]
After evil fans its chaos, the imperial will return to its foundations.
Availing himself of heaven, ordering earth, he will quell the western
  Yi peoples.
He who will control the refractory has a date to be determined.
The craftsman should not worry, sorrow distances danger.
In only five generations—it will be a matter for sorrow.
But there is a limit to the time granted usurpers—the Thearch's seat
  is broken.
We will see changes in profusion, one after another.[47]
Golden chambers reside in this.[48]

Lady Right Blossom announced [the following] for the Gentleman:
Place a single container of musk incense under your neck as a pillow to
drive off watery infusions and stop bad dreams. It would be good to
constantly envision your three passes.[49]

Wherever it says "the Gentleman" it refers to Sima Yu, when he was
Prince of Xiang. The previous was written on one slip in Yang Xi's
handwriting, and the last five graphs were written in vermilion.[50]

精氣神妙參二儀。慎傳凡人賢者施。封天制地無不宜。子能寶祕天知
之。吾道要妙豈相欺〕[51] 自有奇神先兵規。火寸三五天瑞之。隆代迭換

45. The Japanese translation team, which reserves its collective judgment on the
meaning of most of these images, takes this one to refer to Sima Yu's death at the age of
fifty-three *sui*. (See SKKY, 294n5.) I think it could as easily refer to the three sons that
Sima Yu lost to early death.

46. Liu Xiang 劉向 (77–6 BCE) was a scholar, historiographer, and astronomer of
the Han period. It was his son, Liu Xin 劉歆 (d. 23 CE), who was more closely involved
with calendrics and prediction. (See Bokenkamp, "Time after Time," 63–67). But perhaps
I am missing something.

47. To this point, the poem has been divided into lines of seven characters in length.
The final four characters of the 144-character *huiwen* are also part of the poem.

48. We should probably understand this as the Japanese translation team suggests,
as a summary sentence meaning roughly: "This is how the imperial house will fare."

49. The three passes appear in the *Huangting neijing jing* in an injunction to keep
them sealed. Traditional commentaries give several options, but the most relevant here is
likely a point three inches below the navel through which essence or semen was believed
to pass. See DZ 1032, 11.37a–b.

50. I assume that the "last five graphs" refers to the phrase "It would be good to
constantly envision your three passes," absent the final particle.

51. Correcting 期 to 欺 on the basis of the palindrome.

運相推。明匠保德愼無思。驅惡除逆疾尋師。[52]萬金之術龍之熙。隆數卒三失由兒。莫測其源劉向知。有凶撥亂皇復基。乘天命世遂平夷。制逆者誰必定期。匠不足慮憂遠危。　五世之間眞可悲。篡歷有數帝座虧。當見變異紛紛來。金室在茲。枕麝香一具於頸間。辟水注之來。絕惡夢矣。常存三關佳也。右英告公。（凡云公者，皆簡文帝爲相王時也。[53]）

右一條楊書。（五字朱書）

52. Correcting 思 to 師 on the basis of the palindrome.
53. Following the Yu edition in correcting 主 to 王.

CHAPTER FOUR

"Eight Pages of Lined Text"

INTRODUCTION TO THE "EIGHT PAGES OF LINED TEXT"

The following passages were originally part of a single document, eight pieces of paper in length. According to a note by Tao Hongjing, the pages were lined, and the document seems to have been written by two different persons. Yang's calligraphy appeared only on the final page. Nonetheless, Tao Hongjing affirms that, in his opinion, the document originated from Yang Xi. He clearly had other copies of a few of the passages that were in the calligraphy of Yang Xi. And indeed, the gods that feature in these passages are those who regularly appear in Yang's scriptures. The importance of this text, if it can be reconstructed, is that it was written out in scriptural style and provides us with the earliest "edition" of what was held to be the first Buddhist text to arrive in China.[1] As I have reconstructed it, the "eight pages" included:

1. Poems on the theme of dependence and independence discussing the suitability of arranging for a spirit marriage for Xu Mi. (DZ 1016, 3.2b8–5a5)

2. The account of the Han emperor Liu Zhuang's 劉莊 (r. 57–75 CE) dream of a golden man that led to the introduction of

---

1. For this scriptural style, see Cui Zhonghui, *Fojiao chuqi*, 111ff.

Buddhism to the Central Kingdom by land. (DZ 1016, 9.19b7–20b2)

3. A description of the mythical isles of Fangzhu, floating in the Eastern Seas, where Buddhism originated as well as some of the practices appropriate to that place. (DZ 1016, 9.20b.2–23a6)

4. The "Teachings and Admonitions of the Assembled Numinous Powers" 眾靈教戒, a collection of sayings from the gods of Fangzhu that plagiarizes a good part of what came to be known as the Buddhist *Scripture in Forty-Two Sections*. (DZ 1016, 6.6a1–12b7)

As I have indicated, these elements were dispersed in three chapters of the received edition of the *Declarations*. My justification for this reconstruction of the content of the eight pages follows my translation of Tao's note confirming at least part of this ordering, provided in context below.[2]

The contents of this document will seem strange to modern readers. At first sight it is far from clear how these various pieces of poetry and narrative fit together. The document begins with a poetic debate between the Perfected as to whether it is a good idea for Xu Mi to enter into a spiritual marriage with one of the Perfected.[3] Next is a passage copied from some source concerning the arrival of Buddhism, followed by a series of descriptions of the Fangzhu 方諸 Isles. These islands are said to float in the seas to the northeast of China, like Fusang or Penglai, the traditional home of Transcendents.[4] Significantly, the smaller of the Fangzhu Islands is the original home of the teachings of the Buddha.

2. It seems to me that the only hypothetical part of the reconstruction I am making is including the sections on Fangzhu just as they appear in the modern *Declarations* as part of the eight pages. My justification for this inclusion precedes Tao Hongjing's note joining these passages (see pp. 165–168).

3. Xu Mi's name is not mentioned in the poems. We only have Tao Hongjing's explanaton that the "poetry debate" poems were intended to discuss his forthcoming spiritual union, together with the fact that Lady of the Eastern Grove was later promised Xu Mi in marriage. But when they were composed, they might in fact have referred to any person to whom Yang wanted to introduce a Perfected mate. I borrow the term "poetry debate" from Paul W. Kroll's "Poetry Debate," the first translation of this series of poems. My debt to Kroll's elegant translations is too thoroughgoing to acknowledge at every point where I have benefited from his work.

4. See Needham and Lu, *Science and Civilisation*, 5.2:97 and Nienhauser, *Grand Scribe's Records*, 1:142. For a translation of one early account of these locales, not in this case including Fangzhu, see Smith, "Record." In fact, *fangzhu* might be an alternate name for one of the earliest attested isles, *fanghu* 方壺, also known as 壺梁 *huliang*.

The "Way of the Buddha" 佛道 has been practiced there since the division of the heavens from the earth. By implication, it is superior to the Buddhism that has come from foreign lands across dusty inland roads. In addition, we learn here techniques for ingesting solar and lunar emanations that are practiced by the Perfected of these isles. This information is followed immediately by passages cribbed from the early and widely popular Chinese Buddhist apocryphon, the *Scripture in Forty-Two Sections* 四十二章經. As I will show, the main thread linking these disparate bits of text is formed by the deities who pronounce them.

The *Scripture in Forty-Two Sections* is not identified as such in the *Declarations*. In the form it has come down to us in the Buddhist canon, it comprises forty-two sayings presented as the "words of the Buddha" 佛說. Each of the "sections" or "paragraphs" 章 present basic knowledge concerning Buddhist practice and morality in simple language with ample metaphorical illustration. For example, "The Buddha said: The practice of the Way is like holding a burning torch and entering into a dark room: the darkness immediately vanishes and everything is illumined."[5] But Yang Xi has altered the aphorisms to make them accord with his message and put them into the mouths of many of the same Perfected who pronounced on Xu Mi's prospects. Following the single document are a few items that seem to continue it in the same vein. These include new sections that do not appear in the received *Scripture in Forty-Two Sections*.

While Tao Hongjing's note indicates clearly that the passages I have marked as nos. 1 and 4 came from a single document, some later redactor has moved no. 1, the eleven debate poems, to the third scroll of the present work. They seem to fit there with the other Perfected poems in the chapter and, to my knowledge, no one has ever remarked upon the fact that they have been moved. Nonetheless, they do appear out of place in that there is no annotation from Tao Hongjing telling readers which calligrapher was responsible for the copy he had seen, as is common for other entries in the first four chapters. The redactor left that annotation back in what is now chapter 6 of the present work.[6]

---

5. Sharf, "Scripture in Forty-Two Sections," 367.

6. Interestingly, the modern scholar Zhao Yi 趙益 seems to have noticed the discrepancy. He added after the poetic debate the note "To the right, from the graphs *jiaxu* to here, there are eleven pieces. They are written in two hands. 右從「駕欻」來有十一篇，有兩手寫." (Zhao Yi, "*Zhen'gao*," 47). Zhao Yi gives no source for this note, and it does not appear in any of the editions of the *Declarations* that I have been able to check. He seems to have moved the remark from chapter 6.

The passages I have marked nos. 2 and 3—on the Emperor's dream and Fangzhu—fit where I have placed them for several reasons. Most important is the fact that the Emperor's dream serves as a preface to no. 4, the "Teachings and Admonitions," and the Fangzhu section is implicitly tied to it by Tao Hongjing. Further, the revealing deities for the Fangzhu materials are the same high gods who, Tao notes, seem not to have appeared regularly to Yang Xi. Nonetheless, it is significant that they all are associated with Fangzhu in one way or another.

The reason that these diverse messages—from poems addressed to Xu Mi to aphorisms clearly meant for a wider audience—were written out in such a formal fashion is not certain today. Nonetheless, they might be grouped under the rubric "messages from the higher deities of Fangzhu." Further, we can speculate that Tao Hongjing is correct in his assertion that this document seems to derive from the time when "the Perfected first descended to Yang" with information to pass on to the Xus. If that is the case, then the document may represent Yang Xi's first and awe-inspiring transmission to the Xu family. Since the eight pages included the higher deities' permission to train Xu Mi, the passages on the Fangzhu Isles and the simplified meditation for ingesting the rays of sun and moon, it would have been a good advertisement to the kind of materials Yang was receiving from the Perfected.

The formal way that the eight pages were written on lined paper, however, indicates that they were intended as a scriptural treasure in their own right. There are, in fact, mid-fifth-century Buddhist scriptures that were presented in this fashion.[7] Since the eight pages seem to have been done in what was a standard form for the imperial library, and Tao Hongjing cannot recognize the hand in which they were written, they may have been prepared by later Daoists for presentation in the Jin court. Tao Hongjing mentions in his account of the diffusion of the Shangqing manuscripts several times when this might have happened.[8] Be that as it may, Tao Hongjing's notes indicate that these diverse items were once parts of a continuous passage in the *Declara-*

---

7. See Cui Zhonghui, *Fojiao chuqi*, 111–14.

8. Tao Hongjing's postface mentions three occasions when parts of the Shangqing scriptures and bits of the *Declarations* were taken to the court. The first is implied by the close relationship between Yang Xi and Sima Yu, who held the throne briefly during the Jin from 371 to 372. The second was in 465, when Shu Jizhen brought documents to the youthful and impetuous Liu-Song emperor, Liu Ziye 劉子業 (449–66). And the third was in 481, when Lu Xiujing's disciple, Xu Shubiao, provided chapters for the emperor of the Qi dynasty.

tions. And, whether prepared by Yang and the Xus or by later Daoists, these parts of the revelations were linked by their association with Fangzhu and the higher deities residing there.

The inclusion of so much Buddhist material, as well as Tao Hongjing's assertion that the "two ways" (our "Buddhism" and "Daoism") share common goals, leads to further interesting questions. The *Scripture in Forty-Two Sections* seems to have existed in some form as early as 166 CE, when it was cited in a memorial to the emperor.[9] The *Scripture* had as preface the legend of the arrival of Buddhism in China as the result of an imperial dream. These two copies of what must have been earlier Buddhist material were, in fact, what first attracted scholars to the study of the *Declarations of the Perfected*. Already in the twelfth century, the neo-Confucian scholar Zhu Xi 朱熹 (1130–1200) noticed that passages from the *Declarations* "stole ideas from the *Scripture in Forty-Two Sections*."[10] Much later, the famous intellectual modernizer Hu Shi (1891–1962) excoriated Tao Hongjing's editorship of a "superstitious" Daoist work. How could a scholar and proto-scientist like Tao have anything to do with such things? Clearly, Tao Hongjing's thinking had been muddled by religious "superstition."[11] Others, like Tang Yongtong (1883–1945) exploited Yang Xi's "theft" to clarify the editorial history of the early Buddhist work.[12]

Reading Yang Xi's plagiary in context, however, adds to our understanding of the very process by which Buddhism came to be accepted and spread in China. First of all, we learn something important about Buddhism's acceptance among the intelligentsia of the fourth and fifth centuries CE from the facts that (1) Yang thought he could produce a revealed version of this popular early Buddhist scripture and (2) Tao Hongjing, some 125 years later, did not feel that he had to conceal the deed. How was it that one could hope to establish the idea that there was another, superior, Buddhism originating in the Transcendent isles floating in the shrouded Eastern Seas?[13] And what did the creation of unseen links between the foreign religion and time-honored Chinese myth mean for the acceptance of Buddhism?

9. See Sharf, "Scripture," 360–64.

10. See Hu Shi, "Tao Hongjing," 140.

11. Discussed in Hu Shi's "Tao Hongjing," especially 5.131–32.

12. See T'ang Yung-t'ung (Tang Yongtong), "Editions," 149ff. Another early account is Henri Maspero's (1883–1945) "Le songe."

13. For an engaging account of these ancient, water-borne, paradises as expressed in early texts and in the works of a ninth-century CE poet, see Schafer, *Mirages*.

Second, reading Daoist appropriations of Buddhist concepts and practice helps us to understand just what attracted medieval Chinese to the religion. As Daoists sought to naturalize the foreign religion, they naturally "stole" aspects that they believed would solve problems or answer questions for them. In this way, the borrowers paradoxically validated Buddhist ideas and practices and suggested ways in which the religion might accommodate itself to Chinese conditions. One obvious contribution of Buddhism was its introduction of new ways of understanding death and postmortem existence. In the following passages, however, we will notice in addition elements of Buddhist morality and approaches to wisdom that equally attracted early Chinese observers.

Third, once we stop thinking in terms of isms and begin to probe the ways that the teachings of the Buddha really interacted with other systems of thought in early medieval China, we encounter what to the twenty-first century scholar might seem a novel religious understanding. It is one that views human comprehension as always partial and flawed, thus allowing for a number of paths to the "Truth." Rather than seeking for differences and declaring one path right and others wrong, such an understanding seeks for commonalities that might point to the Ultimate, which, at any rate can only be approximated in human language. This is demonstrated here by the fact that, beyond correcting whatever edition of the *Scripture in Forty-Two Sections* he had acquired, Yang Xi was inspired to seek further inspiration from his deities to write his own sections as a continuation.

The Perfected beings who appear in the pages that follow are listed below in order of appearance. The first ten contributed poems to the poetic debate on Xu Mi's divine marriage. Numbers 8, 9, and 10 also appeared in the section on 'Teachings and Admonitions of the Numinous Spirits," the "original" version of the *Scripture in Forty-Two Sections*. Lord Wang of the Western Citadel and the Lady of Dark Purity did not offer opinions on the debate, but the rare appearance of these two high deities does link the section on Fangzhu with the "Teachings and Admonitions."

1. Lady Right Blossom of the Palace of the Cloudy Grove 雲林宮右英夫人, Wang Meilan 王媚蘭 (byname Shenlin 申林), thirteenth daughter of the great goddess Xiwangmu 西王母

2. Lady Wang of the Left Palace of Purple Tenuity 紫微左宮王夫人, Wang Qing'e 王青娥 (byname Yuyin 鬱音), twenty-fourth daughter of Xiwangmu

3. The Perfected of Mount Tongbo 桐柏山眞人, Wang Ziqiao 王子喬.

4. Perfected of Pure Numinosity 清靈真人, Lord Pei 裴君, Xuanren 玄仁

5. Lady Wang the Central Watchlord of the Eastern Palaces 東宮中候夫人, Wang Guanxiang 王觀香, third daughter of the ancient King Ling of Zhou 周靈王 and younger sister (by a different mother) of Wang Ziqiao

6. Lady Li of Splendid Numen 昭靈李夫人, the daughter of Li Qingbin 李慶賓, who is Dao Lord of the Inner Mystery of the Northern Prime 北元內玄道君, and also the little sister of Li Lingfei 李靈飛[14]

7. The Perfected Consort of of Nine Blossoms in the Highest Palace of Purple Clarity 紫清上宮九華真妃, An Yubin 安鬱嬪 (byname Lingxiao 靈簫)

8. Great Void Perfected of the Southern Marchmount 太虛南嶽真人, Master Red Pine 赤松子

9. Azure Lad of Fangzhu 方諸青童君

10. Lady Wang of Purple Prime in the Southern Culmen 南極紫元夫人, Wang Lin 王林 (byname Rongzhen 容真), fourth daughter of Xiwangmu

11. Lord Wang of the Western Citadel 西城真人王君, Wang Yuan 王遠, byname Fangping 方平. This deity is also known as "the Most High" 太上 or "the Overlord" 上宰.[15]

12. Lady of Dark Purity, of the Six Tenuities in the North Sea 北海六微玄清夫人

While he does not doubt that they came from the brush of Yang Xi, Tao Hongjing has some reservations about how this series of revelations came into Yang's hands. Of the latter five deities, he writes, "These three male Perfected and two female Perfected are all the most revered of the Higher Perfected. They seldom descend [to the mortal realms]." He further points out that "The Azure Lad, [Lady] Purple Prime, and the Great Void [Perfected of the Southern Marchmount] never descended together, unless something has been lost." He thus feels that the poems and messages of these deities must have been reported to Yang Xi

14. In translating the titles of this goddess, I followed a suggestion of Kroll, "Poetry Debate," 11.

15. See SKKY, 230, notes 13 and 14.

through one of the other Perfected. And he gives an example where this sort of thing occurred.

. . .

INTRODUCTION TO POEMS ON DEPENDENCE AND INDEPENDENCE

According to Tao Hongjing, the following series of eleven poems debate the question of Xu Mi's suitability for marriage with Lady Right Blossom of the Cloudy Grove. She is the first to compose a verse. To set the question, she draws on the story from the *Zhuangzi* concerning Liezi's vaunted ability to harness the wind and fly. Zhuangzi's critique of Liezi was "Well, he could avoid walking, but there was still something upon which he depended!" 此雖免乎行，猶有所待者也。 Implicitly, this critique is redirected to Xu Mi: If, through marriage to a Perfected being, Xu is able to "fly," is he not still just as dependent as was Liezi on the wind? "Is he, then, really worth our while?" the Perfected implicitly ask. At stake is the question of whether or not any human is worth divine aid in their quest for self-perfection. Lady Right Blossom answers this question in the affirmative. She thus begins her poem with a forthright challenge: "I come for the sake of dependence." In the Daoist world, this is not always a good thing, and the Perfected all voice their own opinions on the matter in ways that I will try to indicate in brief notes to each poem.

Beyond the passage from Zhuangzi, the central metaphor that informs these texts is the idea that the goddesses must cross from the Eastern Isles over the "blue-green waves" of the sea to finally arrive at Mount Mao. This crossing is figured as a move from the celestial to the mundane, to be sure, but it also mimics poems from the *Book of Poetry* that describe how women "lift their skirts" 褰裳 as they cross streams to join lovers on the spring festival held on the third day of the third lunar month.[16] The idea that crossing between existential realms entails a challenging liminal moment is explored in a number of the poems we will encounter later as well.

16. Bokenkamp, "Zhengzha," 61–65.

TRANSLATION: POEMS ON DEPENDENCE AND INDEPENDENCE

(dz 1016, 3.2b8–3.5a5)

This is the song of the Lady of Right Blossom:

Piloting wisps of qi I roam far into the eight directions of Void;
Turning back to feast in chambers of the Eastern Flower.
Amah invites me to the railed balcony of her Watchtower,[17]
Whistling a clear note, I tread the numinous winds.
Now I have come for the sake of dependence—
For this reason, I have traversed the blue-green waves.[18]

駕欻敖八虛。徊宴東華房。阿母延軒觀。朗嘯躡靈風。我爲有待來。
故乃越滄浪。右英王夫人歌。

Lady Right Blossom is the Perfected being who was eventually promised in spiritual union to the mortal Xu Mi. We might paraphrase her poem as follows: I roam independently throughout space, traveling to the extremities of east and west, not by means of mundane wind, mind you, but bits of qi and the spiritual counterpart of wind. Now I cross the muddy waters from my home on the floating isles of Fangzhu for the sake of a human's need for dependency. –Trans.

. . .

This is the song of the Lady of Purple Tenuity in response to Right Blossom:

Mounted on a whirlwind, I travel down the Nine Heavens
To rest my mount on the peaks of the Three Eminences.[19]

17. *Amah* is "a term of affectionate familiarity used to refer to the Queen Mother of the West by her daughters" (Kroll, "Poetry Debate," 579).

18. While the imaginative topographies of the Shangqing scriptures are extremely difficult to fathom, the term "blue-green waves" 滄浪 can be placed with relative accuracy. The name is applied to the oceans that separate gods and mortals, and sometimes to the mountains floating in those oceans where the two might meet. See, for instance, Schipper, *L'empereur*, 100n6, translating DZ 292, 13a–b. It is thus symbolically the intervening river that lovers had to cross to be together on the third of the third month (see Granet, *Fêtes et Chansons*, 103–4), or that had to be traversed by the herd boy and the weaving girl on the ninth of the ninth month (Schafer, *Pacing the Void*, 144–48). In this series of poems, it is the Perfected who must cross the waves into the dust of our world.

19. According to Tao Hongjing, the "Three Eminences" 三秀 are the three peaks of Mount Mao, imagined as blossoms open to the sky. (See DZ 1016, 2.16a1–3.)

As to dependence—I pace back and forth, gazing this way and that;
For independence, one must in fact be still,
But how is it laborious to cross the blue-green waves?
How could it be anything like traversing the Mystic Well?[20]

乘飆遡九天。息駕三秀嶺。有待徘徊眪。無待故當靜。[21] 滄浪奚足
勞。孰若越玄井。　右紫微夫人答英歌。

. . .

Lady Purple Tenuity, the divine instructor who will serve as the intermediary for Yang Xi's union with Consort An, is a frequent visitor to the triple peaks of Mount Mao. She seems willing to find a mate herself. She paces expectantly but has not found someone to depend upon her. She will find such a mate, since humans lack the purity to achieve true independence. For her, the trip is not the main concern. As younger sister, she chides Consort An; the trip to the human world is really not all that difficult. While the exact referent of the term "Mystic Well" is unclear, it is apparently more difficult to cross than the seas between Fangzhu and the human world. Perhaps it refers to a spot in the highest of the Nine Heavens, which she has apparently just visited. Others will have more to say about this journey. –Trans.

. . .

This is the song of the Perfected of Mount Tongbo, Wang Ziqiao:

Once they'd transported me from the Halls of the Gold Court,
I released my steeds in the demesne of the Three Eminences.[22]
Overnight holy plants cloak the floriate peaks,
Chewing them satisfies even the deepest hunger.
I sing on high that this is not a carefree jaunt—
Each time I raise the song of dependence.

20. Given the comparison here, it seems likely that the Perfected use this locution to refer to the "Celestial Well" 天井, a term that refers at once to a spot in the body, images of the stellar cosmos portrayed on tomb roofs, and, in the macrocosm, the lunar lodging known briefly as "well." (See Bokenkamp, *Ancestors and Anxiety*, 143n34; DZ 1139, 7.9a; and Schafer, *Pacing the Void*, 82.) The word I translate here as "mystic" 玄 is commonly glossed "heaven" 天. Whether I am correct or not, the term "Mystic Well" 玄井 is found only in these poems.

21. DZ 783, 3.7a: 盼 for 眪, 靜 for 淨; DZ 980, 18b and DZ 1032, 97.10a–b: 盼 for 眪, 靜 for 淨. I accept the latter variant since "stillness" will be referred to again below.

22. The translation "demesne" is from Kroll, "Poetry Debate," 580.

For the empty hollows to harmonize with numinous tones—[23]
How could this be done independently?

寫我金庭館。解駕三秀畿。夜芝披華〔鋒〕。(謂應作峰字) 咀嚼充長
飢。[24]高唱無逍遥。各興有待歌。[25] 空同酬靈音。無待將如何。右桐
柏山眞人歌。

. . .

Wang Ziqiao, who appears to Yang as a very young man speaking an
incomprehensible language, wearing a sword, and crowned in lotus, is a
sometime visitor to the three peaks of Mount Mao. He knows the wonders
hidden there, but reminds all that coming even to this holy spot in the
human world is not pleasurable. Each visit can have only one purpose, to
instruct needy humans who, despite their fortunate residence, would
never be able to resonate with the holy harmonies of heaven without divine
assistance. –Trans.

. . .

This is the song of the Perfected Pure Numinosity [Lord Pei].

Mornings I roam Mount Mottled Cliffs;
Evenings, I take my rest in the Hall of Lofty Brilliance.[26]
Giving a shake to the reins, I ascend numinous peaks at a walk.
I never draw near the blue-green waves.
Though the Mystic Well's edge be thirty feet distant,

---

23. The term 空同, which I translate as "empty hollows," appears throughout these
poems and throughout Yang's writings more generally. It seems to refer to mountains
containing cavern heavens within, Mount Mao in this case. The *locus classicus* is the
Zhuangzi: "When the Yellow Thearch was established as Child of Heaven for nineteen
years, he traveled throughout the realm. Guangchengzi was on top of [Mount] Empty
Hollows so the Thearch went to see him." 《莊子·在宥》：" 黃帝立爲天子十九年，令行
天下，聞廣成子在於空同之上，故往見之。 Guo Xiang 郭象 (252–312) states that it is
"a mountain directly below the Dipper." (See *Zhuangzi zhu*, SKQS, 20b–21a). We are
clearly dealing with a mythological spot that is cognate with the void of cavernous space
that existed as one of the stages in cosmogenesis, the "Vacuous Grotto" 空洞. (See
Bokenkamp, *Early Daoist Scriptures*, 191–92.)

24. DZ 1132, 1.5a–5b, 峰 for 鋒, 無 for 充. Since Tao's note also gives 峰 as correct,
I follow that.

25. Following the Yu edition variant reading 各 for 冬.

26. These are Lord Pei's normal haunts. According to his biography, he resides on
the easternmost of the three peaks that form Ge Yan 葛衍 Mountain, Mount Mottled Cliff
Root 鬱絕根山. Mount Lofty Brilliance 高暉山 is situated between his abode and Mount
Kunlun, the residence of the Queen Mother of the West. See DZ 1032, 105.10a6–10b5.
Apparently, the source of the brilliance is his hall.

There are no fords or bridges for *my* horses.
On a wisp of qi they travel ninety thousand *li*;[27]
And we'll gaze on one another across the eight extents.
Dependence is not the ultimate Nothingness—
Something is missing from the numinous tones.

朝遊鬱絕山。夕偃高暉堂。振轡步靈〔鋒〕。（謂應作峰字）無近於
滄浪。玄井三仞際。我馬無津梁。儵欻九萬間。八維已相望。有待非
至無。靈音有所喪。
右清靈眞人歌。

Lord Pei's biography was composed by one of his disciples, the Perfected
Deng Yunzi 鄧雲子.[28] He was one of the higher Perfected whose messages were leaked by Hua Qiao and, as we shall see, his message was
rather more subtle than what Hua could handle.[29] Perhaps his experience
with Hua has made him reluctant to have further dealings with humans.
Whatever the case, he here strongly denies any human's ability to correctly harmonize with the tones of heaven, even through reliance on a
Perfected partner. So he just won't descend into the human world at all.
This poem, unlike the others, is not cited in subsequent collections. It
seems that Lord Pei's solipsist argument that interacting with humans is
demeaning and that even harmonizing with another destroys one's com-
munion with ultimate nothingness is not what Daoist practitioners wanted
to believe. –Trans.

. . .

This is the song of the Lady [Wang] the Central Watchlord:

My dragon streamers dance in the Great Void,
As my flying wheels traverse the banks of the Five Marchmounts.
Wherever I am, that's carefree roaming;
When moved, I raise a song of the hidden—
Independence triumphs over dependence—
Whoever I meet will as a result harmonize with me.
But how is [the realm across] the blue-green waves distant enough?

27. A *li* is a measurement of distance equal to approximately one-third of an English
mile.
28. See DZ 1032, 105, Qingling zhenren Peijun zhuan 清靈真人裴君傳. For the
scriptural catalog contained in this text, see Chang, "Xipu," 303–4.
29. On Lord Pei's appearances to Hua Qiao, see Chang and Pettit, *Library of
Clouds*.

Mystic Wells are certainly not numerous.
Mount Mottled Cliff is also but a step or two distant—
All these are gathered within the four seas.
How could any of this compare to leaving behind the sunlit world,
To go through three kalpas in a single pass?[30]

龍旌舞太虛。飛輪五嶽阿。所在皆逍遥。有感輿冥歌。無待愈有待。相遇故得和。[31] 滄浪奚足遼。玄井不爲多。鬱絶尋步間。俱會四海羅。豈若絶明外。三劫方一過。
右中候夫人歌。

. . .

Lady Wang the Central Watchlord appears to Yang from time to time. Tao at one point notes that she seems knowledgeable concerning the affairs of the cavern heavens within Mount Mao, perhaps through her official service in the Eastern Palaces of Fangzhu.[32] She chides Lord Pei for his seeming fear of coming into contact with humans. She reminds the assembled Perfected that their abilities far surpass any concern about crossing the Mystic Well. Perhaps the problem, she hints, is that Lord Pei does not elicit harmony from all those he meets? Further, his pacing of familiar spaces is limiting. The Perfected are able to travel beyond the bounds of the cosmos. They can even traverse impossible stretches of time to encounter entirely new worlds. There are thus plenty of potential dependents whose inner spirits resonate at the very approach of Perfected beings. –Trans.

. . .

This is the song of Lady Li of the Resplendent Numina:

Having made free with the ale, I observe the assembled worthies,
When, with a whoosh, I am circling the four reaches of space.
I do not have awareness of why this is so,
But it is certainly not dependent roaming.

30. Although it here likely just connotes an unimaginably long period of time, the term "three kalpas" 三劫 came to signify a particular thoroughgoing destruction of heaven and earth. According to the *Shangqing Scripture of the True Law of the Three Heavens* 上清三天正法經, this cycle would augur the "great kalpa," when heaven and earth would be overturned, mountains collapse, and metals melt in the seas. (DZ 1032, 2.7b and DZ 1139, 9.4a.)

31. DZ 980, 16a, and DZ 1032, 97.8a: 旂 for 旌 and 喻 for 愈. DZ 1138, 20.5a: 喻 for 愈.

32. DZ 1016, 12.10a1–3.

When we meet I take joy in our encounter;
When we do not I am likewise not downcast.
When we set shadows free in the mystic void[33]
And two meet, they are natural mates.

縱酒觀羣惠。[34]儵忽四落周。不覺所以然。實非有待遊。相遇皆歡樂。
不遇亦不憂。縱影玄空中。兩會自然疇。
右昭靈李夫人歌。

. . .

As Tao Hongjing notes in his postface, Lady Wang the Central Watchlord and Lady Li of the Resplendent Numina have an unclear relationship with human beings, though they may have been intended as possible future mates for members of the Xu family or their acquaintances.[35] Just when we thought every possible argument has been made, Lady Li obliquely recalls for the assembly the troubled status of intentionality in the Daoist Way. As the earliest texts tell us, the Dao is so of itself 自然, without intentionality 無為. Human beings should model their actions on those of the Dao. If they can do so, dependence is not possible. Directionless roaming, should it bring one into contact with a celestial being, effortlessly brings a true union within the Dao. –Trans.

. . .

This is the song of Consort An of Nine Flowers:

I pilot a wisp of qi, setting out from Western Flower
Caught between independence and dependence.
Sometimes I glimpse the peaks of the Five Marchmounts;
Sometimes I bathe in the ford of the Celestial River.[36]
I release my steeds and seek out an empty boat;
Wherever I am, there are threads of attachment.
But suddenly the mustard seed is ten thousand *qing* in size

33. Despite the fact that, as we will see in a moment, the world is but illusion, "set shadows free" 縱影 should likely remind us of the phrase "set phosphors free" *zongjing* 縱景. It is through "piloting their phosphors" 御景, that is the exteriorized gods of their bodies, that the Perfected move freely through space. The term is common in the scriptural literature by, and inspired by, Yang Xi. See, for example: DZ 1331, 22b9; DZ 1323, 15b8. In addition, spiritual marriage is described as *oujing* 偶景, a marriage of phosphors.

34. DZ 783, 2.14b; DZ 980, 17a; and DZ 1032, 97.10a: 慧 for 惠. This is a common phonetic loan.

35. See p. XX in chapter 1.

36. The "celestial river" 天河 is our Milky Way.

And Mount Sumeru sits within.[37]
There is in fact no difference between large and small;
And near and far stem from a single cause.
That one arrives for purposes of dependence,
This one makes a marriage of independence.[38]

駕欻發西華。無待有待間。或眴五嶽峯。或濯天河津。釋輪尋虛舟。
所在皆纏綿。芥子忽萬頃。中有須彌山。小大固無殊。遠近同一緣。[39]
彼作有待來。我作無待親。
右九華安妃歌。

Consort An is the Perfected whose marriage to Yang Xi is depicted in the
opening chapter of the *Declarations*. In her first meetings with him, she
makes clear that they are destined for one another and that it is his great
virtue that makes it so. She describes their union with a number of metaphors connoting the union of equals, and she makes the same claim
here—theirs is a marriage free of dependence.[40] She immediately allies
herself with Lady Right Blossom by beginning her poem in the same way:
"I pilot a wisp of qi. . . ." To arrive at her main stance on such human-
divine unions as theirs from the beginning of the poem in which she
describes herself as "caught between independence and dependence,"
she extrapolates on the religious metaphors Lady Li has introduced. While
the metaphors were derived from Buddhist texts, they seem natural here.
In a world of contingency, where a cosmic mountain might fit in a mustard
seed and far dissolves into near, this and that (a trope drawn from

37. Mount Sumeru is the Buddhist cosmic mountain. The image of a cosmos within a
mustard seed is first found in the *Vimalakīrtinirdeśa sūtra*, translated by Zhi Qian 支謙
(fl. 225 CE). See T 474, 佛說維摩詰經, 14.527c. Citations of this verse turn the magically
shrinking mountain to Mount Kunlun, a more Chinese choice. (See DZ 980, 15b, and DZ
1032, 97.6b.) The earliest surviving citation, found in the *Wushang biyao*, makes the
mountain Penglai and, skipping Lady Li's poem, joins this verse to that of Lady Wang.
This latter error has been corrected by an added note. But this citation also has the per-
sona of the poem "leaping" 躍 the Milky Way rather than bathing in it 濯. (See DZ 1138,
20.19a.)

38. Lady An, Yang Xi's destined celestial bride, provides a Buddhist-style discourse
on contingency to collapse the dependence/independence distinction. The one who
"arrives for purposes of dependence" is Lady Right Blossom, Xu Mi's potential celestial
mate, while the one who "makes a marriage of independence" is Lady An herself.

39. DZ 980, 15b; DZ 1032, 98.6b–7a: 崑崙山 for 須彌山. DZ 1138, 20.19a, merges
this poem with that of Lady Wang. In addition to confirming the reading 須彌山, which
is to be preferred given the Buddhist terms in this verse, this version also contains the
graphic variant 躍 for 濯, which I do not accept.

40. For this scene, see Bokenkamp, "Declarations."

the Zhuangzi) are one. Her independent mate, she deftly concludes, is no different than Lady Right Blossom's dependent mate. –Trans.

. . .

This is the song of the Great Void Perfected of the Southern March-mount:

Independence resides within Grand Nonbeing;
Dependence at the borders of Grand Being.
Large and small share a single wave;
Far and near meet at the same point.
I sound strings at the apex of the mystic empyrean,
My chanted whistle swirls the eight qi.
How could I not, made tipsy on numinous liquors,
Gaze out with joy on the nine margins?[41]
Dependent or independent depends on mystic fate—
The two encompass one another.

無待太无中。有待太有際。大小同一波。遠近齊一會。鳴絃玄霄顛。吟
嘯運八氣。奚不酗靈液。[42] 眄目娛九裔。有無得玄運。二待亦相蓋。
右太虛南嶽眞人歌。

. . .

Master Red Pine's verse begins the final commentaries, rightfully pronounced by the very highest Perfected. There is no word here of his own travels; no sense that he will be visiting Mount Mao. He places the question in a cosmic context, allowing that even one of his far-ranging vision cannot see into the workings of fate. His is so far the most philosophical of the poems. He invokes the standard Daoist *coincidentia oppositorium* in which all contradictions dissolve in the face of the unity from which they emerged. –Trans.

. . .

41. The translation "nine margins" for 九裔 was suggested by Kroll, "Poetry Debate," 15. The term is used by Ge Hong to refer to blessings spread throughout the human realm through good governance. (See DZ 1187, 1.8a.)

42. DZ 1138, 20.10b: 巔 for 顛, 金 for 吟, 酒 for 液. All of these are graphic variants.

This is the song of the Azure Lad of Fangzhu:

Having rested in my oratory on the Eastern Flower,
I set my chariot to soar, circling the eight directions.
Looking down at their place amongst hillocks and anthills,
I do not even hold the Five Marchmounts in high esteem.
Those holy mounds are the same height as the deepest abyss or
    font—
Large and small do construct one another,
But the difference between long and short is not much.
The Grand Cedrela dies in a trice,[43]
So why not comply with the movements of heaven
And set one's spirits free to comply with the empty and cavernous?

偃息東華靜。揚軿運八方。俯眄丘垤間。莫覺五嶽崇。靈阜齊淵泉。
大小互相從。長短無少多。大椿須臾終。奚不委天順。縱神任空同。
右方諸青童君歌。

. . .

The Azure Lad, the deity whose palaces we visit in the passages below,
shifts to another implied audience, the human auditors. His final plea is
not for the assembled Perfected, but for Xu Mi. Following his offering, the
final poems will be summations. The Azure Lad represents the ultimate in
spiritual attainment, yet the greatest he knows is not so different from the
smallest. The example he sets of ultimate freedom to be found in the dis-
cernment of radical relativity is meant to incite emulation. –Trans.

. . .

These are the songs of Lady Purple Prime of the Southern Culmen:[44]

Controlling the whirlwind, I fan the Grand Barrens,
My eight phosphors flying into the lofty and clear.
I look up to the floating, beyond the purple dawn
And look down to observe cut-off precincts so shadowed.

43. The *Cedrela sinensis* tree, with its longevity of up to one hundred fifty years, is
no match for the "Grand Cedrela, which "takes eight thousand years as a spring and eight
thousand as an autumn" 以八千歲爲春，八千歲爲秋。 (See *Zhuangzi zhu*, 1.11, SKQS
edition.)
44. It seems strange that this goddess should chant two poems. It may be that one
name has dropped out. But all the sources that cite these poems give the name of Lady
Purple Primordial for both.

My mysterious thoughts rest within the empty and cavernous,
Above, below, they neither flow nor stop.
When one is independent between both borders,
There is no spot for dependence to be constructed.
If one embodies nonexistence, death is possible;
If one embodies existence, one can nurture life.
The eastern guest joins in our lofty singing,
So why is it worth arguing the two dependences?

控飆扇太虛。八景飛高清。仰浮紫晨外。俯看絶落冥。玄心空同間。
上下弗流停。無待兩際中。有待無所營。體無則能死。體有則攝生。
東賓會高唱。二待奚足爭。 [45]

. . .

The Azure Lad having shifted the performance to a demonstrative mode,
the Lady Purple Prime steps forward to best him in exploding the boundaries between the extremes they have been arguing. Her final line seems to
acknowledge the Azure Lad's preeminence. He is the "eastern guest" from
the isles of Fangzhu whose entry has settled the question. The last couplet
depends on an untranslatable wordplay. What I have translated as "existence" and "nonexistence" are also the "with" and "without" of with dependence and without dependence. She thus implies that, "without" dependence, humans perish; with it, they live. The final line thus refers only to the
"two dependences" that the Perfected have been discussing. Now that she
has issued this decisive view, the argument seems over. But she is not fin-
ished speaking. –Trans.

. . .

Ordering the steeds of my jade brocade cart,
My dancing reins raise us up to dart back and forth.
In the morning I roam to the Vermilion Fire Palace;
In the evening I rest at the Night-gleaming Pond.
Floating my phosphors to the tips of the clear auroras,
The eight dragons are truly in ragged formation.
Whenever I perform an independent ramble;
Dependence is always seen to follow.
We have met on high in the fine one's boudoir,

45. DZ 783, 2.16b; DZ 980, 17b: 滇 for 冥; DZ 1032, 97.11a: 滇 for 冥 and 管 for
營; DZ 1138, 20.10b–11a 空洞 for 空同.

Giving positive and negative views on dependence and independence.
Since existence and nonexistence are not fixed,
Dependence and independence each dissolve naturally.

命駕玉錦輪。儵轡仰徘徊。朝遊朱火宮。夕宴夜光池。浮景清霞杪。
八龍正參差。我作無待遊。有待輒見隨。高會佳人寢。二待互是非。
有無非有定。待待各自歸。 [46]
右南極紫元夫人歌。

The Lady Purple Prime closes the event not only by summing up, but also
by describing, in the manner of countless banquet poems, her forthcoming
journey. She allows, in homage to the thought of the Laozi, that asserting
her independence presupposes, indeed creates, its opposite. Finally, she
describes the event and, playing on words in a way that truly brings in the
cosmic dimension of the argument (the "existence" of dependence and
"nothingness" of nondependence) she amicably dissolves the discussion.
Most difficult here is the term *zi gui*, "return of themselves/naturally,"
which I translate in this context as "dissolve naturally." Since Zhuangzi has
been cited several times in these poems, I think this line might have something to do with his "great return," which is a description of death as departure from the human world.[47] The image had evolved by Yang Xi's time, so
even the Dao has its own "great return" whereby it dissolves back in on
itself, alternating between existence and nonexistence. –Trans.

These songs all seem to have been delivered when the Perfected first
descended [to Yang]. But I doubt that these particular Perfected all
chanted them [for Yang]. The Azure Lad, [Lady] Purple Prime, and
the Great Void [Perfected of the Southern Marchmount] never
descended together, unless something has been lost. Further the matter
of "dependence" refers to [Lady] Right Blossom, not to Consort An.[48]

(按此諸歌詩，並似初降語。而嫌衆眞多高唱。上清童紫元太虛未嘗有
雜降處。恐或遺失耳。有待之説並是指右英事。非安妃也。)

• • •

46. DZ 783, 2.16b–17a; DZ 980, 18a; DZ 1032, 97.11a–b: no variants.
47. See *Zhuangzi zhu*, 22.746.
48. According to Tao Hongjing, then, the question of whether a human's dependence on a deity could lead only to contingent transcendence did not apply to Yang Xi but
did to Xu Mi. Apparently, there were no doubts about Yang's achievements.

INTRODUCTION TO HAN MINGDI'S DREAM

The following section includes Yang Xi's version of the first of two Buddhist textual fragments that appear in the *Declarations of the Perfected*. This is an account of the arrival of Buddhism in China as the result of an emperor's dream. According to this legend, the emperor posthumously known as the Filial and Bright Emperor of the Han 孝明帝 (Liu Zhuang 劉莊, r. 57–75) had a dream of a great spirit with a halo of blinding light which, on inquiry, turned out to be the Buddha. The emperor sent envoys to bring back news of this deity. They returned with the *Scripture in Forty-Two Sections*. This particular legend concerning the coming of the Indian religion to China has the advantage of presenting it as an invited guest, rather than a foreign invader.

As originally written, the story served as a preface to the *Scripture in Forty-Two Sections*. Yang Xi's Perfected did indeed present him with a version of that work. Tao Hongjing, though, questions whether the story of the emperor's dream was actually revealed by the Perfected at all. He doubts the account because it is "roughly the same" as that found in "outside," nonrevealed writings and contains some factual errors that, Tao reasons, the Perfected would not make.[49] At the same time, Tao is concerned to show that the *Declarations* does account for the Way of the Buddha. And in fact the tale seems to stand as "preface" to an account of another sort of Buddhism, that practiced by the Perfected of Highest Clarity on the floating isles of the Eastern Seas known as the Lesser Fangzhu. The account ends with the words "The arrival of Buddha images to the Central Kingdom began with the Lustrous Emperor." There are stupas, but no Buddha statues, on Fangzhu, the original home of the Way of the Buddha. Thus, distinguishing western from eastern Buddhism might be the reason Yang Xi included the account.

According to these passages, Daoist spirits live on what is known as "Greater Fangzhu," while Buddhists superior to those who followed the dusty trade routes through central Asia live on two isles to the east and west of the larger island, known as the "Lesser Fangzhu." Tao, in his notes, is quite intent on pointing to other places in Yang's revelations where he talks about these "Eastern Buddhists" whose practice accords with the Shangqing scriptures. But there is clear evidence that some of

---

49. This, despite the fact that he elsewhere does call out errors.

Yang Xi's practices seen as too closely aligned with Buddhism were later expunged from our received texts.[50]

Following the passages describing Fangzhu, we are provided with an actualization of the sun and moon that the deities of the floating isles use to feed themselves. As a result of this actualization, the rays of the sun and moon are conducted into the body to illumine the internal organs. We are told that the practice comes from the *Scripture of Wisdom* 智慧經 and that the successful practitioner will live to see the age of Great Peace.[51] This method is similar to that found in a Shangqing scripture entitled the *Purple Script Inscribed by the Spirits*. We are told, however, that these two methods can be practiced simultaneously for even better results.

The three deities who appear to provide this actualization method and the passage that follows are (1) Lady Wang of Purple Prime in the Southern Culmen 南極紫元夫人, Wang Lin 王林 (byname Rongzhen 容真), fourth daughter of the Queen Mother of the West; (2) Lord Wang of the Western Citadel 西城真人王君, Wang Yuan 王遠, byname Fangping 方平; and (3) Lady of Dark Purity, of the Six Tenuities in the North Sea 北海六微玄清夫人.[52]

As Tao mentions in his commentary at the end of the passages, these three deities seem seldom to reveal material directly to Yang. They appear only in the poems on dependency and in the "Teachings and Admonitions of the Assembled Numinous Powers" passages parallel to the Buddhist *Scripture in Forty-Two Sections*. Tao thus speculates that these materials were not the result of direct revelation, but were passed to Yang Xi by one of the Perfected who do appear to him regularly.

Here it is enough to note that the appearance of these three Perfected link the present series of passages with the rest of the material written on eight sheets of lined paper in two unknown persons' handwriting. Another link is the short aphorism from Lady Dark Purity that ends the present passage. This reads very much like some of the apothegms found in the *Scripture in Forty-Two Sections*, the Perfected version of which is the "Teachings and Admonitions of the Assembled Numinous Powers." All of this hints at what must have been the underlying story, now obscured by deletions. It seems that Yang's Perfected want us to

50. This may be one reason why Tao Hongjing's set of annotated citations from the Shangqing scriptures, the *Secret Instructions on the Ascent to Perfection* 登真隱訣, DZ 421, is now missing twenty-one of its original twenty-four chapters.

51. See also DZ 421, 2.18a4–5.

52. On this deity, see See DZ 1016, 1.3a1.

understand that the way of the Buddha in fact originated on Fangzhu. If that is so, this Shangqing version of the "conversion of the barbarians" myth has been effectively erased from history.

. . .

TRANSLATION: HAN MINGDI'S DREAM
(dz 1016, 9.19b7–9.20b2)

The Filial and Lustrous Emperor of the Han dynasty dreamt of a Spirit who was sixteen feet tall, with a round light issuing from behind his neck, who was soaring in front of the palace.[53] He took joy at the sight and asked around the court. The wise man Fu Yi 傅毅 (d. 90) responded, saying "I have heard that there is one in India who has achieved the Way and is called 'Buddha.' I have heard that he can fly and that his body emits white beams of light. This spirit must be the one of whom they spoke." The emperor, thus enlightened, sent the envoy Zhang Qian 張騫, the Gentleman of the Feathered Grove Qin Jing 秦景, the Erudite Wang Zun 王遵, and eleven others to visit Sogdiana 大月氏國. There they copied Buddhist scripture in forty-two sections. These were secreted in the fourteenth stone chamber of the Orchid Terrace. They immediately constructed a Buddhist temple north of the road leading out of Loyang's western gate. Also, in the Clear and Cool Terrace of the Southern Palace, they fashioned a Buddhist image and a painting of the Mother of Demons.[54] The emperor was tremendously moved. First he built a "Long-Life Tumulus" [grave for himself] and then he had a Buddha image made for the upper hall of the palace. At this, the kingdom prospered, the people were at peace, and the distant western peoples were respectful and civilized, wishing to send their sons and daughters as officials and concubines. The arrival of Buddha images to the Central Kingdom began with the Lustrous Emperor.

漢孝明皇帝夢見神人，身長丈六，項生圓光，飛在殿前。欣然悅之，遍問朝廷。通人傅毅對曰：臣聞天竺國有得道者，號曰佛。傳聞能飛

53. This story is recounted in the *Mouzi* (see Keenan, *How Master Mou*, 123–26); the *Hongming ji*, T 2102, 52:4c–5a; the *Sishier zhang jing xu* 四十二章經序 T 784, 17:722a; the *Chu sanzang jiji* 出三藏記集 T 2145, 55:42c; the *Gaoseng zhuan* 高僧傳 T 2059, 50:322c–323a; the *Weishu* 魏書, 114.3025–3026, and others.

54. The Mother of Demons 鬼子母 (Skt. Hārītī) was mother of five hundred demons who wished to kill the children of others to make room for her own. Converted by the Buddha, she became a protector of children. For early mentions, see Zhi Qian 支謙 (fl. 222–52) T 128b, 2:839b24 and Dharmarakṣa 竺法護 (239–316) T 186, 3:504a16.

行，⁵⁵身有白光，殆其神乎。帝乃悟。即遣使者張騫、羽林郎秦景、博
士王遵等十四人之大月氏國，採寫佛經四十二章。祕蘭臺石室第十
四。即時起洛陽城西門外道北立佛寺。又於南宮清涼臺作佛形像及鬼
子母圖。帝感非常。先造壽陵。亦於殿上作佛象。是時國豐民安，遠
夷慕化，願爲臣妾。佛像來中國，始自明帝時耳。

This recounting is roughly the same as that found in outside writings.
It seems as if Chang'an has had the Buddha for quite a while. The
[*Traditions of*] *Lord Pei* confirm this. However, the practices of the
Buddha were in India and Kashmir. Sogdiana did not have them.
This is one difference. Now, since [the Perfected] wish to explain how
those on Lesser Fangzhu revere the Buddha, it is appropriate to first
recount this [arrival of Buddhism over the Silk Road]. Note that the
Zhang Qian mentioned here is not the [explorer] of the Former Han
period.[56] It must be another person with the same name and
surname. Fu Yi had the byname Zhongwu 仲武, for which see the
History of the Han.[57] Qin Jing, Wang Zun, and the rest are unknown
today. The temple mentioned here is the White Horse Monastery.
The Luminous Thearch was buried in the Manifest Decorum
Tumulus 顯節陵. Here it says "Long-Life Tumulus" 壽陵. All of the
Han Thearchs, when they were on the throne, constructed their own
tumuli in advance with this name. This is just like the people of the
present day who construct "long-life sepulchers" 壽冢. "Long Life"
was not the name of the Thearch's tumulus. Outside writings also say
that it was the Palace Attendant Zhang Kan 張堪 and the Director
Zhang Yin 張愔 who were sent to India to copy and bring back
scriptures and images as well as monks. [Because of all this,] I
suspect that this account was not revealed by the Perfected. It might
just be some old tale that Lord Yang recounted. But there are
repeated mentions of matters pertaining to the Buddha in the
scriptures and declarations of the Perfected.

此說粗與外書同。而長安中似久已有佛。裴君即是其事。且佛法乃與天
竺罽賓，而月氏無有。與此爲異。今既欲說小方諸奉佛，故先宜敍此
也。按張騫非前漢者。或姓名同耳。傅毅，字仲武，見漢書。秦景王遵
等不顯。此寺名白馬寺。明帝乃葬顯節陵。此云壽陵者，漢諸帝在位
時，皆預造壽陵。猶今世人作壽冢。非陵名也。外書記亦云：遣侍中張
堪，或云郎中張愔，並往天竺，寫致經象并沙門來至。又恐今此說未必
是眞受。猶可楊君疏舊語耳。但眞經誥中自亟有論及佛事也。⁵⁸

55. Correcting 傳 to 傳 with SKKY, 337.

55. Correcting 傅 to 傳 with SKKY, 337.

56. On the Zhang Qian of the Former Han, see Sima Qian, *Shiji* 111.2944, and Ban
Gu, *Hanshu* 61.2687–98.

57. Tao Hongjing had access to histories that are lost today. This seems to be one of
them. See Fan Ye, *Hou Hanshu*, 80.2610–13 for Fu Yi's biography.

58. DZ 1016, 9.20a7–20b2.

INTRODUCTION TO ON FANGZHU

This section differs slightly from that found in the received edition of the *Declarations*. I have added a footnote by Tao Hongjing that seems to have been cut from the text, and I have placed further likely bits of deleted text in the footnotes. The source of Tao Hongjing's deleted note is the lengthy Daoist collection, the *Jade Slips of Great Clarity on the Ultimate Dao of the Celestial Luminaries*天皇至道太清玉冊, compiled and annotated by the Ming Prince Zhu Quan 朱權 (1378–1448).[59] I have elsewhere provided evidence that this footnote was most likely cut due to its Buddhist content.[60] As Tao's note indicates, both the western and eastern lesser Fangzhu Isles were likely once described as home to Buddhist Perfected and Transcendents. In the received text of the *Declarations*, only the westernmost Lesser Fangzhu has Buddhists.

Even without this external evidence, however, Tao Hongjing's eagerness to justify the practice of the "Way of the Buddha" among Shangqing practitioners is apparent. He cites other examples of the "Way of the Buddha" in Yang Xi's revelations and, when the Perfected mistake the date of an archaic Chinese text supposedly practiced by the "Buddhists," he defends the error. The goal of Yang Xi in presenting this data is clear. The real origin of Buddhism lies hidden in the ancient classics of China.

TRANSLATION: ON FANGZHU

dz 1016, 9.20b2–9.23a7)

The Lady [of the Purple Prime] from the Southern Culmen said:[61]

Fangzhu is square, thus its name.[62] It is 1,300 li on each side, so that its circumference is 5,200 li. It is ninety thousand feet in height. There are the Ever-Bright Grand Mountain and Night Moon Lofty Mound, each a circumference of four hundred li, and many small mountains and rivers surrounding them. But the vegetation and trees are all extremely

---

59. On Zhu Quan, his relations with Daoism, and his library, see Richard Wang, *Ming Prince*, prologue and 62–71.

60. Bokenkamp, "Research Note."

61. As usual, this reference occurs at the end of the passage. I suspect that it refers to the utterance that begins here, since Tao has judged the previous passage on the Martial Thearch of the Han unlikely to be revealed material.

62. Fangzhu 方諸 was the name of a square mirror that the Martial Thearch of the Han had built to catch lunar essences. See Major et al., *Huainanzi*, 217, where the term is translated "square mirror."

lush with flowers and fruits glossy and unblemished. The herb of death-lessness grows in abundance and there are sweet springs everywhere. Those who eat and drink of these will not die.[63] The Lord Azure Thearch resides on Mount Eastern Flower, which is two hundred li square and full of the palaces and chambers of Celestial Transcendents and Higher Perfected. Gold, jade, blue and red gems intermingled form their roof ridges and porticoes. There is also the Mountain of Mysterious Cold, upon which there is a detached palace, two hundred li in circumference. On the east and west of Fangzhu there are lesser Fangzhu islands that are each distant from the Greater Fangzhu by three thousand li. The Lesser Fangzhu are each three hundred li on a side and twelve hundred li around. Both of them have palaces of Lord Azure and also many mid-level Transcendents, and numinous birds and beasts.[64] If one looks from Greater Fangzhu to the southeast, the banks of Guiji are about seventy thousand li distant. If one gazes to the northeast, one can see Boiling Valley and the Village of the Towering Trees, both sixty thousand li from Fangzhu.[65]

63. DZ 1483, "*Yuji lingwen zhang* 玉笈靈文章" 11a.7 adds the superfluous comment "all the people are long-lived" 人皆長生. Below, I will catalog only the most significant variants.

64. This is a bit strange, as one would expect attendants to the Azure Lord to be Perfected and not mid-level Transcendents. In fact, DZ 1483, in its citation of this passage, reads "Each [of the Lesser Fangzhu Isles] contains palaces and chambers of the Lord Azure Thearch. Celestial Perfected reside [in both of these palaces]. One source says that they have been there since the separation of earth from heaven. None knows their age. The mountains of this place produce numinous birds and beasts, the names of which are unknown. 亦各別有青帝君之宮室在焉.中有天真居之. 一云開闢有之矣. 莫知其 . 其山出靈鳥靈獸,莫知其名." I suspect that this reading should be accepted. I have not moved it to the main text, only because the clause "one source says" is not a feature of the original revelations. Instead, it could indicate the existence of multiple copies of the *Declarations* at the time this passage was copied. The DZ 1483 citation, dating from the fifteenth century, is thus likely a better witness to the original. One telling detail is the insistence of the cited source that these Perfected have "been there since the separation of earth from heaven." That is to say, they were decidedly *not* converted by the current wave of Buddhist missionaries. The account thus fits with the "conversion of the barbarians" legend: "Buddhism" was original to China.

65. "Boiling Valley" is a mythical locale on the far eastern edges of the world. The *Scripture of Mountains and Seas* 山海經 depicts it as just below the tree that is the launching pad of the morning sun, the Fusang tree. (DZ 1031, 9.2a–b) "Towering Trees" 建木 are marvelous trees growing at the northwestern edges of the known world. They are often associated with the strange peoples who reside beneath them. The *Scripture of Mountains and Seas* describes them as growing on the banks of the Weak Waters and near the home of the Di people 氐人, descendents of the Blazing Thearch who have scales and come back to life spontaneously after they die. (DZ 1031, 10.3a–4a.) The Huainanzi describes it as the sun canopy, which, given the position of the pole star, would have to be in the northwest. (See Major et al., *Huainanzi*, 157.)

Fangzhu is in the southeast and Boiling Valley is in the northeast.[66]
From *yin* [northeast] to *chen* [southeast] is 100,000 li. So, if [in a
square with Guiji at the center] the sides are five and the diagonal
seven, the diagonal would be 140,000 li. Thus Fangzhu would be
70,000 li distant from Guiji.

方諸正四方，故謂之方諸。一面長一千三百里。四面合五千二百里。上
高九千丈。有長明太山，夜月高丘，各周迴四百里。小小山川如此間
耳。但草木多茂蔚。而華實多蒻蕟。饒不死草。甘泉水所在有之。飲食
者不死。青帝君宮在東華山上。方二百里中。盡天仙上眞宮室也。金玉
瓊瑤，雜爲棟宇。又有玄寒山。山上別爲外宮。宮室周二百里中。方諸
東西面又各有小方諸。去大方諸三千里。小方諸亦方面各三百里。周迴
一千二百里。亦各別有青帝君宮室。又特多中仙人及靈鳥靈獸輩。大方
諸對會稽之東南小看，去會稽岸七萬里。[67] 東北看則有湯谷建木鄉，又
去方諸六萬里。[68] （方諸是乙地。湯谷是甲地。則自寅至辰十萬里。方
五隅七言之，邪角十四萬里。故去會稽七萬里也.）

On the Lesser Fangzhu that is to the west, there are many who serve the
Way of the Buddha. There are stupas that are inlaid with gold and jade,
some of which are one thousand feet and many tens of stories in height.[69]
In this place all are filial and do not die, which is brought about by their
consumption of the herbs of deathlessness. They all consume the essences
of the five planets and recite the *Return to the Storehouse Scripture* of
the Xia dynasty and by this means are able to travel by flying.[70]

The Xia dynasty classic is called *Joined Mountains*, that of the
Yin-Shang, the *Return to the Storehouse*.[71] This reference differs.[72]

66. These directions are given according to the diviner's compass. See Kalinowski,
"Topomancie."

67. DZ 1138, citing Gu Huan's 真迹經, omits the character 小, which I accept as a
preferable reading. Still, there is something a bit unclear about this passage.

68. Correcting 十萬 to 六萬 on the basis of sense. See SKKY, 337.

69. The term 浮屠 for stupa occurs elsewhere. See, for instance, Li Daoyuan 酈道元
(d. 527) *Shuijing zhu* 水經注, (SKQS ed. 1.8a4): "King Asoka raised stupas at the spot
where the Buddha achieved nirvana. 阿育王起浮屠于佛泥洹處。"

70. DZ 1483 includes the following phrase before the reference to reading the Xia
dynasty scripture: "[they also consume] the flowers of the sun and moon—the sunbeams
by day and the moon flowers by night 日月之華,晝服日光夜服月華." This seems to be a
reference to the meditation practice appended to this section of the text.

71. *Joined Mountains* 連山 and *Return to the Storehouse* 歸藏 are imaginative
names used for the Confucian *Scripture of Changes* 易經 in earlier ages. See the "Spring
Officers, Grand Diviner" 春官·大卜 of the *Zhouli* 周禮 (SSJZS, 1.802b.)

72. Stating that the information provided by the Perfected differs from that found in
mundane sources is about as close as Tao Hongjing gets to saying that the Perfected
are wrong about something. But he still nuances his conclusion. The force of the next

For another example, the "three disciples," although they revered the
way of the Buddha, did not wear monk-style clothing. People of their
generation knew them as Perfected Bodhisattva Householders.[73]

大方諸之西，小方諸上，多有奉佛道者。有浮圖，以金玉鏤之。或有
高百丈者數十〔曾〕（謂應作層字）樓也。其上人盡孝順而不死。是
食不死草所致也。皆服五星精。讀夏歸藏經。用之以飛行。（按夏曰
連山，殷曰歸藏。與此不同。依如三弟子，雖奉佛道，不作比丘形
服。世人謂在家眞菩薩耳。）[74]

The annotation to the following passage is added by me from a work by the
Ming Daoist and imperial Prince Zhu Quan. This "note" is not marked as
such in the source that provides it. Instead the note follows without separation on the previous paragraph, which is attested in the Declarations.
Further, the entire passage is explicitly marked as coming from the Declarations. This segment is unlikely to be from Yang Xi's hand, however,
since it cites the Nirvāna Scripture that was brought to China in 414 and
subsequently translated by Faxian 法顯 in 417–18 (T 7, 大般涅槃經; see
Zürcher, *Buddhist Conquest*, 105; Ch'ên, Buddhism in China, 89–91).
According to Jan Nattier (personal communication, 20 June 2017), another
possible early source is the so-called Southern version (T 375); that is, the
revision of Dharmakṣema's T 374 by Huiyan/Jñānabhadra et al. Whatever
the Buddhist source of this citation, it is most likely a note by Tao Hongjing
that was cut from the Declarations, and that is how I have presented it. Tao
Hongjing sometimes has relatively positive things to say about Buddhism.
I suspect that the difference is that Tao favored the "Buddhism" that came
from Fangzhu and criticized that which came from the "western foreign-

---

sentence seems to be that just as the disciples of the Three Perfected were not outwardly
marked as Buddhist, so the *Return to the Storehouse* just might have circulated unremarked as a Buddhist text during the Xia.

73. This might be a reference to the Buddhist scriptures written in China that claimed
early Chinese sages to be disciples of the Buddha. Daoan 道安 (fl. 570), in his "Treatise on
the Two Teachings" 二教論, cites one example, a *Scripture on the Dharma Practices of
Stillness and Purity* 清淨法行經, as follows. "The Buddha sent his three disciples to
Zhendan 振旦 [= China] to proselytize. There was the Bodhisattva Scholarly Lad 儒童菩
薩, who was called Confucius, the Brilliant and Pure Bodhisattva 光淨菩薩, who was Yan
Yuan [Confucius's disciple], and Mahākāśyapa 摩訶迦葉, who was Laozi." (T 2103,
8.140a4–8.) Naturally, these Chinese culture heroes were not thought to have worn Buddhist garb. I think it more likely, though, that the text originally read "disciples of the
three *Perfected* 三真弟子," as did the lost bits of Tao's commentary to Tao's *Central Scripture of the Nine Perfected* found at Dunhuang. If so, the phrase refers specifically to "Buddhist disciples of the three Perfected" [Pure Numinosity, Purple Yang, and Mount Tongbo]
(see p. 22 in the introduction).

74. Following the Yu edition in correcting 在眞菩薩家 to 在家眞菩薩. See SKKY, 337.

ers." Nonetheless, even the positive descriptions of Buddhism written by Tao were subsequently cut from the canon.[75] –Trans.

On the Lesser Fangzhu of the East there are many exceedingly strange and numinous treasures.[76] There are White Jade ales and Golden liquor pools.[77] Lord Azure here raises precious celestial beasts. There are also many Transcendents here.[78] They eat the herbs of deathlessness and drink the naturally occurring ales and liquors, so that their bodies thereby emit a golden, gemmy luster. They always blow the reed organ of the Nine Numinosities in order to amuse themselves. Those who are adept can make the reed organ audible for a distance of forty li. The reed organ has thirty keys and the bamboo pipes of two or three feet in length. When they play in unison, the "hundred beasts stamp and dance" and several tens of phoenix pairs come to harmonize with the music.[79]

The music of this kingdom differs greatly from the Buddhist [musical] practice of the western foreigners. The western foreigners "blow the conch of the law and strike the drum of the law."[80] Their music thus differs and their practices even more so. The Nirvāṇa Scripture states: "When life is obliterated, it is obliteration with no remainder: Total obliteration is bliss."[81] In this way, Buddhists take life to be an illusion and regard death as a joyful thing. On Fangzhu,

75. See Bokenkamp, "Research Note."

76. Accepting DZ 1483, 6.24a, 多奇寶甚靈異 for DZ 1016: 多奇靈寶物 "many strange numinous [things] and treasured creatures." The creatures or beasts are mentioned in the following sentence, and 靈寶 is an easy error for a later copyist to make.

77. "White Jade Ale" appears in some versions of the *Traditions of Son-of-Heaven Mu* 穆天子傳. (See the citation at Li Fang, *Taiping yulan* 696.2a. DZ 291, 2.1b has a lacuna where "ale" should appear.)

78. I suspect that this line originally also read "those who revere the Way of the Buddha" 奉佛道者, as on the westernmost isle. However, Zhu Quan's citation gives the text as it appears in the received editions. (See DZ 1483, 6.24a.)

79. The last lines paraphrase a passage from the "Yiji" 益稷 chapter of the *Shangshu*: "When the nine parts of the Shao music for reed pipes is played, the phoenixes come in stately formation. Kui said: "Oh! When I strike the stones or gently tap the stone the hundred beasts lead one another to dance." 簫韶九成，鳳皇來儀。夔曰: 於, 予擊石拊石, 百獸率舞. (SSJZS, 1:144a–b.)

80. This phrase about "dharma conches" 法螺 and "dharma drums" 法皷 shows up in several early Buddhist scriptures.

81. I translate the text as given (生滅滅矣，寂滅爲樂) despite the fact that the likely sources, T 7, 1.204c22, or T 375, 12.693a31, both read 生滅滅已, 寂滅爲樂. Still, this is not the way that a contemporary Buddhist would have interpreted this passage. The Buddhist scholar Stefano Zacchetti kindly offers his version: "once birth and extinction are extinguished, [their] quiet appeasement is a joy!" (personal communication, 24 August 2017). This is clearly not Tao Hongjing's reading.

life is blissful and death is a calamity. This is why [the residents of Fangzhu] call their practices "the methods of the Buddha" and not "the Way of the Buddha."[82]

大方諸之東，小方諸上，多奇靈寶物。有白玉酒金漿汧。青帝君畜積天寶之器物，盡在於此。亦多有仙人。食不死草。飲此酒漿。身作金玉色澤。常多吹九靈簫，[83] 以自娛樂。能吹簫者聞四十里。簫有三十孔。竹長二三尺。九簫同唱，百獸抃儛，鳳凰數十來至和簫聲。（此國之樂也，與西胡之佛法大不侔矣。西胡之法謂吹大法螺、擊大法皷。其樂不同，況其法也。　涅盤經云：生滅滅矣。寂滅為樂。是以生為幻。死為樂。方諸國以生為樂，死為患也。故稱佛法，不稱佛道。）[84]

The palaces of the Greater Fangzhu are the permanent residence of Lord Azure. Those who reside there are all celestial Perfected and higher Transcendents. This is the location of the Dukes, Earls, and Directors of Destiny who know the method of ingesting the rays of sun and moon. Though they have already achieved the Way and become Perfected, they still ingest them.

In the Red City of Mount Huo there are also offices of the Director of Destinies.[85] The Perfected of the Grand Primordial and Lady [Wei] of the Southern Marchmount are resident there.[86] Li Zhongfu 李仲甫 is in the east, and Han Zhong 韓衆 (var. 韓終) is in the south.[87] The remaining thirty-one Directors of Destiny are in [the Palaces of] Eastern Flower. The Lord Azure Lad is called the Great Director of Destinies, since he is the general overseer. Lord Yang himself was [promised the post] "Manager of the Eastern Carts," but I do not know the rank of that post.[88]

82. I am uncertain as to the subject of this sentence. Both Yang Xi and Tao Hongjing use the term "Way of the Buddha." It seems, then, that the remark is based on normal Buddhist usage. Buddhists also often called their religion "the Way of the Buddha," but they used *fa* 法 ["dharma"] in a way that would have seemed strange.

83. From 常多吹 to the end of this paragraph is cited without significant variation in DZ 1138, 20.14b9–15a2.

84. DZ 1483, 6.24a–b.

85. In a note at DZ 1016, 11.6a5, Tao Hongjing notes that the central offices of the Director of Destinies is at Mount Huo.

86. For the shifting location of the Southern Marchmount in Daoist accounts, see Robson, *Power of Place*, 75–84.

87. For the *Declarations* accounts of these two Transcendents, see DZ 1016, 12.3b5 and 12.14b4, respectively. For their status in Transcendent lore more generally, see Campany, *To Live as Long*, 230–32, for Li Zhongfu and Bokenkamp, "The Herb Calamus," for Han Zhong.

88. Tao here refers to the verification found at DZ 1016, 2.8b–9a.

大方諸宮。[89]　青童君常治處也。其上人皆天眞、高仙、太極公卿、諸司命所在也。有服日月芒法。[90]雖已得道爲眞，猶故服之。[91]（霍山赤城亦爲司命之府。唯太元眞人南嶽夫人在焉。李仲甫在西方。韓衆在南方。餘三十一司命皆在東華。青童爲太司命總統故也。楊君亦云東軫執事。不知當在第幾位耳。[92]）

There is no surviving introduction to the following section, which details the meditation called above "method of ingesting the rays of sun and moon" that is practiced by the Perfected and Higher Transcendents of Greater Fangzhu. –Trans.

Directly actualize within your heart an image of the sun as large as a coin.[93] It will be vermilion in color within your heart. Also, actualize it with nine beams which issue forth from the heart and rise up the throat and through the teeth. Then the beams[94] return into the stomach. Do this for a long time. Then, look down and visualize[95] clearly the heart and the stomach issuing qi. Then swallow saliva thirty-nine times and end [the meditation]. Do this three times a day for a year and illness will be eradicated. After five years, the body will shine and, after eighteen years, you will certainly obtain the Way. You will be able to walk at noon without a shadow and to drive off the myriad demons and the thousand types of evil and disastrous qi. Always actualize the sun in your heart and the

89. This and the following paragraph are cited in DZ 1221, 6.6b–7a.

90. Tao Hongjing gives extensive annotation for this practice in DZ 421, 2.16b7–18a5. The graphic changes he proposes here are likely on the basis of the *Zhihui jing* version he possessed that was written in Yang Xi's hand.

91. In addition to the citations in Tao Hongjing's *Dengzhen yinjue*, the text from this passage through the meditation on the sun and moon is cited in DZ 1270, 1a–2a, and DZ 1221, 6.6a–7a, with only minor variations in official titles.

92. Following the Yu edition in reading 位 instead of 住.

93. The detail that it is an image 象 of the sun is added on the basis of logic from the DZ 1032, 23.9b citation. It is possible, though, that some later editor is trying to correct Tao Hongjing's questioning of this passage in his *Secret Instructions:* "I do not know the direction of 'directly actualize.' It is not that the light is descending from heaven into the mouth. The sun appears in the heart." (DZ 421, 2.16b8–9)

94. Tao notes here that "This graph has been obliterated and written over. "Beams" 芒 is not original." What this means in practice is only that the graph has been rewritten at some point, not that it is necessarily incorrect. It may, in fact, simply have been miswritten and corrected by the original calligrapher.

95. Tao notes "This graph is overwritten and not original." Tao's reason for this comment is likely his understanding of how the actualization was to proceed. When one actualized the beams coming from the heart, they were shaped like blades. Reaching the closed teeth, these are to be seen as curling back and going into the stomach. In descent, they are no longer actualized as bladelike beams. (DZ 421, 2.17a3–4.)

moon in your muddy pellet. At night ingest the flowers of the moon just as you ingest the beams of the moon. Actualize the ten rays of white issuing from the middle of the brain down into the throat. The beams do not issue from between the teeth, but circle back into the stomach. This is the method of the residents of Fangzhu and comes from the upper and middle sections of the *Great Wisdom Scripture*. If you are able to employ it constantly, you will be assured of seeing Great Peace.[96]

It seems that this came from the seven-section *Scripture of Devil-Destroying Wisdom*.

直存心中有象太如錢，在心中赤色。又存日有九芒，從心中上出喉至齒間。而 〔d. 芒〕（此字儳。非眞）徊還胃中。如此良久。臨目〔存〕（此字儳。非眞）見心胃中分明，乃吐氣。嗽液三十九過止。一日三爲之。行之一年疾病除，五年身有光彩，十八年必得道。行日中無影，辟百鬼千惡災氣。恆存日在心，月在泥丸。夜服月華，如服日法。存月十芒白色從腦中下入喉。芒亦不出齒間而迴入胃。右此方諸眞人法。出大智慧經上中篇。[97] 常能用之，保見太平。（此即應是消魔智慧七篇之限也。）
右南極夫人所告。

Lord Wang of the Western Citadel announced this to Lord Yang with the instructions that he reveal it to the various Xus.[98]

The practice of this way of causing the sun to reside in the heart and the moon in the Niwan is short, easy, and understandable. You are ordered to practice it without giving up in midcourse. It is a Way that will result in ridding the body of the Three Corpses, the myriad illnesses and harms, refining the cloud-souls and controlling the white-souls.[99] When the sun and moon constantly shine within your body, demons will have no place to hide their forms. This is why Lord Azure Lad practices it. I

96. This implies that one will live through the coming cataclysmic end times and live in the new world to come.

97. In addition to DZ 1221, this paragraph is cited to this point in DZ 1032, 23.9b.

98. This note appended to the passage is another indication that this was revealed early in Yang Xi's relationship with the Xu family. For one thing, Yang seemingly did not specify a single individual but authorizes release to the family as a whole. For another, Yang uses the same strategy—indicating that his Perfected know about a person and have authorized limited revelation to that person—in his dealings with Chi Yin 郗愔 (313–384), who was not among the inner circle of recipients of these revelations.

99. For these constituents of the human body, see Bokenkamp, *Early Daoist Scriptures*, 322–31.

am such a person [who practices this method], and now I announce it to you. You may, with care, secretly show it to those with the will [to practice]. If one is practicing this Way, it will not interfere with carrying out the method of imbibing [essences of the] sun and moon found in the precious writings. In fact, it is very good to carry them out simultaneously. Transcendents practice a thousand such tasks all through the day and night and do not even begin to feel fatigued. From this we understand that through even the most extreme pursuits of self-perfection, life will always be preserved.[100]

The "precious writings" on the sun and moon refer to the practice found in the *Purple Texts*.[101]

行此日在心、月在泥丸之道謂省易可得。旨行無中廢絶者也。除身三尸，百疾千惡，鍊魂制魄之道也。日月常照形中，則鬼無藏形。青童君今故行之。吾則其人也。今以告子。子脫可密示有心者耳。行此道亦不妨行寶書所服日月法也。兼行益善善也。仙人一日一夕行千事，初不覺勞。明勲道之至，生不可失矣。（寶書日月即謂紫文所用者。）

右西城王君告。此並告楊君令以示諸許也。[102]
[Lady] Dark Purity announced:[103]

Practicing the Way should be like shooting an arrow. If the arrow goes straight without deviation, it can hit the target. If one gathers one's will to enter the mountains, one should proceed without hesitation, and then one will achieve the ultimate Perfection.

100. This statement resonates with the views of the fourth-to-sixth-century Daoists whose views we are exploring. It is, in short, a polemical understanding of *miedu* 滅度 [Skt.: nirvāna]: the goal of Daoist practice is never to blink out of existence through achieving *nirvāna*. For a more judicious account of how *nirvāna* was understood and the concept deployed by Buddhists, see Gómez, "Nirvāna."

101. This refers to the methods found in the *Purple Texts Inscribed by the Spirits* 靈書紫文, translated in Bokenkamp, *Early Daoist Scriptures*, 314–22.

102. This passage is reproduced in DZ 421, 2.16b7–19a1 with extensive commentary by Tao Hongjing. It occurs as well in DZ 1032, 45.18b1–19a4; DZ 1221, 6.6a10–7a9; and DZ 1270, 1a9–2a8, lacking only Tao Hongjing's commentary. The only significant variation is that 青君 is given as 青童君 in DZ 1032 and 1270. The DZ 1230 1.5b8–6a4 citation from Li Yanshou, *Taiping yulan*, includes Tao's commentary and also gives the name 青童君, which I accept.

103. This is the Lady Dark Purity of the Six Tenuities in the North Sea 北海六微玄清夫人.

I note that the three Higher Perfected—Lady Purple Prime of the Southern Culmen, Lord Wang of the Western Citadel, and Lady Dark Purity—seem not to have at other times descended [to Yang Xi]. They have provided only one passage of instruction and poetry each in this series of passages.[104] I do not know when these were passed on to Yang. The eight previous passages were all in the calligraphy of Yang Xi.

為道當如射箭。箭直徃不顧，乃能得造堋的。操志入山，唯徃勿疑，乃獲至眞。　玄清告。[105]

(按南極西城玄清三高眞未當有餘降受。唯戒及詩各一條耳。不審此當是何時所喻。)[106]　右八條並楊書。

INTRODUCTION TO THE TEACHINGS AND ADMONITIONS OF THE ASSEMBLED NUMINOUS POWERS

The following passages are plagiaries of and revisions to the Buddhist *Scripture in Forty-Two Sections*, considered by many medieval Chinese the first Buddhist scripture translated into Chinese.[107] Where the original text has each "section" or paragraph headed by the words "the Buddha said," the following are attributed to the deities of Fangzhu. Each speaker delivers several "sections" of the Buddhist scripture. I have divided the *Declarations* paragraphs to match the usual numbering of the Buddhist text for easier comparison. The order follows that of the canonical *Declarations*, however.

. . .

TRANSLATION: THE TEACHINGS AND ADMONITIONS OF THE ASSEMBLED NUMINOUS POWERS
(dz 1016, 6.6a1–6.12b7)

I received an announcement from Azure Lad of Fangzhu that said: It is bitter for a person to act according to the Way, but also bitter not to do so. Human beings' existence—from death to old age, from old age to

---

104. On the participation of these Perfected, see p. 128.
105. This passage appears at DZ 296, 24.6b1–3 and at DZ 1032, 106, 3b4–6 without change.
106. Emending 二高眞 to 三高眞 on the basis of meaning.
107. The Chinese text of the "Scripture in Forty-Two Sections" is compared with the canonical *Declarations* version in Bumbacher, "Buddhist Sūtra."

illness, from guarding their health until death—is immeasurably bitter. Their minds are vexed and they accumulate transgressions and are ceaselessly born and reborn.[108] The bitterness is indescribable.[109] Not to mention the fact that many do not even get to live out their heavenly allotted years. To act in accord with the Dao is also bitter. One must maintain clarity and stillness to actualize the Perfected, guard the mysterious to retain in thought their numinosity, assiduously seek out a master, and pass through hundreds of trials, all the while keeping one's heart from sinking and maintaining a firm and inexhaustible will. All of these things are also the extremes of bitterness.

If you can view the position of feudal lord as if you were only a passing guest, view treasures of gold and jade as if they were tiles or stones, view the beauty of damasks and brocades as if they were tattered cotton—only then may you be pronounced ready to begin inquiring into the Dao.[110]

方諸青童見告曰：人爲道亦苦，不爲道亦苦。[111]惟人自生至老，自老至病，護身至死，其苦無 量。心惱積罪，生死不絕，其苦難説。況多不終其天年之老哉。爲道亦苦者。清淨存其眞、守玄思其靈、尋師軔 軻、履試數百、勤心不墮、用志堅審、亦苦之至也。視諸侯之位如過客，視金玉之寶如磚石，視紈綺[之麗]如弊帛者，始可謂能問道耳。[112]

The Azure Lad of Fangzhu said:

Those who act according to the Dao are able to pluck out the roots of passion and desire. It is like plucking at a string of pearls. If you pluck them off one by one, they will eventually be gone. If one lessens and

108. DZ 458, 1.1a, removes the reference to the Buddhist doctrine of rebirth and records this line as "until death it does not cease" 至死不絕. On the Shangqing method for overcoming rebirth, see Bokenkamp, "Research Note."

109. Excluding the name of the speaker, the passage to this point corresponds to section 35 of the Buddhist *Scripture in Forty-Two Sections*. See Sharf, "Scripture," 370. The following lines concerning the bitterness of practicing the Dao do not appear in the received Buddhist text.

110. This passage corresponds to paragraph 42. Sharf translates this passage as a proclamation of the Buddha's own detachment from worldly concerns, but the Daoist text adds a clause at the end, making the whole statement conditional and applicable to any practitioner. See Sharf, "Scripture," 371. My translation follows DZ 458, 1.1b, which adds the words 之麗 to the line on fabrics, restoring the implicit parallelism.

111. DZ 458, 1.1a, adds a phrase at this point. "The reason it is bitter not to practice the Dao is that. . ." 不爲道亦苦者.

112. Cited at DZ 458, 1.1a–b.

eradicates evils encroaching from outside, they will eventually be gone. When this occurs, one achieves the Dao.[113]

Or, to draw a nearby analogy, it is like a heavily loaded ox walking through the mud. When the ox reaches the limits of fatigue, it does not even dare to look left or right. Its only desire is to get out of the mud and rest. Gentlemen of the Dao regard emotions and desire as worse than that mud.[114] They keep their minds focused on the Dao so that they can avoid the various sorts of suffering. In this way they also achieve the Dao.[115]

I respectfully note that there is no example of the Upper Minister [Azure Lad] descending to give a verbal revelation [to Yang Xi].[116] We have only the above two announcements and one poem. I suspect that Lord Yang did not visit [the Upper Minister] in audience to personally receive and record [these revelations].[117]

方諸青童君曰：[118] 人之爲道能拔愛欲之根者，譬如摘懸珠。一一摘之會有盡時。稍去外惡會有盡時。盡則得道矣。又近喻牛負重行泥中。疲極不敢左右顧。趣欲離泥以蘇息。道士視情慾，甚於彼泥中。直心念道，可免衆苦，亦得道矣。（謹案上相都無降唉事。唯有此二告及歌詩一首。恐未必是楊君親所瞻奉受記也。）

Lord Wang of the Western Citadel announced: It is difficult for a person to escape the three evil paths [of rebirth] to become human.[119] Even if one becomes human, it is difficult to escape from being reborn female to be reborn male. Even if one is reborn male, it is difficult to have the six senses and four limbs all complete. Even if one is physically complete, it is difficult to be born in the Central Kingdom. And, even if one is born

113. To this point, this passage corresponds to section 40.

114. DZ 458, 1.2b, has "gentlemen of ultimate attainments" 達士 rather than "gentlemen of the Dao" 道士.

115. This passage corresponds to section 41, with "gentlemen of the Dao" 道士 replacing "*sramanera*" 沙門 of the Buddhist text.

116. The Azure Lad holds the full title Lord Azure Lad of the Fangzhu Palaces, Upper Minister to the Sage of the Latter Age, Lord Li 後聖李君上相方諸宮青童君. (See DZ 442, 9a, translated in Bokenkamp, *Early Daoist Scriptures*, 354.) His connection with the imminent end of the world cycle is important.

117. That is to say, Tao doubts that the high deity Azure Lad appeared to Yang. Instead, he thinks, these revelations must have been supplied by another deity. The Azure Lad is often cited in the *Declarations*, as for instance when he and three other high lords exchange poems on Mount Kunlun on the autumnal equinox (DZ 1016, 3.9a), but he seems never to appear directly in Yang's visions.

118. Cited at DZ 458, 1.2b without Tao's commentary.

119. As Sharf notes ("Scripture," 370), the usual three evil paths 三惡道 are rebirth in the hells, as a hungry ghost, or as an animal. But see Tao Hongjing's note to this passage.

in the Central Kingdom, it is difficult to meet with a father, mother, and Lord of the Kingdom who possess the Dao. Even if one meets with a Lord who possesses the Dao, it is difficult to be born into a family that studies the Dao and gives rise to your heart of benevolence and goodness. Even if one develops an inclination toward goodness, it is difficult to keep faith with the Dao and live long. Even if one keeps faith with the Dao and lives long, it is difficult to be born into the *renchen* age of Great Peace.[120] Should you not strive [to achieve these things]?

The "three evil paths" are rebirths other than human, that is, as bird, beast, or insect.

西城王君告曰：夫人離三惡道得爲人難也。既得爲人，去女爲男難也。既得爲男，六情四體完具難也。六情既具，得生中國難也。既處中國，值有道父母國君難也。既得值有道之君，生學道之家，有慈仁善心難也。善心既發，信道德長生者難也。既信道德長生，值太平壬辰之運爲難也。可不勗哉。（三惡道者，生不得作人，得作鳥獸蟲畜之三惡也。）

The Most High [Lord Wang] asked of practitioners of the Way: "How long is a person's life span?"[121] One responded "a number of days." The Most High said, "You are not yet capable of acting according to the Way." One responded, "A mandated life span lasts about the length of a meal." The Most High said, "Depart from me. You have not yet spoken of acting according to the Way." Yet another said, "It is within the space of a breath." The Most High said, "Excellent! You may be said to be someone who acts according to the Way."[122] Of old I heard these words and now I tell them to you. If you skillfully study the Way, you may be fortunate enough to escape this breath of a life.

Even though you, my disciple, are a million li distant from being like me, if in your heart you maintain my precepts, you will certainly achieve

120. This passage corresponds to section 36, with these differences: DZ 1016 adds "four limbs" 四體 to the six senses; replaces "born upholding the Buddha's way" 值奉佛道 with "to meet with a father, mother, and Lord of the Kingdom who possess the Dao" 值有道父母國君; changes "bodhisattva's family" 菩薩家 to a "family that studies the Dao" 學道之家; alters "faith in the three honored ones" 心信三尊 with "[a family] that gives rise to your heart of benevolence and goodness" 有慈仁善心; and substitutes "the *renchen* age of Great Peace" 太平壬辰之運 for "a generation with a Buddha" 佛世.

121. Correcting, with DZ 458, 1.2a, 幾日 to 幾許.

122. This passage to this point corresponds to section 37 of the *Scripture in Forty-Two Sections* with the following changes: "Most High" for "the Buddha" 佛 and "practitioners of the Way" 道人 for śramaṇas 沙門.

the Way.[123] If you work diligently at the jade scriptures and precious writings, you will certainly achieve the status of a Transcendent. One who remains my loyal retainer yet harbors evil in his mind will never achieve the Dao.[124]

For a person to practice the Way, recite scriptures, and practice rituals of the Dao is like eating honey—one's mouth is filled with sweetness, one's six storehouses are unblemished, and there is a lingering savor.[125] One who can practice in this fashion will achieve the Dao.[126]

There is also no account of the Overlord [= Most High Lord Wang] descending to Yang. From him, we have only the above and the method of ingesting the rays of the sun and moon.

太上問道人曰：人命在幾日間？或對曰：在數日之間。太上曰：子未能爲道。或對曰：人命在 飯食之間。太上曰：子去矣，未謂爲道。或對曰：在呼吸之間。太上曰：善哉。可謂爲道者矣。吾昔聞此言，今以告子。子善學道，庶可免此呼吸。弟子雖去吾〔教〕（謂應作校字。皆猶差懸也）千萬里。心存吾戒，必得道矣。研玉經寶書，必得仙也。處吾左側者，意在邪行，終不得道也。人之爲道，讀道經行道事者，譬若食蜜。遍口皆甜，六腑皆美，而有餘味。能行如此者得道矣。（上宰亦無降楊事。有此及服日月芒事耳。）

The Great Void Perfected of the Southern Marchmount, Lord Red Pine, said: If a person has committed many transgressions and does not confess them, they will stop in his or her heart. Transgression returns to the transgressor like rivers return to the sea, daily growing deeper and wider. If one recognizes one's faults, repents them, and does good deeds, the

123. Tao's note corrects 教 to 校 and explains the phrase as meaning "distant from" in the sense of "far from emulating." This is distinct from the Buddhist passage, the point of which is that physical closeness to the Buddha does not determine holiness.

124. This paragraph corresponds to paragraph 38 of the Buddhist text, with the addition of the sentence: "If you work diligently at the jade scriptures and precious writings, you will certainly achieve the status of a Transcendent" 研玉經寶書，必得仙也. The Declarations also omits the concluding sentences that Sharf ("Scripture," 371) translates: "The gist lies in practice. If one is close to me but does not practice, of what benefit are the myriad divisions [of the path]." I take "by my left side," which I have translated "loyal retainer," to mean "among the highest ranked of my followers."

125. The "six storehouses" 六腑 are (1) the stomach, (2) the gall bladder, (3) the urinary bladder, (4) the large intestine, (5) the small intestine, and (6) the "three burners" 三焦, cavities situated in the abdomen.

126. This paragraph corresponds to section 39, with the additions: "recite scriptures and practice rituals of the Dao" 讀道經行道事 and "there is a lingering savor" 有餘味.

transgressions will be erased, goodness will accumulate and one will achieve the Dao.[127]

If someone meets me with evil intent, I should repay him with goodness. In this way, the qi of good fortune and virtue will always remain with me, while the evil qi of multiple misfortunes will revert to him. This is the practice of one who studies the Dao.[128]

太虛眞人南嶽赤君告曰：人有衆惡而不自悔，頓止其心。罪來歸己如川歸海。日成深廣耳。有惡知非，悔過從善，罪滅善積，亦得道也。夫人遇我以禍者，我當以福往。是故福德之氣恆生於此。害氣重殃還在於彼。此學道之行也。

He also announced: "An evil person trying to harm the worthy is like spitting at heaven. Heaven is not sullied; the foulness falls on one's own body.[129] It is like kicking dust into the wind. The dust does not sully it, but returns to cover one's own body. The Way cannot be destroyed; ill-omened [behavior] will destroy the self.[130]

又告曰：惡人害賢，猶仰天而唾。唾不洿天，還洿己〔刑〕。（凡刑字皆應作形。）逆風揚塵，塵不洿彼，還灌其身。道不可毀，禍必滅己。

The Great Void Perfected [further] stated: Feeding one hundred ordinary persons is not as good as feeding one good person. Feeding a thousand ordinary persons is not as good as feeding a student of the Dao. Those who reside in reclusion in the mountains and forests are even more to be included in this category.[131]

127. This paragraph corresponds to no. 4 of the *Scripture in Forty-Two Sections*, with only inconsequential variants.

128. This passage corresponds to no. 5 of the *Scripture in Forty-Two Sections*. The *Declarations* has deleted the sentences that Sharf ("Scripture," 365) translates "I counter with the four virtues of benevolence, [compassion, joy, and equanimity]. The more he approaches me with malice, the more I reach out with kindness."

129. Tao notes that 刑 "corporal punishment" should be read as 形 "body" here and subsequently.

130. This paragraph corresponds to no. 7 of the *Scripture in Forty-Two Sections*. The Buddhist version of this passage keeps the focus on the inability of the evil to injure the good. It is thus possible that a 者 has been omitted from Yang's text, so that the final passage should read: "A person of the Way cannot be destroyed; ill-omened [behavior] will destroy the perpetrator." But DZ 458, 1.3a, and DZ 1032, 98.8b both record the line as given here.

131. This paragraph corresponds to a part of no. 9 of the *Scripture in Forty-Two Sections*. The *Declarations* adds "those who reside in reclusion in the mountains and forests are even more to be included in this category" 寒栖山林者。益當以 爲意, while changing "one who keeps the five precepts" 持五戒者 to "student of the Dao" 學道者. It

There is likewise no further record of Lord Red[pine] transmitting material other than this.

太虛眞人曰：飯凡人百不如飯一善人。飯善人千不如飯一學道者。寒栖山林者，益當以 爲意。（赤君亦無復別授事。）

The Lady Purple Prime announced:

There are five difficult things in the human realm. It is difficult to donate if one is poor. It is difficult to study the Dao if one is powerful and rich. It is difficult to manage one's destiny to avoid death. It is difficult to be able to view the cavern scriptures. Finally, it is difficult to live during the *renchen* year of the Sage of the Latter [Heavens].[132]

Long ago I asked the Most High what causes one to have the ability to know inborn destiny.[133] He replied, "The Dao and its powers are formless. There is nothing to be gained by knowing [one's destiny]. One need only be true to one's will and practice the Dao. It is like polishing a mirror. The dirt is removed, but the brightness remains and one is able to see one's form. Through cutting off the six senses and holding to emptiness and purity, one can likewise see the truth of the Dao and also know one's inborn destiny."[134]

---

also naturally leaves out account of stream-winners, the pratyekabuddha, etc. But, most surprisingly, it skips the final enjoinder to filiality found in the Buddhist text.

132. This paragraph corresponds to no. 10 of the Buddhist version, with "cavern scriptures" 洞經 replacing "scriptures of the Buddha" 佛經 and the *renchen* year once again replacing the generation with a Buddha. Li Hong, Sage Lord of the Latter Heavens, is the god who was to appear in the *renchen* year to gather the "seed people," those who had faithfully practiced the Dao before the destruction of heaven and earth. The seed people would form the basis of the new populace in a reconstituted realm after the cleansing apocalypse. See Bokenkamp, *Early Daoist Scriptures,* 156–57.

133. "Inborn destiny" translates 宿命, which in Buddhist texts is a translation for *karman.* In the fragments collected in the *Zhen'gao,* Yang Xi uses the term in only one other context, which, as Strickmann has shown, deals with the previous life of Xu Mi. (See DZ 1016, 3.14a5, and Strickmann, *Chinese Magical Medicine,* 44–47.) I retain the clumsy translation because Yang also seems not to have believed that all must be reborn. That is to say, other-directed rebirth is avoidable for the Shangqing Daoist. Even in the passage just mentioned, he discusses Xu's rebirth as "the beginnings of [your] inborn destiny" 宿命之始, indicating that the term was not fully integrated into his vocabulary. It thus seems likely that various constituents of fate are meant in this instance, to include previous lives only in some cases.

134. This paragraph corresponds to no. 11 of the *Scripture in Forty-Two Sections.* The major difference is that the *Declarations* replaces "the emotion of desire" 欲情 with all six emotions. One standard list includes joy 喜、 anger 怒、 sadness哀、 happiness 樂、 love 愛、 and hate 惡 (see *Baihutong* 白虎通, *Hanwei congshu* 漢魏叢書 edition,

He also said: "If one thinks of the Dao, practices the Dao, and keeps faith with the Dao, one obtains the roots of faithfulness, which lead to limitless good fortune."[135]

紫元夫人告曰：天下有五難。貧窮惠施難也。豪富學道難也。制命不死難也。得見洞經難 也。生值壬辰後聖世難也。我昔問太上：何緣得識宿命？太上答曰：道德無形，知之無益。要當守志行道。譬如磨鏡，垢去明存，即自見形。斷六情，守空淨，亦見道之眞，亦知宿命矣。又曰：念道行道信道，遂得信根。其福無量也。

Lady Purple Tenuity announced:[136]

Practicing the Dao is like carrying a torch into a dark room. The darkness is erased and only brightness remains. Through studying the Dao and meditating on the correct, ignorance is erased and only the correct remains.[137]

Wealth and sexual desire act on the self like honey on a sharp knife attracts a child. Its sweetness is not enough to fill the mouth, and it will cut the child's tongue.[138]

紫微夫人告曰：爲道者譬彼持火入冥室中。 冥即滅而明獨存。學道存正，愚癡即滅而正常存也。財色之於己也，譬彼小兒貪刀刃之蜜。其甜不足以美口，亦即有截舌之患。

Lady Dark Purity announced:

Emotional ties to wife, children, and household are worse than the shackles of prison.[139] When one is shackled in prison, a pardon is possible, but the desire for wife and children, though more dangerous than a tiger's mouth,[140] is entered into willingly. There is no pardon for this crime.[141]

171a). These are also associated with the six senses. (See Han Ying, *Hanshi waizhuan* 韓詩外傳, 474.)

135. This paragraph corresponds to paragraph no. 17 of the *Scripture in Forty-Two Sections*.

136. DZ 458, 1.3b, also lists the Lady of the Purple Prime as the author of this paragraph.

137. These sentences correspond to paragraph 14, but the last sentence changes from "leaving nothing unseen" 得無不見 to "only the correct remains" 正常存也.

138. This paragraph corresponds to no. 20 of the *Scripture in Forty-Two Sections*, with no significant variation.

139. Following DZ 458, 1.3b10, in reading 家宅 for the 寶宅 of DZ 1016.

140. Tao notes at this point: "One copy in a different hand lacks the above nineteen characters. I fear that they were [carelessly] omitted."

141. This paragraph corresponds to no. 21 of the *Scripture in Forty-Two Sections*, with no significant variation.

The entanglements of emotion are like carrying a torch and walking into the wind. The stupid, not daring to let go of the torch, have their hands burnt. The poisons of desire, anger, and ignorance reside in the self.[142] If one does not eradicate these evils by practicing the Dao, then danger and disaster will result, just like that stupid person who burns his hands.[143]

One who practices the Dao is like wood in water. If it goes with the flow, touching the bank neither on the left nor on the right; if it is not picked up by humans or blocked by demons or spirits; and, further, if it does not rot away, then I can guarantee that it will enter the sea. If a person who practices the Dao is not misled by foul desire, is not driven to distraction by the many perversions, and strives to advance without doubtful hesitations, I guarantee that person will achieve the Dao.[144]

玄清夫人告曰：夫人係於妻子寶宅之患，甚於牢獄桎梏。牢獄桎梏會有原赦，而妻子情慾，雖有虎口之禍，（有此一異手寫本。無此十九字。恐是脫漏）己猶甘心投焉，其罪無赦。情累於人也，猶執炬火逆風行也。愚者不釋炬火必燒手。貪欲、恚怒、愚癡之毒（又闕此十五字。於辭有不應爾。貪嗔癡所謂三毒）處人身中。不早以道除斯禍者，必有危殆。猶愚癡者火燒手之謂也。爲道者猶木在水。尋流而行，亦不左觸岸，亦不右觸岸，不爲人所取，不爲鬼神所遮，又不腐敗，吾保其入海矣。人爲道，不爲穢慾所惑，不爲衆邪所誑，精進不疑，吾保其得道矣。

The Lady of the Southern Culmen said: Human worry is born from attachment, and once worry is born, there is fear. Without loving attachment there is no worry, and without worry there is no fear.[145]

Once there was a person who was chanting scriptures very mournfully at night. When his sorrow reached its limit, an idea was born within him and he grieved so much that he longed for death. The Most High

142. At this point in the text, Tao notes "That copy also lacks the fifteen graphs above, so its sentences do not fit together. Greed, anger, and ignorance are called the 'three poisons.'"

143. This paragraph corresponds to no. 23 of the *Scripture in Forty-Two Sections*. The *Declarations* replaces "passion and desire" 愛欲 with "entanglements of emotion" 情累, as does DZ 458, 4a.

144. This paragraph corresponds to no. 25 of the *Scripture in Forty-Two Sections*. The *Declarations* copy leaves out only "and if it is not stopped by a countercurrent" 不爲洄流所住, which appears in the Buddhist version after "not blocked by demons of spirits" 不爲鬼神所遮.

145. This paragraph corresponds to no. 31 without significant variation.

Perfected transformed himself into a commoner and went to question him. "Do you often pluck the lute?" The man responded, "At home I often played it." The Perfected asked, "And what was it like when the strings were too loose?" The man replied, "The lute made no sound, neither high pitched nor mournful." He then asked, "And what if the strings were too tight?" The man replied, "Then the sound was cut off and very mournful." Then the Perfected asked, "What was it like when the strings were tightened correctly?" The man replied, "Then all of the notes were in harmony and the music sounded forth wondrously." The Perfected said, "The study of the Dao is just like that. You must control your heart and adjust its tendencies just as though you were playing the lute. Then you may achieve the Dao."[146]

The greatest of attachments is that to sex. There is no dodging this transgression and no pardon for it either. Fortunately, there is only one such desire. Were there two, no one in the world could ever achieve the Dao.[147]

For one who studies the Dao, there is no greater hidden merit than that of compassionate giving and saving [the destitute]. There is no greater aspiration than to preserve one's body and uphold the Dao.[148] The good fortune [derived from these deeds] is extremely great and the life they confer very stable.[149]

146. This paragraph corresponds to no. 33, with the following variations: (1) the Buddhist text has the Buddha summon a monk 沙門 to do his bidding, while the *Declarations* features the Most High transforming himself into a commoner 太上真人忽作凡人; (2) the *Declarations* makes clear that "controlling the heart and adjusting its tendencies" 執心調適 is "just like plucking the lute" 亦如彈琴, a clarification that would not need to be made were the text taught orally. On the early use of this lute metaphor by Celestial Master Daoists, see Bokenkamp, *Early Daoist Scriptures*, 80–81.

147. This paragraph corresponds to no. 22, with the addition of "no pardon for it either" 其事無赦, which does not appear in the Buddhist text. The oblique reference to unseen judges does, however, correspond well to Daoist conceptions of otherworldly justice.

148. DZ 458, 1.5a, has "There is no greater calamity than to preserve one's body and uphold the Dao" 患莫大於守身奉道. The context does not fit this reading, so it must be a copyist's error caused by the similarity of handwritten forms of 志/患.

149. This paragraph corresponds to the first part of no. 8 of the *Scripture in Forty-Two Sections*. The opening sentence of the *Scripture* is clarified somewhat by the Daoist "reading" of it. Mistranslated in Sharf ("Scripture," 8), it seems to read: "For those who labor at the Way, universal love, compassion, and the performance of virtue are not so great as spreading the mustering of will to uphold the Way. The good fortune gained thereby is very great. If you see someone spreading the Way and you joyfully aid him, you will also gain favorable recompense." The problem seems to be the verb 施, which has the technical meaning of *dāna* "giving" in Buddhist writings but here and in the Daoist rewrite is used in its more normal sense of "promulgate, spread." The *Declarations* replaces merit 德 with "hidden

If someone is evil to me and I do not accept that evil, it will return to
him and the disaster brought about will be visited on his body, just as
shadow follows an object and an echo follows sound.[150]

南極夫人曰：人從愛生憂。憂生則有畏死。無愛即無憂。無憂則無畏。
昔有一人夜誦經甚悲，　　　悲至意感。忽有懷歸之哀。太上眞人忽作凡
人，徑往問之：子嘗彈琴耶？答曰：在家時嘗彈之。眞人曰：絃緩何
如？答曰：不鳴不悲。又問絃急何如？答曰：聲絕而傷悲。又問緩急得
中如何？答曰：衆音和合，八音妙奏矣。眞人曰：學道亦然。執心調
適，亦如彈琴。道可得矣。愛慾之大者，莫大於色。其罪無外，其事無
赦。頼其有一。若復有二，普天之民莫能爲道者也。夫學道者，行陰德
莫大於施惠解救。志莫大於守身奉道。其福甚大，其生甚固矣。有人惡
我者，我不納惡，惡自歸己。將禍而歸身中，猶〔景〕（謂應作影字）
響之隨形聲矣。

Above are the "Teachings and Admonitions of the Assembled Numinous Powers."

右衆靈教戒所言。 [151]

These three male Perfected and two female Perfected are all the most
revered of the Higher Perfected. They seldom descend [to the mortal
realms]. I suspect that those who did descend recounted the above,
just as they did the chants of the Four Lords who assembled at the
Redgem Terrace on the autumnal equinox.[152] It is not necessarily the
case that they personally presented these sayings to Lord Yang [Xi].

按此三男眞二女眞並高眞之尊貴者。降集甚希。恐此是諸降者，敍説
其事，猶如秋分日 瑶臺四君吟耳。非必親受楊君也。

---

merit" 陰德, the performance of secret good deeds intended not to earn earthly recompense but postmortem reward and breaks the sentence in two by changing "maintain
will" 守志 to "maintain the body" 守身 and adding a second comparative clause ("There
is no greater aspiration than to . . ." 志莫大於). The definition of *merit* is also missing
from the *Declarations*.

150. This paragraph corresponds to a sentence from no. 6 of the *Scripture in Forty-
Two Sections*, without significant variation.

151. From the beginning of this section to this point is entirely copied in DZ 458,
1.1a–5a, with the textual variation noted in the previous notes. I suspect that this "subti-
tle" was *not* added by Yang or by Tao, but inserted by a later editor to separate off the
additions by Yang Xi that appear below.

152. The chants of the Four Lords—the Azure Lad, the Perfected of Clear Vacuity
Wang Bao, the Perfected of the Western Citadel Wang, and the Perfected of the Heaven of
Lesser Existence Wang Zideng—are recorded at DZ 1016, 3.9a–b. As Tao notes, the
poems were not personally delivered but were reported by a lesser Perfected, Lady Right
Blossom, who often appeared to Yang.

If in your mind you frequently roam the mountains and lakes and entrust your effulgences to the Transcendents and Perfected, numinous qi will increase the pleasure of your distant travels and mountain spirits will delight in your long-ago conversion. In this way, the hundreds of ailments will not detain you and the many deviant forces will not encroach upon you. When you burn incense, it causes your cloud- and white-souls to be regulated. Through constantly smelling the qi carried by fragrant winds, they will after a long time become enlightened. Once this happens, you may enter the Dao. Having entered the Dao, you will become Transcendent and eventually complete Perfection.[153]

數遊心山澤，託景仙眞者，靈氣將愍子之遠樂，山神將欣子之向化。是故百疾不能干，百 邪不得犯。屢燒香左右者，令人魂魄正。而恆聞芳風之氣，久久乃覺之耳。覺之則入道。入道則得仙。得仙則成眞。

The text, from the eleven "Songs on Dependence," through the "admonitions" down to this point, is entirely written on eight pieces of lined paper in [two] alternate hands. After this, half a line of text has been torn away, leading to the remainder of the line that begins "In stillness, observe heaven and earth . . ." in Yang's hand.[154] Yang must have written more in continuation before this, but some later person continued it differently. This is [also?] why there is no way to know what Yang wrote with respect to the thirty-four graphs missing before ["In stillness, observe heaven and earth . . .]."

(從前卷有待歌詩十篇接戒來至此，，凡八紙，並更手界紙書。後截半行書字，即是楊書 "淨覩天地" 行。 此前當並有楊續書。後人更寫別續之耳。所以前脫三十四字，楊所書， 今未知何事。)

Despite the fact that the title has seemingly been moved, this note marks the end of the text copied by two different hands on eight pages of lined paper. After the first sentence of Tao Hongjing's note, which is fairly clear, it is difficult to visualize just what he had in front of him.[155] It is clear that the copy Tao saw began with the "Songs on Dependence" and continued on past the section marked at the end with the words "Above are the

153. Preceding this paragraph, I have deleted three lines of text (DZ 1016, 6.10a8–10b1 and DZ 458, 1.5a6–8) that relate information for Xu Mi from his departed wife Tao Kedou. This paragraph may well be a continuation of that message, but its more general tenor mandates its inclusion here.

154. That line, also seemingly cribbed from the *Scripture in Forty-Two Sections*, now follows this note in the received *Declarations*.

155. I want to thank Chang Chao-jan 張超然, Jessey Choo, and Hao Chunwen 郝春文 for their help in discussing this passage. The final result is solely my responsibility.

teachings and admonitions of the assembled spirits." Beyond this, the note is a bit puzzling. I have placed the section beginning "In stillness, observe heaven and earth," which in the received edition of the *Declarations* appears after this note, under the heading "Related Fragments." What Tao means by "Yang must have written more in continuation before this" is a statement that is not entirely clear to me. Tao cannot be referring only to the missing half line before "in stillness, observe heaven and earth" because he is able to calculate that thirty-four characters were missing. This would likely be two lines of text. Whatever the case, the "in stillness" passage Tao saw in Yang's hand is now part of the Buddhist *Scripture in Forty-Two Sections.*

Hu Shi 胡適, in his vitriolic account of the *Declarations,* points out that two gaps in the manuscript Tao noted above (see footnotes 140 and 142) total thirty-four characters.[156] Hu wants to use Tao's differing responses to these lacunae to prove that Tao falsified the *Declarations,* writing both the text *and* the commentary himself. Hu's biases to the side, he may be correct that the "missing" thirty-four graphs refer to these two gaps in the manuscript. But since scripture copies tended to have lines of seventeen graphs in length, another possibility is that Yang himself had written 34 characters or two lines of text at the end of the manuscript, right before the half line ending "In stillness, observe heaven and earth."[157] But we can be relatively certain that the inclusion of the final "section" in Yang's hand at the end of the eight pages indicates that this passage, like those we will see later, was Yang's original composition, altered to read "observe impermanence" in later Buddhist versions of the text.

My primary justifications for the material that I have included between the end of the dependence/independence poems and the "Teachings and Admonitions of the Assembled Numinous Powers" are threefold: (1) the revealing deities for these sections overlap, yet these are not deities who appear frequently elsewhere in the Declarations; (2) the fact that Tao notes this, remarking frequently that these deities only reveal this particular body of material; (3) the mechanics of how much text could have been included on "eight pages" during the Jin period. Hu Shi, noting the distance between this footnote and the first line, argues that "the ancients . . . copied two to three thousand characters per sheet of paper."[158] While this

---

156. See DZ 1016, 6.9a1 and 6.94. For Hu Shi's opinion, see *Hu Shi wenji,* vol. 5, 137ff.

157. Unfortunately, the Japanese translation team is silent on all of these issues. See their translation at SKKY, 233.

158. *Hu Shi wenji,* 5:137.

would seem to solve the problem, there is ample reason to doubt the statement. Hu Shi did not specify which "ancients" he meant, but the number seems impossibly high. Fortunately for me, the Dunhuang studies expert Hao Chunwen 郝春文 of Capitol Normal University agreed to discuss the problem with me, consulted other scholars, and provided the following data (the translation is mine):

> There are two different sizes of paper from the Jin. The first was 23.5 to 24 cm high and the second 26 to 27 cm high. The length of both types was between 43 and 46 cm. On each page, one could write twenty to thirty lines of text. Calculating from a line length of around seventeen graphs per line, each page would hold around four hundred to five hundred characters. Thus Hu Shi's statement that each sheet could hold two to three thousand characters is definitely wrong. My source for this information is Pan Jixing's 潘吉星 early study based on actual examples.[159] In his recent book, Pan writes "Each scroll is formed from pieces of paper of the same height that had been glued together to form a long scroll, sometimes meters in length. Before copying, each page had been prepared by drawing columns in diluted ink so that each line would be straight. These lines were called "dark strand columns" 烏絲蘭. Each page has a certain number of lines, between twenty and thirty, and there is 1.5 to 2 cm between lines. Each line has a certain number of graphs, most are seventeen graphs in length. . . . So each page holds from four hundred to five hundred graphs, not including small characters [as notes]."[160] Du Weisheng 杜偉生 writes: "Sheets of paper in the Dunhuang documents that have come down to us are mostly 45 to 50 cm in length and 25 to 26 cm tall."[161] If each line takes up something like 2 cm, then the paper Du describes would also allow for twenty to thirty lines, and with each line having approximately seventeen graphs, each page would hold around four to five hundred graphs. Thus, the calculations of the two authors are largely the same.[162]

Depending on what size the sheets of paper used, then, the "eight lined pages" would total between thirty-two hundred and four thouand graphs. The two sections Tao mentions ("Dependence Poems" and "Admonitions"), without his annotations, comprise 2026 graphs. With the Fangzhu passages I have speculated were part of the package, the total is 2098 graphs. But, according to Tao's note, there seems still to have been enough room on the eighth page for Yang Xi to "continue" with his own paragraphs. Further, if spaces were left above god names and after the end of each poem in the section on the "Dependence/Independence Poems," it is possible

159. Pan Jixing, "Dunhuang shishi," 39–47. Pan writes specifically of paper length during the Eastern Jin.

160. Pan Jixing, *Zhongguo zaozhi shi*, 137. This information comes from the chapter on papermaking in the Six Dynasties period.

161. Du Weisheng 杜偉生, "Dunhuang yishu yongzhi," 70.

162. Hao Chunwen, personal communication, 8 January 2019.

that three thousand graphs could nearly fill eight pages. It might also be possible that something else is missing. –Trans.

. . .

INTRODUCTION TO RELATED FRAGMENTS

Following Tao's note and the end of the section labeled "Above are the Teachings and Admonitions of the Assembled Numinous Powers," more passages in the same format appear. These include two that appear in received editions of the Buddhist *Scripture in Forty-Two Sections*, raising the intriguing possibility that some items from Yang Xi's plagiary might have been copied into early editions of that Buddhist work. These are also attributed to the deities introduced at the head of this section and might have been part of a longer work that Yang was planning. The final passages are even more resolutely "Daoist" in outlook. I have thus included them here.

. . .

TRANSLATION OF RELATED FRAGMENTS

In stillness, observe heaven and earth and think of flying in transcendence. In stillness, observe the mountains and streams and think of flying in transcendence. In stillness, observe the ten thousand things and think on the benevolence of what covers us and bears us.[163] If you are able to control your heart and mind in this way, you will achieve the Dao.[164]

Human life is like an illusion.[165] We are placed here between heaven and earth for only a short period of time. If one is able to control one's qi and strengthen one's spirits, working hard to infuse oneself with Perfection, one will be able to achieve the longevity of the Dao. Once the Dao

163. "What bears and what covers" is a metaphor for earth and sky.

164. To this point, this passage is a rewording of no. 16 of the *Scripture in Forty-Two Sections*. (Omitted in Bumbacher, "Buddhist Sūtra"; see T 784, 17:723a16.) The Scripture advises contemplating "impermanence" 非常, whereas the *Declarations* urges the remembrance of "flying Transcendents" 飛仙 and "the compassion of what covers us [the heavens] and what bears us [the earth]" 覆載慈心.

165. The poet Tao Qian 陶潛 (365–427) may have been influenced by this line when he wrote "Human life seems an illusion / In the end we return to empty nothingness" 人生似幻化，終當歸空無。 ("Returning to my Gardens and Fields to Reside," no. 4 歸園田居詩之四, in *Tao Yuanming ji* 陶淵明集, 2.5a, SKQS).

is achieved, one may accompany heaven and earth in their place within great nothingness. If one is able to comprehend the void, embodying nothingness, then one may accompany great nothingness in its place within the utterly still. If one is able to comprehend stillness, then "one might look at you without seeing you; listen to you without hearing you."[166] Then it will be easy to free yourself from the roots of life and death;[167] easy to seek out extended longevity. What you seek can be obtained, what you free can be enduring.

靜觀天地念飛仙。[168] 靜觀山川念飛仙。靜觀萬物念覆載慈心。常執心如此，得道也。 人生者 如幻化耳。寄寓天地間少許時耳。若攝氣營神，苦辛注真，將得道久。道成則同與天地共寓在太無中矣。若洞虛體無，則與太無共寄寓在寂寂中矣。能洞寂者，則視之不見，聽之不聞。[169] 死生之根易解，久長之年易尋。尋之可得，解之可久。

One is able to endure in the Dao through nurturing life; what can always endow extended roaming is the ability to ingest qi. When one's qi is full, life endures and one may then nurture life. Through nurturing to completion, one joins with the Perfected and then may achieve longevity. One may then ascend to the single realm of living qi and hope for the perfect stillness that comes from nurturing to fullness.[170] Then one will see that the ten thousand things, heaven and earth, are all mere fabrications. Should one not labor to achieve this? Once your qi is full you may drive off demons and perversities. Once you have nurtured it to completion you may drive off the myriad injuries. This is what is meant when [the *Daode jing*] states: "Entering military conflict, you will not meet weapons; traveling in the mountains, you will not encounter tigers or rhinoceri."[171]

夫可久於其道者養生也。常可與久遊者納氣也。氣全則生存，然後能養至。養至則合真， 然後能久。[172]登生氣之二域，望養全之寂寂。視

---

166. Paraphrasing section 14 of the *Daode jing*. The verb *dong* 洞, which I have translated as "comprehend" in these two sentences, means "pass through" and likely also implies full embodiment rather than a mere mental state.

167. "Life and death" here likely should be understood to refer to rebirth.

168. This and the following four paragraphs are cited in DZ 458, 1.5b–7a.

169. To this point, this paragraph is cited in DZ 1138, 100.9a.

170. Both DZ 1016 and DZ 458, 1. 6a, have "the two realms of living qi" 生氣之二域, a concept that occurs nowhere else. I follow DZ 1138, 100.9a, and DZ 1032, 57.1b, both of which speak only of a single realm.

171. Yang here paraphrases chapter 51 of the *Daode jing*.

172. In this and the previous sentence, I follow DZ 1138, 100.9a. DZ 458, 1.6a, reads 養生 for 養至 and DZ 830, 1b, reads 養志.

萬物玄黃盡假寄耳。豈可不懃之哉。氣全則辟鬼邪。養全則辟百害，
入軍不逢甲兵，山行不觸虎兕。此之謂矣。

Studying the Dao is like recalling breakfast—anyone can do it. Cherishing qi is like cherishing one's face—everyone accomplishes it. But the
face can be destroyed, and qi likewise can be lost. The main point to
remember is that what humans cherish is always visible in the face. You
should worry that it be destroyed, for your four limbs are next. Among
those who always cherish qi as the first priority in [cultivating] their
bodies, I see few who wither and become emaciated.

I note that the qi discussed here is likely the essence and qi of sexual
cultivation, not the qi one breathes.

學道常如憶朝食， [173]　未有不得之者也。惜氣常如惜面目，未有不全者
也。然面目亦有　毀壞者，猶氣亦有喪失。要人之所惜，常在於面目。
慮有犯穢，次及四肢耳。若使惜氣常爲一身之先急，吾少見其枯悴矣。
（案此所云氣，蓋是房中精氣之氣。非呼吸之氣。）

Following the profane in seeking fame is like burning incense: Everyone
enjoys its fine fragrance, but none realizes that its smoldering consumes
it. Once it is fully burnt away, the fine fragrance dissipates.[174] As name
is established, the body perishes. For this reason, those of high attainments laugh at them and keep their distance. In this way they maintain
the stillness and purity.

人隨俗要求華名譬若燒香。衆人皆聞其芳，然不知薰以自燔。燔盡則
氣滅。名立則身絕，　是故高人哂而遠之，遂爲清淨。[175]

As a thing, life is comparable to sun, moon, heaven, and earth.[176] These
four images exist in correspondence with life after life. If life is lost, the
four images are likewise obliterated. It is not that the four images are
obliterated in themselves; the loss of life destroys them. If one could
achieve immortality, then the four images would be eternally preserved.
It is not that the four images achieve immortality; it is because of the self

173. I follow DZ 1032, 57.18a, and DZ 824, 2.3a2–3, in correcting "the intention to
study the Way" 學道之心 to "studying the Way" 學道.

174. To this point, this paragraph corresponds to no. 19 of the *Scripture in Forty-Two
Sections*. (Omitted in Bumbacher, "Buddhist Sūtra"; see T 784, 17:723a22.)

175. In addition to DZ 458, this passage is also cited in DZ 1403, 20b–21a.

176. The topic posed here "life as a thing" 生之爲物, was first posed by Yan Zun
嚴遵 (59–24 BCE) in his *Daodejing zhigui* (DZ 693, 9.8b). On this commentary, see
Robinet, *Les commentaires*, 11–24.

that is eternally preserved that they continue to exist. Eternal life can also arise in the imageless realm, so how could the four images in themselves be enough to account for it?[177] When disasters threaten and misfortune arises, the body is destroyed and qi perishes. What causes this to occur? It seems to arise from an excess of speech, from not maintaining unity, and from plotting in hopes of escaping disaster. This is how the nest of the mysterious falls with the dropping branch, and one hundred victories are lost in a single defeat. How valued the talent who can pass through to Transcendence! How can his destruction be brought on by top-knotted youths?

This was spoken by Lady Southern Marchmount.

The phrase "top-knotted youths who bring destruction" 豎子致弊 seems to refer to an incurable ailment residing in the chest and refers to the story of Duke Jing of Jin's dream.[178] If not, then it must be some other story about a youth.

生之爲物，[179] 譬日月天地。此四象正與生生爲對。失生則四 象亦滅。非四象之滅，生滅之也。若使常生，則四象常存。非四象之常存，我能常生故也。常生亦能生於無景。何四象之足計哉。災遘禍生，形壞氣亡，起何等事耶？似由多言而不守一，多端而期苟免耳。是以玄巢頹枝以墜落。百勝喪於一敗矣。惜乎通仙之才，安可爲豎子致弊也。（豎子致弊，蓋爲膏肓之患不除。借取晉景公之夢。不爾則是別有小兒事也。）

南嶽夫人所言。

The following was spoken by the Lady of Purple Tenuity:

Swan geese and egrets travel to the south with outstretched wings soaring into the distance. Only after having reached tens or hundreds of wild spots will those birds declare it sufficient. But quails and pigeons sigh at the distances they have traveled, while the Great Peng bird laughs that those quails and pigeons have only gone a foot or two. Since each

177. My translation of "imageless realm" for 無景 is conjectural. Yang Xi nowhere else uses the term, and it occurs most often as a way of writing 無影 "shadowless," a sign of transcendence in some stories. (See DZ 1016, 9.22a7.)

178. Duke Jing, after inviting a famed physician to cure his illness, dreamt that two top-knotted boys embodied his ailment and were discussing where in the Duke's body to hide to avoid detection. When the physician arrived, he confirmed that the illness was incurable, since it had moved to that spot. (See the Zuo zhuan 左傳, Chenggong 成公 10, SSJZS, 2:1906c.)

179. This paragraph is cited at DZ 458, 1.6b.

is satisfied with their own lot, they are content with the truth they know. Thus, the three sorts of birds have nothing to discuss. What need is there for them to criticize one another?[180]

The previous eight passages were in the calligraphy of Yang Xi.[181]

鴻鷺對南旅，以遏扇揚翮。[182] 在於十百之野，彼鳥自謂足矣。然鸚鳩歎其眇邈。大鵬晒鴻舉之〔指〕（謂應作咫字）尺耳。苟安其安而是非自足。故三鳥不相與議焉。何譏之乎。

紫微言。

右八條竝楊書。

---

180. While the birds used as examples differ somewhat, this is a meditation on the opening chapters of the *Zhuangzi*. For the critical birds, including the mythical Great Peng bird 大鵬, see Graham, *Chuang-Tzŭ*, 43–44; for the contingent nature of this/that or true/false (是/非), Graham, 52–53. Putting these two insights together, the Perfected conclude that the birds simply cannot speak to one another, which has obvious implications for their relations with humans.

181. This note seems to indicate that the passages from 6.10a9 are in Yang's hand. I have moved the first of these (concerning the three visits with Tao Kedou) to the section on the death of Xu Mi's wife in volume 2.

182. This paragraph is cited at DZ 458, 1.7a.

Works in the Daoist Canon

Daoist works are cited from the *Zhengtong daozang* 正統道藏 (1445), published by the Commercial Press of Shanghai in a thread-bound, photo-reproduced edition from 1923 to 1926. These texts will be cited by numerical order, preceded by the abbreviation "DZ." Passages within the work are further specified by chapter, page, followed by *a* for recto and *b* for verso, and in some cases, line numbers. For information on the dates and contents of these works, see Schipper and Verellen, *The Taoist Canon* (University of Chicago Press, 2004). In addition to a title index, that work includes an index organized by DZ number.

DZ No.

22   *Yuanshi wulao chishu yupian zhenwen tianshu jing* 元始五老赤書玉篇真文天書經

253 *Jinque dijun sanyuan zhenyi jing* 金闕帝君三元真一經

291 *Mu tianzi zhuan* 穆天子傳

292 *Han wudi neizhuan* 漢武帝內傳

296 *Lishi zhenxian tidao tongjian* 歷世真仙體道通鑑

300 *Huayang yinju neizhuan* 華陽陶隱居內傳

302 *Zhoushi mingtong ji* 周氏冥通記

304 *Maoshan zhi* 茅山志

392 *Shangqing huoluo qiyuan fu* 上清豁落七元符

421 *Dengzhen yinjue* 登真隱訣

434 *Xuanlan renniao shan jingtu* 玄覽人鳥山經圖

442　*Shangqing housheng jun lieji* 上清後聖道君列紀

458　*Shangqing zhongzhen jiaojie dexing jing* 上清眾真教戒德行經

543　*Taishang cibei daochang xiaozai jiuyou chan* 太上慈悲道場消災九幽懺

682　*Daode zhenjing zhu* 德真經註

693　*Daode zhenjing zhigui* 道德真經指歸

783　*Yongcheng jixian lu* 墉城集仙錄

824　*Songshan Taiwu xiansheng qi jing* 嵩山太无先生氣經

830　*Fuqi jingyi lun* 服氣精義論

980　*Zhuzhen gesong* 諸真歌頌

1016　*Zhen'gao* 真誥

1025　*Guigu zi* 鬼谷子

1031　*Shanhai jing* 山海經

1032　*Yunji qiqian* 雲笈七籤

1050　*Huayang Tao yinju ji* 華陽陶隱居集

1129　*Daojiao yishu* 道教義樞

1138　*Wushang miyao* 無上秘要

1139　*Sandong zhunang* 三洞珠囊

1185　*Baopu zi neipian* 抱朴子內篇

1187　*Baopu zi waipian* 抱朴子外篇

1221　*Shangqing lingbao dafa* 上清靈寶大法

1230　*Taiping yulan* 太平御覽

1248　*Sandong qunxian lu* 三洞群仙錄

1270　*Zhengyi fawen xiuzhen zhiyao* 正一法文修真旨要

1323　*Dongzhen taishang basu zhenjing fushi riyue Huanghua jue* 洞真太上八素真經服食日月皇華訣

1331　*Dongzhen shangqing Shenzhou qizhuan qibian wutian jing* 洞真上清神州七轉七變舞天經

1369　*Shangqing huaxing yinjing dengsheng baoxian shangjing* 上清化形隱景登昇保仙上經

1376　*Shangqing taishang dijun jiuzhen zhongjing* 上清太上帝君九真中經.

1378　*Shangqing Jinzhen yuguang bajing feijing* 上清金真玉光八景飛經

1382　*Shangqing jiudan shanghua taijing zhongji jing* 上清九丹上化胎精中記經.

1403　*Shangqing xianfu qionglin jing* 上清僊府瓊林經

1483　*Tianhuang zhidao taiqing yuce* 天皇至道太清玉冊

Works Cited

Andersen, Poul. "The Practice of *Bugang*." *Cahiers d'Extrême-Asie* 5 (1990): 15–53.

Aramaki Noritoshi 荒牧典俊. "'Shinkō yizen shoshinkō no hennen mondai' ni tsuite" 真誥以前の編年問題について. In Yoshikawa Tadao, *Rikuchō dōkyō no kenkyū* 六朝道教の研究, 55–100.

Ban Gu 班固 (32–92) et al. *Hanshu* 漢書. Beijing: Zhonghua, 1962.

Barbezat, Michael David. "'He Doubted that These Things Actually Happened': Knowing the Otherworld in the *Tractatus de Purgatorio Sancti Patricii*." *History of Religions* 57, no. 4 (May 2018): 321–47.

Barolini, Teodolinda. *The Undivine Comedy: Detheologizing Dante*. Princeton, NJ: Princeton University Press, 1992.

Barrett, T. H. "Gu Huan." In Pregadio, *Encyclopedia of Taoism*, 1:451–52.

Baxter, William H. *An Etymological Dictionary of Common Chinese Characters*. Self-published, 2000.

Benn, Charles D. "Wushang Biyao." In Pregadio, *Encyclopedia of Taoism*, 2:1062–66.

Boileau, Gilles. "Wu and Shaman." *Bulletin of the School of Oriental and African Studies* (University of London) 65, no. 2 (2002): 350–78.

Bokenkamp, Stephen R. *Ancestors and Anxiety: Daoism and the Birth of Rebirth in China*. A Philip E. Lilienthal Book in Asian Studies. Berkeley: University of California Press, 2007.

———. "Declarations of the Perfected." In *Religions of China in Practice*. Princeton, NJ: Princeton University Press, 1996.

———. *Early Daoist Scriptures*. Taoist Classics 1. Berkeley: University of California Press, 1997.

———. "Ge Chaofu." In Pregadio, *Encyclopedia of Taoism*, 1:440–41.

———. "The Herb Calamus and the Transcendent Han Zhong in Taoist Literature." *Studies in Chinese Religions* 1, no. 4 (19 November 2015): 293–305.

———. "Lu Xiujing, Buddhism, and the First Daoist Canon." In *Culture and Power in the Reconstitution of the Chinese Realm, 200–600*, edited by Audrey Spiro and Patricia Ebrey, 181–99. Cambridge, MA: Harvard University Press, 2001.

———. "Research Note: Buddhism in the Writings of Tao Hongjing." *Daoism: Religion, History and Society* 《道教研究學報：宗教、歷史與社會》, no. 6 (2014): 247–68.

———. "Scriptures New and Old: Lu Xiujing and Mastery." In *Xinyang, shijian yu wenhua tiaoshi* 信仰, 實踐與文化調適 *Belief, Practice and Cultural Adaptation, Papers from the Religion Section of the International Conference on Sinology*, edited by Kang Pao 康豹 (Paul Katz) and Liu Shufen 劉淑芬, 2:449–74. Taipei: Zhongyang yanjiu yuan, 2013.

———. "Sisters of the Blood: The Lives of the Daoist Nuns behind the Xie Ziran Biography." *Daoism: Religion, History and Society* 《道教研究學報：宗教、歷史與社會》, no. 8 (2016): 7–33.

———. "Sources of the *Ling-pao* Scriptures," in *Tantric and Taoist Studies*, vol. 21 of *Mélanges chinois et bouddhiques*, edited by Michel Strickmann, 2:434–86. Brussels: Institut Belge des Hautes Études Chinoises, 1983.

———. "Stages of Transcendence: the *Bhūmi* Concept in Taoist Scripture," in *Chinese Buddhist Apocrypha*, edited by Robert E. Buswell, 119–47. Honolulu: University of Hawai'i Press, 1990.

———. "Time after Time: Taoist Apocalyptic History and the Founding of the T'ang Dynasty." *Asia Major*, third series, vol. 7, pt. 1 (1994): 59–88.

———. "Zhengzha, qujie, he qucong: Zhen'gao shige de yingyi" 掙扎、曲解和屈從：《真誥》詩歌的英譯 [Struggle, Accommodation, Surrender: Translating the Poetry of the Zhen'gao into English]. In *Daojiao xiulian yu keyide wenxue tiyan* 道教修煉與科儀的文學體驗, 54–73. Hong Kong: Fenghuang chubanshe, 2018.

Botterill, Steven. Review of *The Undivine Comedy: Detheologizing Dante*, by Teodolinda Barolini. *Italica* 71, no. 3 (1994): 404–5.

Bourguignon E. (1970) "Hallucination and Trance: An Anthropologist's Perspective." In *Origin and Mechanisms of Hallucinations*, edited by W. Keup, 183–90. Boston: Springer, 1970.

Buchan, David, and Edward D. Ives. "Tale Roles and Revenants: A Morphology of Ghosts." *Western Folklore* 45, no. 2 (1986): 143–60.

Bujard, Marianne. "Daybooks in Qin and Han Religion." In Harper and Kalinowski, *Books of Fate*, 305–35. Leiden, the Netherlands: Brill, 2017.

Bumbacher, Stephan Peter. "A Buddhist Sūtra's Transformation into a Daoist Text." *Asiatische Studien* 60, no. 4 (2006): 799–831.

———. *The Fragments of the Daoxue Zhuan: Critical Edition, Translation, and Analysis of a Medieval Collection of Daoist Biographies*. Europäische Hochschulschriften. Reihe XXVII, Asiatische und Afrikanische Studien, Bd. 78. Frankfurt am Main: Peter Lang, 2000.

Buswell, Robert E., ed. *Encyclopedia of Buddhism*. New York: Macmillan Reference USA/Thomson/Gale, 2004.

Bynum, Caroline Walker. "The Female Body and Religious Practice in the Later Middle Ages." In *Fragments for a History of the Human Body*, 1:161–219. New York: Zone, 1989.

Cahill, Suzanne Elizabeth. *Divine Traces of the Daoist Sisterhood: "Records of the Assembled Transcendents of the Fortified Walled City" by Du Guangting (850–933)*. Magdalena, NM: Three Pines Press, 2006.

———. *Transcendence and Divine Passion: The Queen Mother of the West in Medieval China*. Stanford, CA: Stanford University Press, 1993.

Campany, Robert Ford. *Dreaming and Self-Cultivation in China, 300 BCE– 800 CE*, forthcoming.

———. *Making Transcendents: Ascetics and Social Memory in Early Medieval China*. Honolulu: University of Hawai'i Press, 2009.

———. *To Live as Long as Heaven and Earth: A Translation and Study of Ge Hong's Traditions of Divine Transcendents*. Daoist Classics 2. Berkeley: University of California Press, 2002.

———. "Shangqing jing de biaoyan xingzhi 上清經的表演性質' [The Performative Nature of Shangqing Daoist Scriptures]." In *Daojiao xiulian yu keyi de wenxue tixian* 道教修煉與科儀的文學體驗, 25–53. Nanjing: Fenghuang chubanshe, 2017.

Chang Ch'ao-jan 張超然. "Xipu, jiaofa ji qi zhenghe: Dongjin nanbeichao daojiao shangqing jingpai de jichu yanjiu" 系譜、教法及其整合：東晉南朝道教上清經派的基礎研究. PhD diss., National Chengchih University, Taipei, 2008.

Chang Ch'ao-jan 張超然, and Jonathan Pettit. *A Library of Clouds: Rewriting Daoist Scriptures in the Fourth and Fifth Centuries, CE*. Honolulu: University of Hawai'i Press, forthcoming.

Chen Guofu 陳國符. *Daozang yuanliu kao* 道藏源流考. Beijing: Zhonghua shuju, 1963.

Ch'ên, Kenneth. *Buddhism in China, a Historical Survey,* Princeton Studies in the History of Religions. Princeton, NJ: Princeton University Press, 1964.

Chen Shihua 陳世華. "Tao Hongjing shumu zhuanmingwen faxian ji kaozheng" 陶弘景書墓磚銘文發現及考證. *Dongnan wenhua,* 6 (1987) 54–59.

Chen Shou 陳壽 (233–97). *Sanguo zhi* 三國志. Beijing: Zhonghua, 1962.

Corbett, George, and Heather Webb, eds. Introduction to *Vertical Readings in Dante's "Comedy,"* 1st ed., edited by George Corbett and Heather Webb, 1:1–12. Cambridge, UK: Open Book Publishers, 2015. http://www.jstor.org/stable/j.ctt17w8gx0.6.

Cruse, Mark. "Matter and Meaning in Medieval Books." *The Senses and Society* 5, no. 1 (March 1, 2010): 45–56.

Cui Zhonghui 崔中慧. "Fojiao chuqi xiejingfang shezhi lice" 佛教初期寫經坊設置蠡測. *Taida Foxue yanjiu* 臺大佛學研究 32 (2016): 99–134.

Du Weisheng 杜偉生. "Dunhuang yishu yongzhi gaikuang ji qianxi" 敦煌遺書用紙概況及淺析. In *Rongshe yu chuangxin: guoji Dunhuang xiangmu diliuci huiyi lunwenji* 融攝與創新：國際敦煌項目第六次會議論文集, edited by Lin Shitian 林世田 and Alastair Morrison, 69–74. Beijing: Beijing tushu guan, 2007.

Eliade, Mircea. *Shamanism: Archaic Techniques of Ecstasy*. Bollingen Series 76. Princeton, NJ: Princeton University Press, 1974.

Espesset, Grégoire. "Tao Hongjing." In Pregadio, *Encyclopedia of Taoism*, 2:968–71.

Faivre, Antoine. "Sir Arthur Conan Doyle et Les Esprits Photographiés." *Ethnologie Française* 33, no. 4 (2003): 623–32.

Falkenhausen, Lothar, von. "Reflections on the Political Role of Spirit Mediums in Early China: The Wu Officials in the Zhouli." *Early China* 20 (1995): 279–300.

Fan Ye 范曄 (398–445). *Hou Hanshu* 後漢書. Beijing: Zhonghua shuju, 1971.

Fang Xuanling 房玄齡 et al. *Jinshu* 晉書. Beijing: Zhonghua shuju, 1974.

Feher, Michel, Ramona Naddaff, and Nadia Tazi. *Fragments for a History of the Human Body*. Zone (Series) 3. Brooklyn, NY: Zone Books; distributed by the MIT Press, 1989.

Gómez, Louis O. "Nirvāṇa," in Buswell, *Encyclopedia of Buddhism*, 2:600–605.

Graham, A.C. *Chuang-Tzŭ: The Seven Inner Chapters and Other Writings from the Book Chuang-Tzŭ*. London: Allen & Unwin, 1981.

Granet, Marcel. *Fêtes et Chansons Anciennes de La Chine*. Paris: E. Leroux, 1919.

Hamburger, Jeffrey F. "Speculations on Speculation: Vision and Perception in the Theory and Practice of Mystical Devotions." In *Deutsche Mystik im Abendländischen Zusammenhang*, 353–408. Tübingen, Germany: Max Niemeyer Verlag, 2000.

Han Ying 韓嬰 (fl. 150 BCE). *Hanshi waizhuan jianshu* 韓詩外傳箋疏. Edited by Qu Shouyuan 屈守元. Chengdu: Bashu shushe, Sichuan sheng xinhua shudian, 1996.

Hao Chunwen 郝春文. "Dunhuang xiebenxue yu Zhongguo gudai xiebenxue" 敦煌寫本學與中國古代寫本學. *Zhongguo Gaoxiao Shehuikexue* 中國高校社會科學, 2 (2015): 67–74.

Harper, Donald and Kalinowski, Marc. *Books of Fate and Popular Culture in Early China*. Leiden, the Netherlands: Brill, 2017.

Heinze, Ruth-Inge, and Richard Noll. "More on Mental Imagery and Shamanism." *Current Anthropology* 27, no. 2 (1986): 154.

Hu Shi 胡適. (1891–1962). "Tao Hongjing de zhengao kao" 陶弘景的《真誥》考. In *Hushi wenji* 胡適文集, edited by Ouyang Zhesheng 歐陽哲生, 5:126–42. Beijing: Beijing daxue chubanshe, 1998.

Hyland, Elizabeth Watts. "Oracles of the True Ones: Scroll One." PhD diss., University of California, Berkeley, 1984.

Kalinowski, Marc, ed. *Divination et société dans la Chine médiévale: étude des manuscrits de Dunhuang de la Bibliothèque nationale de France et de la British Library*. Bibliothèque nationale de France, 2003.

———. "Topomancie." In Kalinowski, *Divination et société*, 557–612.

Karlgren, Bernhard (1889–1978). *The Book of Odes*. Stockholm: The Museum of Far Eastern Antiquities, 1974.

Keenan, John P. *How Master Mou Removes Our Doubts: A Reader-Response Study and Translation of the Mou-Tzu Li-huo lun*. Albany: State University of New York Press, 1994.

Keightley, David N. *Shamanism, Death, and the Ancestors : Religious Mediation in Neolithic and Shang China (ca. 5000–1000 B.C.)*. Beijing: Zhongguo shehui kexue chubanshe, 1984.

Kleeman, Terry F. *Celestial Masters : History and Ritual in Early Daoist Communities*. Cambridge, MA: Harvard University Asia Center, 2016.

———. *A God's Own Tale: The Book of Transformations of Wenchang, the Divine Lord of Zitong*. SUNY Series in Chinese Philosophy and Culture. Albany: State University of New York Press, 1994.

Knechtges, David R. *Wen Xuan, or, Selections of Refined Literature*. Edited by Tong Xiao 蕭統 during 501–531 CE. Princeton Library of Asian Translations. Princeton, NJ: Princeton University Press, 1982.

Kroll, Paul W. "In the Halls of the Azure Lad" 105 (1985): 75–94.

———. "A Palindrome Poem of the Mid-Seventh Century." presented at the Annual Meeting of the Western Branch of the American Oriental Society, Seattle, 1998.

———. "A Poetry Debate of the Perfected of Highest Clarity." *Journal of the American Oriental Society* 132, no. 4 (2012): 577–86.

Lagerwey, John. *Wu-shang pi-yao : somme taoïste du VIe siècle*, vol. 124. Paris: Publications de l'École française d'Extreme-Orient, 1981.

Ledderose, Lothar. "Some Taoist Elements in the Calligraphy of the Six Dynasties." *T'oung-Pao* 70, no. 4 (1984): 246–78.

Legge, James (1815–97). *Li Chi: Book of Rites, An Encyclopedia of Ancient Ceremonial Usages, Religious Creeds, and Social Institutions*. 2 vols. New York: University Books, 1967.

Lewis, I. M. *Ecstatic Religion: A Study of Shamanism and Spirit Possession*. 3rd ed. London: Routledge, 2003.

———. "Spirit Possession and Deprivation Cults." *Man* 1, no. 3 (1966): 307–29.

Li Fang 李昉 (925–96), et al. *Taiping guangji* 太平廣記. Beijing: Zhonghua, 1961.

———. *Taiping yulan* 太平御覽. Beijing: Zhonghua, 1960.

Li Yanshou 李延壽 (fl. 629). *Nan shi* 南史. Beijing: Zhonghua shuju, 1975.

Liu Zuguo 刘祖国 and Fan Yanli 范艳丽. "*Zhen'gao jiaozhu* kanwu zhaji" 《真诰校注》勘误札记 - Some Tentative Doubts on Punctuations and Annotations of Zhen'gao. 安徽理工大学学报：社会科学版 17, no. 3 (2015): 48–51.

Lo, Vivienne. "Crossing the Nei Guan 內關 'Inner Pass': A Nei/Wai 內外 'Inner/ Outer' Distinction in Early Chinese Medicine." *East Asian Science, Technology, and Medicine* 17 (2000): 15–65.

Lopez, Donald S., Jr., ed. *Religions of China in Practice*. Princeton, NJ: Princeton University Press, 1996.

Luhrmann, T. M. "Hallucinations and Sensory Overrides." *Annual Review of Anthropology* 40 (2011): 71–85.

———. *When God Talks Back: Understanding the American Evangelical Relationship with God*. 1st ed. New York: Alfred A. Knopf, 2012.

Lü Pengzhi 呂鵬志. *Tangqian daojiao yishi shigang* 唐前道教儀式史綱. Beijing: Zhonghua shuju, 2008.

Maeda Shigeki 前田繁樹. *Shoki dōkyō kyōten no keisei* 初期道教經典の形成. Tokyo: Kyūko, 2004.

Major, John S., Sarah A. Queen, Andrew Seth Meyer, and Harold D. Roth. *The Huainanzi: A Guide to the Theory and Practice of Government in Early Han*

China, by Liu An 劉安 *(179–122 BCE)*. New York: Columbia University Press, 2010.

Maspero, H. "Le songe et l'ambassade de l'empereur Ming: Étude critique des sources." *Bulletin de l'École Française d'Extrême-Orient* 10, no. 1 (1910): 95–130.

Mather, Richard B. *A New Account of Tales of the World = Shih-Shuo Hsin-Yü by Liu Yiqing* 劉義慶, 2nd ed. Michigan Monographs in Chinese Studies, no. 95: 403–44. University of Michigan, Center for Chinese Studies, Ann Arbor, 2002.

———. "Chinese Letters and Scholarship in the Third and Fourth Centuries: The Wen-hsüeh p'ien of the *Shih-shuo-hsin-yü.*" *Journal of the American Oriental Society* 84, no. 4 (1964): 348–91.

Miller, James. *The Way of Highest Clarity: Nature, Vision, and Revelation in Medieval China.* Magdalena, NM: Three Pines, 2008.

Mugitani Kuniō 麥谷邦夫. "Liang tianjian shiba nian jinian youming muzhuan he tianjian nianjian de Tao Hongjing" 梁天鑑十八年紀年有銘墓磚和天鑑年間的陶弘景. In *Riben dongfang xue* 日本東方學, edited by Takada, 80–97. Beijing: Zhonghua shuju, 2007.

———. *Shinkō sakuin* 眞誥索引. Kyoto: Kyōto Daigaku Jinbun Kagaku Kenkyūjo, 1991.

———. "Sun Youyue." In Pregadio, *Encyclopedia of Taoism*, 2:928–29.

———. "Tō Kōkei nenpu kōryaku 陶弘景年譜考略." *Tōhōshūkyō* 東方宗教, nos. 47/48 (1976): 30–61, 56–83.

Nasti, Paola, and Claudia Rossignoli, eds. *Interpreting Dante: Essays on the Traditions of Dante Commentary.* The William and Katherine Devers Series in Dante and Medieval Italian Literature. Notre Dame, IN: University of Notre Dame Press, 2013.

Nattier, Jan. *Once upon a Future Time: Studies in a Buddhist Prophecy of Decline.* Nanzan Studies in Asian Religions 1. Berkeley, CA: Asian Humanities Press, 1991.

Needham, Joseph. *Science and Civilisation in China.* Vol. 6, pt. 1, *Botany.* Cambridge: Cambridge University Press, 1986.

Needham, Joseph, and Gwei-Djen Lu. *Science and Civilisation in China.* Vol. 3, *Mathematics and the Sciences of the Heavens and the Earth.* Edited by Nathan Sivin. Cambridge: Cambridge University Press, 1959.

———. *Science and Civilisation in China.* Vol. 5, pt. 2, *Spagyrical Discovery and Invention: Magisteries of Gold and Immortality.* Cambridge: Cambridge University Press, 1974.

Newman, Barbara. "What Did It Mean to Say 'I Saw'? The Clash between Theory and Practice in Medieval Visionary Culture." *Speculum* 80, no. 1 (2005): 1–43.

Nienhauser, William H., trans. *The Grand Scribe's Records*, vol. 1. Bloomington: Indiana University Press, 1991.

Nissinen, Martti, and Risto Uro. *Sacred Marriages: The Divine-Human Sexual Metaphor from Sumer to Early Christianity.* Winona Lake, IN.: Eisenbrauns, 2008.

Noll, Richard, Jeanne Achterberg, Erika Bourguignon, Leonard George, Michael Harner, Lauri Honko, Åke Hultkrantz, et al. "Mental Imagery Cultivation as a Cultural Phenomenon: The Role of Visions in Shamanism [and Comments and Reply]." *Current Anthropology* 26, no. 4 (1985): 443–61.

Ōfuchi, Ninji 大淵忍爾. *Tonkō dōkyō zurokuhen* 敦煌道經圖錄編. Tokyo: Fukubu Shoten, 1979.

Ohnuma, Reiko. "The Gift of the Body and the Gift of Dharma." *History of Religions* 37, no. 4 (1998): 323–59.

———. *Head, Eyes, Flesh, and Blood: Giving Away the Body in Indian Buddhist Literature.* New York: Columbia University Press, 2007.

Ou-yang Xiu 歐陽修 (1007–72), Song Qi 宋祁 (998–1061) et al., *Xin Tangshu* 新唐書. Beijing: Zhonghua shuju, 1975.

Pan Jixing潘吉星. "Dunhuang shishi xiejingzhi de yanjiu." 敦煌石室寫經紙的研究. *Wenwu* 文物 (March 1966): 39–47.

———. *Zhongguo zaozhi shi* 中国造纸史. Shanghai: Renmin chubanshe, 2009.

Pettit, J. E. E. "Learning from Mao Shan: Temple Construction in Early Medieval China." PhD diss., Indiana University, Bloomington, 2013.

Pettit, J. E. E., and Chang, Chao-jan, *A Library of Clouds: The Scripture of the Immaculate Numen and the Rewriting of Daoist Texts.* Honolulu: University of Hawai'i Press, 2020.

Pongratz-Leisten, Beate. "Sacred Marriage and the Transfer of Divine Knowledge: Alliances between the Gods and the King in Ancient Mesopotamia." In Nissinen and Uro, *Sacred Marriages,* 43–73.

Porkert, Manfred. *Biographie d'un taoïste legendaire: Tcheo Tseu-yang,* vol. 10. Paris: Mémoires de l'Institut des Hautes Études Chinoises, 1979.

Pregadio, Fabrizio, ed. *The Encyclopedia of Taoism.* London: Routledge, 2008.

Raz, Gil. "Creation of Tradition: The Five Talismans of the Numinous Treasure and the Formation of Early Daoism." PhD diss., Indiana University, Bloomington, 2004.

———. *The Emergence of Daoism: Creation of a Tradition.* New York: Routledge, 2012.

———. "The Way of the Yellow and the Red: Re-Examining the Sexual Initiation Rite of Celestial Master Daoism." *Nan-Nü,* no. 10.1 (2008): 86–120.

Robinet, Isabelle. *La révélation du Shangqing dans l'histoire du taoïsme.* Publications de l'Ecole française d'Extrême-Orient, vol. 137. Paris: Adrien-Maisonneuve, 1984.

———. *Les commentaires du Tao Tö King jusqu'au VIIe siècle.* Paris: Collège de France, Institut des Hautes Études Chinoises., 1977.

———. *Taoism: Growth of a Religion.* Stanford, CA: Stanford University Press, 1997.

———. *Taoist Meditation: The Mao-Shan Tradition of Great Purity.* SUNY Series in Chinese Philosophy and Culture. Albany: State University of New York Press, 1993.

———. "Ziyang Zhenren." In Pregadio, *Encyclopedia of Taoism,* 2:1303–4.

Robson, James. *Power of Place: The Religious Landscape of the Southern Sacred Peak (Nanyue) in Medieval China.* Cambridge, MA: Harvard University Asia Center, 2009.

Schafer, Edward H., *Mao Shan in T'ang Times.* Boulder, CO: Society for the Study of Chinese Religions, 1989.

———. *Mirages on the Sea of Time: The Taoist Poetry of Ts'ao T'ang*. Berkeley: University of California Press, 1985.

———. *Pacing the Void: T'ang Approaches to the Stars*. Berkeley: University of California Press, 1977.

———. "The Transcendent Vitamin, Efflorescence of Lang-Kan." *Chinese Science*, no. 3 (1978): 27–38.

Schipper, Kristofer Marinus. *Concordance du Tao-Tsang: titres des ouvrages*. Publications de l'École française d'Extrême-Orient ; vol. 102. Paris: École française d'Extrême-Orient, 1975.

———. *L'Empereur Wou des Han dans la legende taoiste*. École Francaise d'Extrême Orient, 1965.

Schipper, Kristofer Marinus and Franciscus Verellen, eds. *The Taoist Canon: A Historical Companion to the Daozang* [= *Dao Zang Tong Kao*]. 3 vols. Chicago: University of Chicago Press, 2004.

Sharf, Robert, "The Scripture in Forty-Two Sections," in Lopez, *Religions of China in Practice*, 360–71.

Shen Yue 沈約 (441–513). *Song shu* 宋書. Beijing: Zhonghua shuju, 1974.

Sima Qian 司馬遷 (145–86 BCE). *Shiji* 史記. Beijing: Zhonghua shuju, 1962.

Smith, Thomas E. *Declarations of the Perfected. Part One, Setting Scripts and Images into Motion*. St. Petersburg, FL: Three Pines Press, 2013.

———. "Record of the Ten Continents." *Taoist Resources*, no. 2.2 (1990): 87–119.

Sowell, Madison U. Review of *The Undivine Comedy: Detheologizing Dante*, by Teodolinda Barolini. *Renaissance Quarterly* 51, no. 2 (1998): 612–13.

Stein, Rolf Alfred. *The World in Miniature: Container Gardens and Dwellings in Far Eastern Religious Thought*. Translated by Phyllis Brooks. Stanford, CA: Stanford University Press, 1990.

Strickmann, Michel. *Chinese Magical Medicine*. Edited by Bernard Faure. Stanford, CA: Stanford University Press, 2002.

———. "The Mao Shan Revelations: Taoism and the Aristocracy." *T'oung-Pao* 63 (1977): 1–64.

———. "On the Alchemy of T'ao Hung-Ching." In *Facets of Taoism: Essays in Chinese Religion*, edited by Holmes Welch and Anna K. Seidel, 123–92. New Haven, CT: Yale University Press, 1979.

———. *Le Taoïsme du Mao Chan: chronique d'une révélation*. Mémoires de l'Institut des hautes études chinoises, 0337–792X, vol. 17. Paris: Presses Universitaires de France, 1981.

———. "A Taoist Confirmation of Liang Wu Ti's Suppression of Taoism." *Journal of the American Oriental Society*, 98 (1978): 467–74.

T'ang Yung-t'ung. "The Editions of the Ssŭ-shih-êrh-chang-ching." *Harvard Journal of Asiatic Studies* 1, no. 1 (1936): 147–55.

Taves, Ann. "History and the Claims of Revelation: Joseph Smith and the Materialization of the Golden Plates." *Numen* 61, no. 2–3 (18 March 2014): 182–207.

Thurston, Herbert. "Summer Land: The Valhalla of the Spiritualists." *Studies: An Irish Quarterly Review* 16, no. 62 (1927): 231–44.

Wang Jiakui 王家葵. *Dengzhen yinjue jijiao* 登真隱訣輯校. Beijing: Zhonghua shuju, 2011.
———. *Tao Hongjing congkao* 陶弘景叢考. Jinan: Qilu shushe, 2003.
Wang Ming 王明. *Daojia he daojiao sixiang yanjiu* 道家和道教思想研究. Chongqing: Zhongguo shehui kexueyuan, 1984.
Wang, Richard G. *The Ming Prince and Daoism Institutional Patronage of an Elite*. New York: Oxford University Press, 2012.
Watson, Burton, trans. *The Complete Works of Chuang Tzu*. New York: Columbia University Press, 1968.
Wile, Douglas. *Art of the Bedchamber: The Chinese Sexual Yoga Classics Including Women's Solo Meditation Texts*. Albany: State University of New York Press, 1992.
Wu, Hung. *Monumentality in Early Chinese Art and Architecture*. Stanford, CA: Stanford University Press, 1995.
Xiao Tong 蕭統 (501–31). *Wen xuan* 文選. Hong Kong: Shangwu, 1974.
Xiao Zixian 蕭子顯 (487–537). *Nan Qishu* 南齊書. Beijing: Zhonghua, 1972.
Yan Changgui. "Daybooks and the Spirit World." In Harper and Kalinowski, *Books of Fate*, 207–47. Leiden: Brill, 2017.
Yan Kejun 嚴可均 (1762–1843). *Quan Shanggu Sandai Qin Han Sanguo Liuchao wen* 全上古三代秦漢三國六朝文. Taibei: Shijie, 1961.
Yan Zhitui 顏之推 (531–591). *Yanshi jiaxun jijie* 顏氏家訓集解. Edited by Wang Liqi 王利器. Shanghai: Guji, 1980.
Yoshikawa Tadao 吉川忠夫. *Rikuchō dōkyō no kenkyū* 六朝道教の研究. Tokyo: Shunjūsha, 1998.
Yoshikawa Tadao 吉川忠夫 and Mugitani Kuniō, eds. *Shinkō kenkyū: yakuchū hen* 真誥研究：譯注篇. Kyoto: Kyōto daigaku jinbun kagaku kenkyūjo, 2000.
Zhao Yi 趙益. *Liuchao Sui Tang daojiao wenxian yanjiu* 六朝隋唐道教文獻研究. Nanjing: Fenghuang, 2012.
———. "*Zhen'gao* yu Tang shi" 《真誥》與唐詩. *Zhonghua wenshi luncong* 中華文史論叢, no. 86 (2007): 97–112.
Zhou Ye 周冶. "Nanyue Furen Wei Huacun Xinkao" 南嶽夫人魏華存新考. *Shijie zongjiao yanjiu* 世界宗教研究, no. 2 (2006): 65–71.
Zürcher, E. *The Buddhist Conquest of China: The Spread and Adaptation of Buddhism in Early Medieval China*. Leiden: Brill, 2007.

Index

Abbey for Veneration of the Void, 67,
67n101
Abbey of the Flourishing Yang, 31
Abbey of the Pervasive Dao, 19. See also
Wushang biyao
Abbey of Vermilion Yang, 32
Abbey to Revivify the Age, 31
Academia Sinica website, 25
Accounts Clerk (Xu Hui), 26, 41–42, 47,
48n55, 49, 54, 90, 118. See also Xu Hui
actualization methods, 15–17, 15n40; for
ingesting mists, 50, 50n64; of ingesting
the images of the sun and moon, 50,
50n64; for ingesting the rays of the sun
and moon, 50, 50n64, 125, 142, 150,
151–53, 151n95, 158; "Mysterious
White," 50; for retaining the black and
the white, 50n64, 118n41
admonitions, 7. See also "Teachings and
Admonitions of the Assembled
Numinous Powers"
alcohol, regulations regarding, 58n80
An, Consort, of the Nine Blossoms (An
Yubin/Lingxiao/Perfected Consort Nine
Blossoms in the Highest Palace of Purple
Clarity), 40, 41, 94; appearance in
"eight pages of lined text," 128; as first
to descend, 51–52; song of dependence
and independence, 135–36; spiritual
marriage to Yang Xi, 43, 43n45,
94n180, 99, 131, 136, 136n38, 140

Analects, 106n35
ancestral practice, 16–17
Annals of the Sage Lord of the Dao of the
Latter Heavens, 76, 76n138
Apocalypse of John, 2
Aramaki Noritoshi, 8–9
astronomical portents, 116, 116n28, 118.
See also Big Dipper
attachment, 135, 162, 163
autograph manuscripts: collection of Tao
Hongjing, 6–7, 31, 69n113; collection
of Gu Huan, 6–7; copyists of, 45–49,
51, 54; of the Xu family, 6, 31, 46, 54,
76
Azure Lad of Fangzhu (Azure Lord): on
achieving the Dao, 155–56; appearance
in "eight pages of lined text," 128;
appearances in Declarations, 156,
156n117; attendants of, 146n64; on the
bitterness of human existence, 154–55;
connection with end of world cycle,
156n116; full title of, 156n116; as Great
Director of Destinies, 150; among most
revered of Higher Perfected, 128, 164;
palaces of, 146, 150; practice of
actualization method of sun and moon,
152; question of descent to Yang Xi,
128, 140, 156, 156n117, 164; raising of
celestial beasts, 149; rejoinder of Lady
Purple Prime, 139; song of dependence
and independence, 138, 139, 140

bamboo, 39, 111, 115–16, 116nn23–24
Baopuzi, 92. *See also* Ge Hong
Bencao gangmu, 31
Big Dipper: attraction of the essences of, 111; Literary Glory constellation, 115, 115n19; as "northern trigger," 115n22; pacing the stars of, 71n118, 73n128; references to, 38n30, 117n33; and Returning to the Origin, 75n134; sixth star, 116n25; stars of, 30n2, 35, 35n22, 36n24, 66n99, 115, 115n20
binomial compounds, 104
birdcage as symbol of office holding, 106n37
blame and blessing, 33, 33n16
Blazing Thearch, 80, 146n65
"blue-green waves," 129, 130, 130n18, 131, 132, 133
Blue Register Text, 37–38, 37n29
Boiling Valley, 146–47, 146n65
Bokenkamp, Stephen, *Ancestors and Anxiety*, 8
Book of Changes, 106n40, 116n26, 147n71; "Appended Words," 106n34
Book of Mormon, 2
Book of Poetry (*Shijing*), 112, 129; "Chou mou" ode, 115n20; "Zhongsi" ode 5, 117n33
Book of the Jin (*Jinshu*), 3, 3n4, 109, 109n5, 118, 118n38
boundedness of the self, 18n46
Buddhism: anti-Buddhist treatise *Yixia lun*, 6n14; arrival in China, 122–23, 126–27, 141, 143, 144; arrival of Buddha images, 141, 143–44; compatibility with Daoist teachings, 19–20, 21, 22, 127; concept of the underworld, 4; in Consort An's song of dependence and independence, 136nn37–39; contingency in, 136, 136n38; converts from Daoism, 70, 74; Daoist borrowings from, 3; in the *Declarations*, 18–24, 22n64–66, 126, 141; doctrine of rebirth, 155n108; of early Chinese sages, 148n73; Eastern variety from Fangzhu, 23–24, 123–24, 126, 141, 148; expunged from texts, 19, 19nn51,54, 24, 142, 145, 149, 155n108; origins in China, 145, 146n64; proscriptions under Yuwen Yong, 21; in Tao Hongjing's annotations, 21–23, 22n64, 148–49; in Tao's *Secret Instructions*, 18–19; temple construction, 143, 144; view of life and death, 127, 149. *See also* Fangzhu isles: Buddhists of; Way of the Buddha

Buddhist canon, 20, 27
Buddhist scriptures, 149n80, 160n132; obtained from India, 144; and the "eight pages of lined text," 122, 125; written in China, 148n73. *See also Scripture in Forty-Two Sections*
Buddho-Daoist debate, 19n54

Cai Mai, 61
Cai Mo, 87
Cai Yong, "Memorial Stele for Grand Marshal Li Runan," 80n151
calendric predictions and taboos, 17n45, 38n31, 120n46
calligraphy: of Chi Yin, 47; Daoist, for dictation from gods, 46; determination of, by Tao Hongjing, 43, 45, 45n51, 46; of the family of Yang Quan, 99; grass (cursive) and running style, 45, 99, 101, 117n34; on slips for Elühua account, 101; Tao family, 30, 43; of the three lords, 45–48; tracing of, 64, 70, 88; of the two Wangs, 47, 70, 70n115; used for revelations, 2, 47; of Xu Hui, 47; of Xu Mi, 41, 47; of Yang Xi, 6, 45, 47, 101, 114n17, 122, 154, 172
Campany, Robert F., 15n40
cavern heavens, 39n33, 52, 132n23, 134
cavern residences and palaces, 34, 51
Cedrela tree, 138, 138n43
Celestial Master Daoism, 10, 14n39, 65n95, 86n169, 91, 96n185, 107n44; libationers, 59n82, 96–96; lute metaphor, 163n146
Celestial River (Milky Way), 135, 135n36, 136n37
Celestial Well, 131n20. *See also* Mystic Well
Central Scripture of the Nine Perfected, 18n50; commentary by Tao Hongjing, 18–20, 21, 148n73
Central Watchlord. *See* Wang, Lady, the Central Watchlord
Changsha, Prince of, 73n127
chanting, 23, 57, 63, 162
Chart for a Mystical Overview of Man-Bird Mountain, 72n123
Chen Baoguang, *Sandong qunxian lu*, 100, 101
Chen Changle, 71
Chen Lei, 71
Chen Shihua, 20–21, 22n66
Chi Yin, 47, 152n98
Chijiangzi, 74n130
Chu Boyu, 59, 59n84, 74

Chu Zhongyan, 74
"clarity and stillness," 15, 15n42, 155
Classic of the Unadorned Woman, 65n95
cloud-souls, 16, 152, 165
Comprehensive Mirror of Historical Perfected and Transcendents, 55n72
Conan Doyle, Arthur, 17–18n46
Confucius, 106nn34–35; as Bodhisattva Scholarly Lad, 148n73
constellations. *See* astronomical portents; Big Dipper; Eastern Barrier constellation; Palace of Purple Tenuity
"conversion of the barbarians" legend, 23, 143, 146n64
cross-referencing, 8
Cui Yuan, 79
cun, use of term, 15, 15n40

Dai Faxing, 69
Dai Kui, "In Praise of Mountains," 104
Dai Qing, 67
Dai Shizhi, 92
Dai Yanxing, 69
danchen, 19
Dante Alighieri, *Divine Comedy,* 2, 2nn1–2
Dao Xuan, *Guang hongming ji,* 20n56
Daoan, "Treatise on the Two Teachings," 148n73
Daode jing, 15, 15n42, 100n8, 169, 169n166; commentaries, 170n176; Han Feizi's discussion of, 35n20
Daoism: adoption of Buddhist aspects, 3, 127; ban of, 20, 32; intentionality in, 135; regulations, 58n80. *See also* Buddhism; Celestial Master Daoism; Daoist practice; Shangqing Daoism
Daoist canon: biography of Tao Hongjing, 30; citation of, 27, 173; contribution of Lu Xuijing, 31, 67, 67n101; unpunctuated, ix; works of Tao Hongqing, 3, 18
Daoist lineages, 58n80, 59, 59n83
Daoist practice: achieving the Dao, 155–56, 157–58, 158–59, 165, 168–69; cherishing qi, 170; compared to playing the lute, 163; difficulty of, 155, 160; Higher Perfected on, 154–64; physical cultivation, 10; pursuit of Perfection, 5; by women, 11, 88n171. *See also* actualization methods
Daoist scriptures: fabricated, 59–60, 59n83, 69; illicit copying of without transmission, 55–58; loss of, 57–58; revealed by Perfected, 38, 44–45, 53–78; stored in gourds, 74, 74n131. *See also* Daoist

canon; Shangqing scriptures; *and names of individual scriptures*
Dao Lord of the Inner Mystery of the Northern Prime (Li Qingbin), 128
Dark Purity, Lady of the Six Tenuities in the North Sea: and actualization practice, 142; aphorism on practicing the Way, 142, 153; appearance in "eight pages of lined text," 127, 128; on emotional ties and Daoist practice, 161–62; among most revered of Higher Perfected, 128, 164
deathlessness, herbs of, 146, 147, 149
Decisive Lyrics of the Winding Immaculate, 75, 75n137
Declarations of the Perfected (Zhen'gao): base text of, 25; Buddhism in, 18–24, 22n64–66, 126, 141; as classic of imaginative literature, 2; as collection of fragments, 1, 29, 49; dating of, 3; dating of the revelations, 37–38, 39–40, 42; division into twenty scrolls, 33n15; as glimpse of family life, 6; pages dropped from, 101; purgation of Buddhist-seeming material, 24; rearrangement of, 8–9, 21, 122–23, 124–26; "Record of the Palaces of Fengdu," 49, 77n141; as religious literature, 2–3; seven-chapter division by Tao, 7, 29, 33–34, 35–36, 35n19; sixth chapter, 52; Strickmann's characterization of sections, 7; translations of, 1, 8, 24–25; "Transmitted by the Dao" section, 49, 49n60; twenty-chapter form, 29, 35, 35n19; versions of, 146n64. *See also* "eight pages of lined text"; "Poems of Elühua"; postface; Tao Hongjing
Deng Yunzi, 133
Dengzhen yinjue. See Secret Instructions on the Ascent to Perfection
dependence and independence, 131, 136, 136n38, 139, 140. *See also* "Poems on Dependence and Independence"
destiny-day, 30
Dharmakṣema, 148
dhyāna, 19
Diagram of the Seven Primal Stars, 71, 71n118
didacticism, 15
Di people, 146n65
Directors of Destiny: announcement of Xu Mi's departure, 87; Azure Lad as, 150; governing spirit, 75n134; Mao Ying as, 90n176; Mao Zhong as Protector of

Directors of Destiny *(continued)*
Destinies, 94n180, 97, 97n191; offices of, 150, 150n85; Wei Huacun as, 9, 54; Yang Xi as, 94
dixia zhu (rulers below the earth), 51n65
Dong Zhongmin, 67, 67n104
Dongguan, Daoists of, 93
dreams: "Dream Incantation," 50, 50n63; of Ma Lang, 61–62; as means of transmissions from Perfected, 13; records of, 13; of Xu Hui, 76n140. *See also* "Han Mingdi's Dream"
drugs: herbs of deathlessness, 146, 147, 149; for release by means of substitute corpse, 99, 100, 103
Du Daoju, 56, 56n74, 62, 69n110
Du family of Qiantang, 68–69, 69n110. *See also* Du Daoju; Du Gaoshi; Du Jingchan
Du Gaoshi, 69, 70n114
Du Guangting, *Yongcheng jixian lu,* 117n36
Du Jingchan, 56n74, 68–69, 69n110
Du Weisheng, 167
Du Zigong, 69n110
Dunhuang manuscripts: Buddhist scriptures, 23; paper size of, 167; *Secret Instructions* fragment containing Tao's annotation of *Central Scripture of the Nine Perfected,* 18, 21, 148n73; Tao Hongjing's writings on pharmaceuticals, 31n9

Eastern Barrier constellation, 116, 116n28, 118
Eastern Flower, Mount, 146
Eastern Flower palaces, 94, 94n180, 130, 138, 150
Eastern Grove, Lady of, 123n3. *See also* Right Blossom, Lady, of the Cloudy Grove
Eastern Seas, islands of, 21, 24, 101, 112. *See also* Fangzhu isles
Eight Immaculates, 75n135; *Songs of Yin and Yang of the Eight Immaculates,* 75, 75n135
"eight pages of lined text": Buddhist material, 122, 123, 124, 126; contents of, 122–23; graphs per page, 166–68; Hu Shi on, 166–67; "On Fangzhu," 145–55; Perfected beings in, 127–28; poetic debate on spiritual marriage of Xu Mi, 123, 123n3, 124, 124n6, 129; presented as scriptural treasure, 125; rare revelations from Higher Perfected, 128, 154, 166; reconstruction of, 123, 123n2, 165–66; related fragments, 166,

167–72; text written in two different hands, 122, 124n6, 125, 165; text in the hand of Yang Xi, 165–66, 168–72. *See also* "Han Mingdi's Dream"; "Poems on Dependence and Independence"; "Teachings and Admonitions of the Assembled Numinous Powers"
eight phosphors of the three primes, 75nn134–35
Eliade, Mircea, 12
elixirs, 21, 32, 57, 71
Elühua: account of, in *Declarations,* 100, 101, 101n11; as banished Transcendent, 101–2, 103; descent of, 40, 102, 107; gave Yang Quan drug for release from the world, 99, 100, 103; gifts and revelations to Yang Quan, 98–99, 101–3; as nine hundred years old, 100, 101, 103; original surname of, 98, 102, 102n16; poems of, 101, 102, 102n13, 104–7
emotions, 15, 156, 160n134, 161–62
"empty hollows," 132, 132n23
existence and nonexistence, 139, 140

Fajing, *Zhongjing mulu,* 35n22
Falin, "Treatise on Contending over the Correct," 74n131
famines, 65, 73, 79
Fan, Lady, 74n130
Fan Miao, 37n29, 76n140. See also *Traditions of Lady Wei*
Fan Miaoluo, 77
Fan Ye, 57, 57nn77–78
Fang Xuanling, *Jinshu* (Book of the Jin), 3, 3n4, 109, 109n5, 118, 118n38
Fangzhu isles: Buddhists of, 21–22, 22n65, 23, 123–24, 141, 144, 145, 147, 149–50; crossing from, 131; descriptions of, 123, 145–46; Daoists of, 22n65, 141; distance from Guiji, 146, 147; "eastern guest" from, 139; gods of, as speakers in *Scripture in Forty-Two Sections,* 154; Greater Fangzhu, 22n65, 141, 146, 150, 151; as home of Buddhism, 24, 123, 143; language of, 24n69; Lesser Fangzhu, 22–23, 22n65, 141, 144, 145, 146, 146n64, 147, 149; mountains of, 145, 146; name of, 21n62, 123n4, 145, 145n62; "On Fangzhu," 145–54; palaces of, 94n180, 134, 146, 150; Perfected and Transcendents of, 24, 125, 126, 130, 149–50; practice of method for ingesting the rays of the sun and moon, 151–53;

sections regarding, 123n2, 125–26; vegetation and trees, 145–46

fanwen (languages of Buddhism), 24n69

Fan Xian (Transcendent Fan), 71, 71n120

Faxian, 148

Fengdu, 4, 5, 7, 51, 51n65; palaces of, 33n16, 49, 77, 77n141

filiality, 92, 160n131

First Farmer sacrifices, 38, 38n31

five and seven, 36, 36n24

Five Man-Bird Talismans, 72, 72n123

Five Marchmounts, 80n151, 133, 135, 138

five phases, 36n24, 60, 119n44

five qi, 115, 115n19

Five Spirits and Twenty-four Spirits of the Great Immaculate, 75, 75n134

Five Talismans of Lingbao, 31, 72, 72nn122–23, 94

five vital governing spirits, 75n134

flying, 106n39, 129, 143, 147, 168, 168n164

Flying Paces Scripture, 73, 73n128

Forty-four Prescriptions on Plain Yellow Silk, 60n85

four images, 170–71

Four Lords, chants of, 164, 164n152

Fu Jian, 84, 84n162

Fu Yi (Zhongwu), 143, 144

Fuhe. *See* Li, Lady (Fuhe/Junrong)

Fusang island, 21n62, 123

Fusang tree, 146n65

Gan Zhuo, 85, 85n165

Ge Can, 72

Ge Chaofu, 58–59, 58n81

Ge Hong, 85, 85n166, 92, 116n25, 137n41

Ge Jingxian, 73

Ge Ti, 85, 85n166

Ge Wan'an, 92

Ge Xiang, 81

Ge Xuan, 58n81

Ge Yongzhen, 73

Ge Yan Mountain, 132n26. *See also* Mottled Cliff, Mount

Golden Flower Mountain, 66n96

Golden Perfected, 75, 75n137

Gold Flower, 75, 75n137

gourds, scriptures stored in, 74, 74n131

Grand Clarity, 4

Grand Tenuity, 116n28

Grand Unity, 75n134

Grand White (Venus), 118, 118n39

great kalpa, 134n30

Great Peace, 142, 152, 157

Great Peng bird, 171, 172n180

great return, 140

Great Void Perfected of the Southern Marchmount (Master Red Pine): appearance in "eight pages of lined text," 128; among most revered of Higher Perfected, 128; question of descent to Yang, 128, 140; song of dependence and independence, 137, 140; on transgressions and achieving the Dao, 158–59; transmissions of, 160

Great Wisdom Scripture, 152

Gu Huan (Xuanping): asked to see *Five Talismans of Lingbao*, 72; corrections adopted by, 46, 49n59; dates for two Xus, 52; mistakes by, 79, 88, 89, 91, 91n177, 93; placement of Consort An and *Traditions of Xu Mai*, 51–52; scriptures selected by, 69; slips omitted by, 52; texts received from Zhang Lingmin, 75; *Traces of the Perfected*, 6–7, 37, 37n28, 49n61, 50, 69n111; *Yixia lun*, 6n14

Guang bowu zhi, 117n31

Guiguzi, Tao Hongjing's commentary to, 46

Guiji, 88, 146, 147

Guiji, Prince of (Sima Daozi), 39, 39n35, 110, 118

Guo Xiang, 132n23

Guoyu, 86n167

hallucination, 14–15, 17

Han Feizi, 35n20

"Han Mingdi's Dream": Buddha in, 122–23, 141, 143; links to other material on eight sheets of lined paper, 142; revelation by Perfected, 142, 144; texts containing, 143n53; translation of, 143–44. *See also* Liu Zhuang (Han Mingdi)

Han Zhong, 150

Hao Chunwen, 167

hapax legomenon phrases, 106n36

He Cidao (He Chong), 83

He Daojing, 63, 64–65, 70; sexual alchemy practice, 65, 65n95

He Faren, 76

He Yan, "Rhapsody on the Hall of Great Blessings," 115n22

heavens, 3–4, 4n6, 41n41; Huayang cavern heavens, 52; Nine Heavens, 115n21, 131; Six Heavens, 75n137

Heaven's Eye Mountain, 69

heqi (merging of pneumas) ritual, 10–11

Hereditary Consort of the Purple Clarity
Palace (Wang Ziqiao), 112. *See also*
Perfected of Mount Tongbo
"hiding away through transformation," 71,
71n119
hierogamy, 10, 10n21
Higher Perfected, 35, 125, 133, 137, 146;
rare revelations from, 128, 154, 156,
164, 166. *See also* Azure Lad of
Fangzhu; Dark Purity, Lady of the Six
Tenuities in the North Sea; Great Void
Perfected of the Southern Marchmount;
Purple Prime, Lady, of the Southern
Culmen; Perfected of Pure Numinosity;
Perfected of Pure Vacuity; Wang, Lord,
of the Western Citadel
Highest Purity, 4n6
History of the Han, 144, 144n57
Hong Sheng, 85
Honoring the Prime temple, 73n127
Houtang Mountain, 65
Hu Qian (fortune-teller), 109, 109n5, 111
Hu Shi, 25, 126, 166–67
Hua family of Jinling, 81, 89, 92, 96–97
Hua Qi, 82, 89
Hua Qiao; Daoist practice, 40n38, 96;
descendants of, 96; found guilty, 96, 97,
97n191; leaking of secret messages, 40,
96, 96n188, 133; passing of messages
for Xu Mi, 40, 96, 97; *Traditions of
Zhou Ziyang* by, 97; worship of profane
spirits, 96, 96n187
Hua Zhuan, 82
Hua Zirong, 11
huahu (conversion of the Western
barbarian) stories, 23, 143, 146n64
Huainanzi, 146n65
Huan Wen, 84, 84nn161–62
Huang Yan, 85, 85n164, 91
Huangting neijing jing, 120n49
Huayang cavern heavens, 52
Huiyan, revision of T 374, 148
Huizi (Hui Shi), 105, 105n30
humans: bitter existence of, 154–55;
dependence of, 134, 135, 139; life as
illusion, 23, 135n33, 149, 168,
168n165; life span of, 157; rebirth as,
156; reliance on Perfected to harmonize
with heaven, 132, 133; union with the
Dao, 135
Huo, Mount, offices of Directors of Destiny,
150, 150n85
Huoluo Talismans, 66, 66n99, 67
Hyland, Elizabeth, 25

illness, 7, 8, 17
immortality, 170–71
Inciting Notary of Jiaozhou, 80
index of scriptures, 72
Inner Chapters of Zhuangzi, 35, 35n22,
36n26. See also *Zhuangzi*
*Inner Traditions of Wang [Bao], Perfected
of Pure Vacuity*, 59, 73, 73n126
intentionality, 135
*Intimate Traditions of Recluse Tao of
Huayang* (Jia Song), 30, 30n2
isle of the dead. *See* Fengdu

Jade Beams of the Golden Perfected,
75n137
Jade Clarity, 4
Jade Lads, 76n138
Jade Luminary, 22, 22n63
Jade Maidens, 64
*Jade Slips of Great Clarity on the Ultimate
Dao of the Celestial Luminaries*, 145
Ji clan of Xuancheng, 84
Ji Quan, 85
Jia Song, 30n1; *Intimate Traditions of
Recluse Tao of Huayang*, 30, 30n2
Jiang clan, 80
Jiang Fuchu, 70n114
Jiang Hongsu, 69, 70n114
Jiang Mountain, 66n96
Jin'an Commandery, 56, 56n75
Jianwen Emperor. *See* Sima Yu
Jing, Duke, of Jin, 171, 171n178
Jing Mountain, 71, 77
Jingzhou, 82; paper from, 49
Jinling, 82, 85, 96n186; Hua family of, 81,
89, 92, 96
Jinshu (Book of the Jin), 3, 3n4, 109,
109n5, 118, 118n38
Jiuyi, Mount, 103, 103n20
Jiyang Parish, 96, 96n185
Joan of Arc, 14
Joined Mountains classic, 147, 147n71
jun (lord), 32, 32n13
Jurong County, 54, 72, 73, 81, 85; Xu
family of, 54, 70, 70n114, 78–79, 81,
93, 95n184

karman (inborn destiny), 160, 160n133
Kleeman, Terry, 25, 45n49, 56n74, 96n185
Knechtes, David R., 115n22
Kong Chunzhi, 56n75
Kong Dan, 82n157
Kong Ji, 68–69n110
Kong Mo (Mozhi), 56–57, 56n75

Kong Tan, 82
Kong Xiuxian, 56–57, 57n77
Kong Xixian, 56–57, 57n77
Kong Yingda, 36n22
Kong Zao, 68, 69n110
Kong Zong, 77, 77n142
Krakucchanda (*Liuqin*), 22, 22n63
Kroll, Paul, 21n62, 25, 123n3
Kunlun, 110, 110n8
Kunlun, Mount, 132n26, 136n37, 156n117
Kyōto University study group, 8, 24, 26,
    35n20, 41n41, 106n36, 116n24,
    117n33, 120nn45,48

Langye, Prince of, 54. *See also* Sima Yu
Laozi, 100n9, 140; as Mahākāśyapa,
    148n73
leaking of celestial secrets, 40, 59, 63, 65,
    96, 96n188, 102, 133
lector difficultor principle, 26
Leiping, Mount, 54, 90, 94
Lewis, I. M., 12
Li Daoyuan, *Shuijing zhu,* 147n69
Li Dong, 86n168, 95–96
Li Guozhi, 67, 68n106
Li Hong, 76n138, 87n170, 160n132
Li, Lady (Fuhe/Junrong), 39, 109, 110, 113,
    114, 118, 118n37
Li, Lady, of the Resplendent Numina, 44,
    128, 134–35, 136, 136n37
Li Lingfei, 128
Li Lingrong, 109. *See also* Li, Lady (Fuhe/
    Junrong)
Li Qingbin (Dao Lord of the Inner Mystery
    of the Northern Prime), 128
Li Yanshou, *Taiping yulan,* 153n102
Li Zhongfu, 150
liberation methods, 91, 94
Liezi, 106n39, 129
"life as a thing," 170n176
life as illusion, 23, 135n33, 149, 168,
    168n165
Ling, King of Zhou, 128
Lingbao scriptures, 58, 58n81, 59n83, 60,
    67n101, 72nn122–23; *Five Talismans of
    Lingbao,* 31, 72, 72nn122–23, 94. *See
    also* Lu Xiujing
linked lapels and joined phosphors, 10, 43,
    43n45. *See also* spiritual marriage
Literary Glory constellation, 115, 115n19
Liu Bao, 79
Liu Dabin, 68n107
Liu Hong, 78
Liu Hu, 79

Liu Pu, 72n122, 94
Liu Xia, 77
Liu Xiang, 120, 120n46
Liu Xin, 120n46
Liu Yikang (Prince of Pengcheng),
    57nn77–78
Liu Yu, 67n101
Liu Zhuang (Han Mingdi): dream of,
    122–23, 125, 141, 143–44; tomb of,
    143, 144
Liu Ziye, 66, 66n98, 125n8
Liuqin (Krakucchanda), 22, 22n63
Liu-Song dynasty, 30, 69n110, 125n8
Loft for Illuminating the Numinous, 68,
    68n107, 69, 71, 72, 73, 74, 75, 77
Lofty Brilliance, Mount, 132, 132n26
Long Mountains of Dongyang, 68
Lotus sūtra (Lotus Flower of the Wondrous
    Dharma), 29, 35, 35n22
Lou Daoji, 69
Lou Fazhen, 69
Lou Huiming, 65–66, 66n96, 68, 69, 70, 76
Lu, Mount, 67, 67n102, 72
Lü Pengzhi, 74n133, 84n160
Lu Xi, 115n18
Lu Xiujing: activities on Mount Lu,
    67n102; established Abbey for
    Veneration of the Void, 67, 67n101;
    catalog of Lingbao scriptures,
    72nn122–23; disciples of, 31, 31n6, 67,
    68n106, 125n8; on Krakucchanda, 22;
    on mixing of Lingbao scriptures with
    imitations, 59n83; scriptures acquired
    by, 31, 67, 72
Lu Yun, 115n18
Luan Ba, 74n130
Luhrmann, T. M., 14, 17, 18n46
Luo Yu, 103. *See also* Elühua
lute metaphor, 163, 163n146

Ma family, 64. *See also* Ma Han; Ma Hong;
    Ma Lang
Ma Han, 55, 55n72, 64, 70, 70n116;
    Daoist practice, 63
Ma Hong, 64, 66, 68
Ma Lang (Wengong), 55, 55n72, 61–65
Ma Zhen, 64
Ma Zhi, 64, 70
Mao, Middle Lord (Certifier of Registers
    Mao Gu), 38, 39, 39n37, 86, 95
Mao, Mount (Mao Shan): administrative
    hierarchy of, 7; cavern heavens of,
    132n23, 134; Daoist establishments on,
    32, 70n114, 73n127; early fourteenth-

century monograph on, 55n72; grave of Tao Hongjing, 20–21, 22n66; inner topography of, 7, 39n37; location of, 31n7; as name for Shangqing scriptures, 4n6; Perfected visitors to, 129, 131, 132, 137; residents of, 31, 73; study center for women, 11, 88, 88n171, 90, 95; Tao Hongjing's residence and burial place, 20–21, 22n66, 31; triple peaks of, 130, 130n19, 131, 132; Yang Xi's meditation chamber, 1, 2, 13, 31

Mao Ying (Director of Destinies), 90n176

Mao, Younger Lord (Mao Zhong), 94n180, 97, 97n191

marriage: metaphors for, 10, 43n45; proposal of Elühua to Yang Quan, 99; sacred, 10, 10n21; time for, 115n20. See also spiritual marriage

Maspero, Henri, 126n12

Mather, Richard, 5

meditation: Buddhist and Daoist postures, 22; for controlling the movements of the cloud-souls, 15–16; descriptions of, 113, 147n70; for ingesting the rays of the sun and moon, 125, 151–52; "oratory" for, 1, 62, 62n88; Yang Xi's meditation chamber, 1, 2, 13, 31

mediums, 11–12, 17, 99, 99n3, 112. See also Yang Xi

Mei Lingwen, 72

Meng Anpai, 55n72

"mental imagery cultivation" (Noll), 13–14, 17

merging qi, 65n95

miedu (nirvāna), 153n100

moon, references to, 118n39. See also sun and moon

Most High Perfected, 128, 157–58, 160, 162–63, 163n146. See also Wang, Lord, of the Western Citadel (Wang Yuan)

Mother of Demons (Hārītī), 143, 143n54

Mottled Cliff, Mount, 132, 132n26, 134

mountains and rivers, 34

Mugitani Kuniō, 25

music: on Lesser Fangzhu, 23, 149; lute playing metaphor, 163, 163n146; references to, 149nn79–80

mustard seed, cosmos within, 135–36, 136n37

Mysterious Record of the Seven Sages, 22n64

Mystical Isles, 103, 103n22

Mystic Well, 131, 131n20, 132, 134

names and titles, 26

Nattier, Jan, 148

New Account of Tales of the World (Shishuo xinyu), 5–6

Newman, Barbara, 14, 14n35

Nine Blossoms. See An, Consort, of the Nine Blossoms

Nine Heavens, 115n21, 130, 131

nine margins, 137, 137n41

Nine Numinosities, 149

nirvāna, 153n100

Nirvāna Scripture, 148, 149

Noll, Richard, 13–14, 17

Nonpareil (governing spirit), 75n134

Northern Zhou Daoist reformation, 21, 24

numinous passes, 114, 115n18

old age, 9, 63, 100, 154

"On Fangzhu," 145–54

oratories, 1, 62, 62n88

oujing ("mating of the phosphors"), 10, 135n33. See also spiritual marriage

Overlord. See Wang, Lord, of the Western Citadel (Wang Yuan)

pacing the stars of the Dipper, 71, 71n118, 73n128

Palace of Mutation and Promotion, 88, 88n171, 90, 95

Palace of Purple Tenuity (constellation), 118n39

palaces and bureaus of the spirits, 34

palindromes, 113–14, 114n16, 118–19

Pan Jixing, 167

Pan Ni, "Rhapsody on the Mulberry Tree," 104

Pan Wensheng (Pan Hong), 69, 70n114

Pan Yuanwen, 30, 30n2

paper, 1, 2, 41n39, 49, 50, 50n64; lined, 23, 24, 125, 142, 165; used for "eight pages of lined text," 166–67. See also slips

Peach Vigor (governing spirit), 75n134

Pei, Lord. See Perfected of Pure Numinosity

Pei Qingling, 96

Peng Zu, 65, 65n95

Penglai, 21n62, 123

Penglai, Mount, 136n37

Perfected: announcements of, 12, 52, 53; appearance in "eight pages of lined text," 127–28; Buddhist practice by, 21, 22n66, 23, 144, 148, 148n72; character assessments by, 6, 43; communications of, 4–5, 7; descent of, 12, 51, 94, 125; as emanations of the Dao, 4n6; garb of,

12; human and nonhuman, 9–10, 12; lineages of, 34; mistakes by, 145, 147n72; predictions for Yang Xi and Xus, 32; ranks and careers, 4, 34; referred to as *jun* (Lord), 32, 32n13; residence in Fangzhu, 150; revelation of Eastern Buddhism of Fangzhu, 23–24; transmission of scriptures, 53–54; traces of, 6–7, 37; women as, 11, 127–28; Yang as medium for, 1–2, 4–5, 11–13, 54, 112. *See also* "eight pages of lined text"; Fangzhu isles; Higher Perfected; Most High Perfected; Transcendents; Yang Xi

Perfected Bodhisattva Householders, 148

Perfected Consort Nine Blossoms in the Highest Palace of Purple Clarity. *See* An, Consort, of the Nine Blossoms

Perfected Forebears, 78; translation of "Genealogy of the Perfected Forebears," 78–97

Perfected of Mount Tongbo (Wang Ziqiao): appearance in "eight pages of lined text," 128; disciples of, 22n66; as Hereditary Consort of the Purple Clarity Palace, 112; song of dependence and independence, 131–32; visitor to peaks of Mount Mao, 132

Perfected of Pure Numinosity (Lord Pei Xuanren), 22n66, 50n63, 97, 128, 132, 132n26; argument against interacting with humans, 133, 134; biography of, 133; messages through Hua Qiao, 97, 133, 133n29; song of dependence and independence, 132–33; *Traditions of Lord Pei*, 144

Perfected of Pure Vacuity (Wang Bao), 37n29, 59n82, 164n152; *Inner Traditions*, 59, 73, 73n126

Perfected of the Grand Primordial, 150

Perfected of the Heaven of Lesser Existence (Wang Zideng), 164n152

Perfected of the Southern Marchmount. *See* Great Void Perfected of the Southern Marchmount; Wei Huacun (Lady Southern Marchmount)

Perfected Scripture of the Great Cavern, 57

Perfected Scriptures, 53–78; *Traditions*, 66

Perfected Texts Written in Red, 72, 72n123

Perfected verse, 5, 104. *See also* "Poems of Elühua"; "Poems on Dependence and Independence"; poetry debate

Pheneas, 18n46

phosphors: joined, and linked lapels, 10, 43, 43n45; mating of (*oujing*), 10, 135n33; piloting, 135n33; setting free (*zongjing*), 135n33

physiognomizing, 109–10, 109n7

Pingyu (Runan), 79, 79n145, 80

"Poems of Elühua," 101, 102, 102n13, 104; translation of, 104–7. *See also* Elühua

"Poems on Dependence and Independence," 122, 129, 142; spacing of text, 167; Tao Hongjing on, 140, 140n48; translation of, 130–40

poetry debate, 123, 123n3, 124, 124n6, 129

postface: additional notes to, 39–53; "Account of the Perfected Scriptures from Beginning to End," 53–78; "Aiding Health and Prospects," 33; "Aiding the Collation of Perfected Gleanings," 34; on the composition of revelations and fragments, 42–43; "Genealogy of the Perfected Forebears," 78–97; "Grasping the Aid of the Perfected," 34; as introduction to *Declarations*, 29–30; "Investigating Pivotal Spiritual Locales," 34; "Revealing the Hidden and Subtle," 34; sections of, 29–30, 33–34; on Shangqing documents taken to the court, 125n8; on Tao Hongjing's devotion to the teachings of the Perfected, 32; three-word section titles, 33n14; "Transmitting Subjects and Images," 33, 33n15; "Verifying Destinies and Transmission Recipients," 33

Prolegomena on the Ingestion of Atractylodes, 50, 50n63

prominent families of the Eastern Jin, 5

promotion and demotion, 4, 5; Palace of Mutation and Promotion, 88, 88n171, 90, 95; study centers for, 4, 11

prophecies, 110, 113–14; on progeny of Sima Yu, 108, 110–11, 113, 114–21

Protector of Destinies, 94n180, 97, 97n191

punctuation, 25

Purple Prime, Lady, of the Southern Culmen (Wang Lin/Rongzhen): and actualization practice, 142; appearance in "eight pages of lined text," 128; on attachment, 162; on Fangzhu, 145–46; among most revered of Higher Perfected, 128, 164; on practice of the Dao, 160–61, 161n136; question of descent to Yang, 128, 140, 154, 164; songs of dependence and independence, 138–40, 138n44

Purple Tenuity, Lady. *See* Wang, Lady, of the Left Palace of Purple Tenuity (Wang Qing'e)
Purple Texts Inscribed by the Spirits, 76n138, 142, 153

qi: beings formed of, 4; of calligraphy, 46–47; ingesting, 169; realms of, 169, 169n167; of sexual cultivation, 170
Qi Jingxuan, 69, 71
Qiantang, 62, 62n87, 77; Du family of, 68–69, 69n110
Qin Jing (Gentleman of the Feathered Grove), 143, 144
Qu'a, 95, 95n184
Queen Mother of the West, 130, 132n26; daughters of, 112, 127, 128, 130n17, 142

rebirth, 4, 155n108, 156–57, 160n133, 169n167
Record of Rituals, 16–17
Red City of Mount Huo, 150
Red Lord of the Southern Marchmount, 22, 22n64
Red Pine, Lord. *See* Great Void Perfected of the Southern Marchmount
Redwall Mountain, 60n84, 67n104
reed organs, 23, 77n142, 149, 149n79
release by means of a corpse, 71n119, 99, 99n4, 100, 103
religious visions, 13–15, 14n35, 17, 18n46
Rendai, Mount, 92
Returning to the Origin, 75, 75n134
Return to the Storehouse Scripture, 147, 147n71, 148n72
revelatory literature, 2–3
Right Blossom, Lady, of the Cloudy Grove (Wang Meilan/Shenlin): advice for Sima Yu, 112–13, 120; appearance in "eight pages of lined text," 127; correspondence with Senior Officer Xu Mi, 44, 45; prophecy by, 95n182; song of dependence and independence, 129, 130, 136; spiritual marriage to Xu Mi, 43, 99, 113, 123n3, 129, 130, 136n38, 137, 140; transmission to Yang Xi of poems from Higher Perfected, 164n152
Robinet, Isabelle, 25, 75n137

Śakyāmuni, 20, 21, 23
Sandong qunxian lu (Chen Baoguang), 100, 101
Schafer, Edward, on *cun,* 15n40

scriptural transmission by secret oath, 60, 60n85
Scripture for Treasuring the Spirts, 50n63
Scripture in Forty-Two Sections: Fangzhu version, 24, 154; legend of, 141, 143; and passages in the "eight pages of lined text," 142, 168; plagiarized in *Declarations,* 123, 126, 154, 165n154; and "Teachings and Admonitions of the Assembled Numinous Powers," 123, 127, 142, 154; version in the Buddhist canon, 124, 166, 168, 168n164; Yang Xi's citations and insertions, 15, 23, 32, 124, 127, 166, 168. *See also* "Teachings and Admonitions of the Assembled Numinous Powers"
Scripture of Devil-Destroying Wisdom, 152
Scripture of Flying Paces along the Celestial Mainstays of the Seven Primes, 73, 73n128
Scripture of Mountains and Seas, 146n65
Scripture of the Nine Perfected, 18n50; commentary by Tao Hongjing, 18–20, 21, 148n73
Scripture of the Yellow Court, 57, 76, 76n140, 115n18
Scripture of Wisdom, 142
Scripture on the Dharma Practices of Stillness and Purity, 148n73
Secret Instructions on the Ascent to Perfection (Dengzhen yinjue), 18–19, 18n47, 21, 21n61, 23, 31, 35–36, 48, 151nn91,93; Buddhist material removed from, 24; missing chapters, 18, 31n8, 48n57, 142n50
Secret Method for Return to the Origin, 75
secret oath, 60, 60n85
seed people, 76n138, 160n132
Senior Officer. *See* Xu Mi
seven-day week, 36n24
Seven Lots from the Bookbag of the Clouds, 55n72
seven primal stars, 30n2, 66n99, 71, 71n118. *See also* Big Dipper
seven regulators, 35, 35–36n22
seventh-generation ancestors, 78, 79, 79n146, 88–89n173
seventh-generation descendants, 95, 95n183
sex: attachment to, 163; sexual arts, 65, 65n95; sexual cultivation, 170
shamanism, 11–12, 16
Shan County, 55, 55n71, 64–65, 69; mountains of, 57–58, 65, 92; as residence of Xu family, 82

Shangqing Daoism, 24n69, 30n2, 71n118; lineage of, 55n72; revelations, 98–99, 99n6; translation of Shangqing, 3–4, 4n6

Shangqing scriptures, 4n6, 6; Buddhism in, 24, 141–42; *Forty-four Prescriptions on Plain Yellow Silk,* 60n85; *Gold Flower,* 75, 75n137; imaginative topographies of, 130n18; inauthentic, 59–61; practice of, 62, 64–65, 75n134; *Purple Texts Inscribed by the Spirits ,* 142; *Shangqing Scripture of the True Law of the Three Heavens,* 134n30; taken to the court, 125n8; of Yang Xi, 3–4, 38. See also *Declarations of the Perfected; Secret Instructions on the Ascent to Perfection*

Shangshu: Shundian chapter, 35n22; Yiji chapter, 149n79

Shangyu, 74, 74n132

Shanyin, 64, 69, 77

Sharf, Robert, 155n110, 156n119, 158n124, 159n128

Shen Chong, 82, 82n157

Shen Ou, 77

Shen Yue, *Treatise on the Equality of the Sages,* 20, 20n56

shijie (release from the world by means of simulated corpse), 99, 71n119, 99, 99n4, 100, 103

Shijing (Book of Poetry), 112, 129; "Chou mou" ode, 115n20; "Zhongsi" ode 5, 117n33

Shishuo xinyu (New Account of Tales of the World), 5–6

shu, technical meaning in Daoism, 41n42

Shu Jizhen, 66, 125n8

Sima Daozi (Prince of Guiji), 39, 39n35, 110, 118

Sima Dezong, reign of, 89

Sima Pi, reign of, 38

Sima Rui, 82

Sima Yan, reign of, 89, 93

Sima Yao (Emperor Filial Martiality): birth of, 39, 108, 110, 116, 118; in instructions from Perfected on how to engender an heir, 111; posthumous temple name, 39n35, 116n27; reign of, 87

Sima Yu (Jianwen of the Jin): appointment of Yang Xi, 54, 54n70, 93; circle around, 99, 107n43; concubines of, 109; court of, 98; death of, 120n45; as minister, 54, 91; progeny of, 39, 108–10, 113, 118; referred to as the Gentleman, 114, 114n17, 118, 120; relationship with Xu family, 87, 91,

98n2, 111; relationship with Yang Xi, 93, 125n8; revelations for, 99n3, 108, 111, 113–14; "Sons of Sima Yu," 114–21, 114n17

Sima Yue, 83

Siming, Mount, 77

Six Heavens, demons of, 75n137

six senses, 156, 157n120, 160, 160–61n134

six storehouses, 158, 158n125

slips (*tiao*), 41, 41n39, 50, 50n64, 52, 66, 107n42; for "Sons of Sima Yu," 114n17

Smith, Joseph, 2n3

Smith, Thomas E., 25

Sogdiana, 143, 144

Songs of Yin and Yang of the Eight Immaculates, 75, 75n135

"Sons of Sima Yu": on four slips in calligraphy of Yang Xi, 114n17; translation of, 114–21

Southern Marchmount, location of, 150n86. See also Great Void Perfected of the Southern Marchmount; Wei Huacun (Lady Southern Marchmount)

Southern version, 148

spirit actualization. *See* actualization methods

spiritual marriage: as marriage of phosphors, 10, 43, 43n45, 135n33; of Xu Mi, 43, 99, 113, 122, 123, 123n3, 124, 124n6, 129, 130, 136n38, 137, 140; of Yang Xi and Consort An, 43, 43n45, 94n180, 99, 131, 136, 136n38, 140. *See also* "Poems on Dependence and Independence"

Strickmann, Michel: on Hua Qiao, 96n187; "Mao Shan Revelations," 41n41, 53, 58n79, 68–69n110, 69n113, 99n6; on Tao Hongjing's Buddhism, 32; work on *Declarations,* 7, 25, 68n107

stupas, 141, 147, 147n69

"submerged trigger," 114, 115n18

Su Daohui, 76

Su Jun rebellion, 82

Sumeru, Mount, 136, 136n37

Sun En rebellion, 55n71

Sun Hong (Yanda), 86

Sun Quan, 80n154

Sun Xiu, 86, 86n169

Sun Youyue, 31, 31n6, 72, 75

sun and moon, 110, 118, 119n32, 153n102; flowers of, 147n70; methods for ingesting the rays, 50, 50n64, 125, 142, 150, 151–53, 158; "precious writings" on, 153

superstition, 126
Supervisor of Deities, 95–96, 96n185

Taiping guangji, 101n11
"Talisman of the Six Jia," 86, 86n168
talismans, 47, 54, 73–74, 74n130, 88, 94;
    calligraphy of, 64; Huoluo Talismans,
    66, 66n99, 67; tracing of, 64, 69, 70.
    See also *Five Man-Bird Talismans; Five
    Talismans of Lingbao*
*Talismans of the Central Yellow [God] for
    Controlling Tigers and Leopards*,
    73–74, 74n130, 94
*Talismans of the Duke of the Western
    Marchmount for Interdicting Mountain
    [Demons]*, 73, 74n130
Tamba Yasuyori, *Ishimpō*, 65n95
Tang Yongtong, 126
Tao Hongjing: accused of falsifying
    Declarations, 166; annotations of, 3,
    18–19, 22n64, 23, 25, 68n109;
    attention to detail, 5, 64n90; attitude
    toward Buddhism, 20–21, 24, 32, 126,
    141, 148–49; biography of, 30–31,
    30n2, 99n5; chronological account of
    scriptures transmitted to Yang, 53–78;
    collection of material for *Declarations*,
    1, 6–7, 23, 31, 41n39, 42, 51, 67–68,
    69n113; color coding and editing marks
    used by, 43, 48, 48n58, 53, 53n69;
    commentary on the *Central Scripture of
    the Nine Perfected*, 18–20, 21, 148n73;
    commentary to *Guiguzi*, 46; comparison
    of Buddhism and Daoism, 35n20;
    determination of copyists, 45–46,
    45n51; disciples of, 70n114; doubts
    about descent of Higher Perfected,
    12–13, 128, 140, 142, 154, 156,
    156n116, 158, 164; doubts about
    revelation of Han Mingdi dream, 141,
    142, 144; father of, 43, 99n5; guesses
    regarding names, 26; introduction to
    Daoism, 31, 31n6; knowledge of
    calligraphy, 43, 45, 45n51, 46, 70; life
    and scholarship, 18–20, 31; organiza-
    tion of material, 7–8, 9, 29, 49, 50,
    51–52; postface of, 5, 7, 29, 32; refusal
    to serve Xiao Yan, 32; reliance on Gu
    Huan, 6–7; residence and burial on
    Mount Mao, 20–21, 22n66, 31; storage
    of scriptures, 68n107; style name of,
    36n23; tasks of reconstruction, 50n62;
    treatment of prediction of Sima Yu
    progeny, 108–11; view of Yang Xi,

140n48; writings on pharmaceuticals,
    31, 31n9; work on *Scripture in
    Forty-Two Sections*, 23; on Yang Quan,
    100. See also *Declarations of the
    Perfected*; Loft for Illuminating the
    Numinous; postface; *Secret Instructions
    on the Ascent to Perfection*
Tao Jun, 82
Tao Kedou: attended women's study center,
    11, 88, 90n175; communications with
    Xu Mi after her death, 11, 165n153,
    172n181; death of, 8, 11, 88, 95; and
    the Hua family, 102; lawsuit from
    beyond the grave, 8, 11; marriage to Xu
    Mi, 88
Tao Qian (Yuanming), 106n37, 168n165
Tao Wei, 88, 95
Tao Yi, 30, 30n2
"Teachings and Admonitions of the
    Assembled Numinous Powers," 123,
    125, 142; additions by Yang Xi,
    164n151; translation of, 154–65. See
    also *Scripture in Forty-Two Sections*
"ten thousand images," 35, 35n21
*Text on the Inner Aspirations of the
    Ninefold*, 115
three beneficial friendships, 106n35
three corpses, ridding the body of, 152
Three Eminences, 130, 130n19, 131, 132
three evil paths, 156, 156n119, 157
threefold respect, 86, 86n167
three kalpas, 134, 134n30
three Lords: autograph manuscripts
    transcribed by, 54; calligraphy of, 45–48;
    notes and letters, 34; oral instructions
    from, 74; paper used by, 49; revelations
    written out by, 54, 67; scrolls written out
    by, 49; other writings by, 52. See also Xu
    Hui; Xu Mi; Yang Xi
Three Ministers, 78n144, 80, 80n151
Three Offices, 11
three passes, 120, 120n49
Three Perfected of Shangqing, 22, 22n66,
    148n72; Buddhist disciples of, 22,
    22n66, 148n73. See also Perfected of
    Mount Tongbo; Perfected of Pure
    Numinosity
three stars, 115, 115n20
three-word titles, 33n14, 36–37
Tiantai Mountains, 60n84, 67n104
tiao (slips), 50n64, 107n42. See also slips
Tiao, Mount, 70
Tongbo, Mount, 131. See also Perfected of
    Mount Tongbo

"top-knotted youths who bring destruction," 171, 171n178
tracing, 64, 69, 70, 88
Tractatus de Purgatorio Sancti Patricii, 2
Traditions, 66
Traditions of Divine Transcendents, 74n130
Traditions of Lady Wei, 37–38, 37n29, 59, 76, 76n140. *See also* Wei Huacun
Traditions of Lord Pei, 144. *See also* Perfected of Pure Numinosity
Traditions of Lord Wang, 59, 73, 73n126. *See also* Perfected of Pure Vacuity
Traditions of Son-of-Heaven Mu, 149n77
Traditions of the Divine Transcendents, 5
Traditions of Xu Mai, 51–52, 52n66
Traditions of Zhou Ziyang (Hua Qiao), 97, 97n192
Transcendents: achieving status of, 4, 57, 158, 158n124; banished (earth-bound), 51n65, 101; family background of, 51; in Fengdu, 51, 51n65; island abodes of, 101, 103n22, 123; of Fangzhu, 123, 146, 146n64, 149, 150, 151; palaces of, 146; ranks and careers, 34. *See also* Elühua
Transcendent Watchlord, 43. *See also* Xu Mi
Treasuring the Spirits in Activity and Repose, 50, 50n63
"triggering deities," 116, 116n25
twenty-four spirits, 75n134
two mechanisms, 119, 119n43
two verifications, 41, 64, 64n93, 66, 90

underworld, 1–2, 4, 5; courts and lawsuits, 8, 11. *See also* Fengdu; Palace of Mutation and Promotion
Upper Clarity, 3–4. *See also* Shangqing Daoism; Shangqing scriptures
Upper Minister, 156. *See also* Azure Lad of Fangzhu
Upper Minister star, 116, 116n28, 118
Upper Scripture of the Most High on the Mysterious Perfected of the Bright Hall, 50, 50n63
Ursa Major. *See* Big Dipper

Vacuous Grotto, 132n23
variant texts, 26
Verellen, Franciscus, 55n72
vermilion gates, 105, 105n32
vermilion writing, 120
vertical reading, 2, 2n2

Village of the Towering Trees, 146, 146n65
Vimalakīrtinirdeśa sūtra, 136n37
visionary experiences, 7, 12, 13–15, 14n35, 17, 18n46

Wang Bao. *See* Perfected of Pure Vacuity
Wang Dao, 87
Wang Daotai, 58, 58n79
Wang Dun, 82n157, 85, 85n165
Wang Guanxiang, 112. *See also* Wang, Lady, the Central Watchlord
Wang Huilang, 63, 76–77
Wang Huizhi (Ziyou), 86
Wang Jiakui, 20n56, 21n61, 25, 32, 118n37; on using revelations to raise social status, 98n1, 99, 107n43
Wang, Lady, the Central Watchlord (Wang Guanxiang): announcement and prophecy for Sima Yu, 39, 114–16, 116n24, 117–18; appearance in "eight pages of lined text," 128; appearances to Yang Xi, 134, 135; reports on cavern heavens, 39n33; as sister of Wang Ziqiao, 112; song of dependence and independence, 133–34, 136n37, 39; unclear status of, 44, 112, 112n11
Wang, Lady, of the Left Palace of Purple Tenuity (Wang Qing'e/Yuyin): appearance in "eight pages of lined text," 127; as Craftsperson, 43; failure to partner with humans, 44; as intermediary for Yang Xi's union with Consort An, 131; mate for, 131; poems by, 112, 117; on practice of the Dao, 161; song of dependence and independence in response to Right Blossom, 130–31; on three sorts of birds, 171–72, 172n180; visitor to triple peaks of Mount Mao, 131
Wang Lin (Rongzhen). *See* Purple Prime, Lady, of the Southern Culmen
Wang Lingqi, 58, 58n80; effort to start his own lineage, 58n80, 61; fabricated corpus of, 59–61, 63, 70
Wang, Lord, of the Western Citadel (Wang Yuan/Fangping): and actualization practice, 142, 152; as Most High Perfected, 128, 157–58, 160, 162–63, 163n146; appearance in "eight pages of lined text," 128; on escaping the three evil paths, 156; and the method of ingesting the rays of the sun and moon, 158; question of descent to Yang Xi, 128, 154, 158

Wang Meilan (Shenlin), 112. *See also* Right Blossom, Lady, of the Cloudy Grove

Wang Qing'e (Yuyin). *See* Wang, Lady, of the Left Palace of Purple Tenuity

Wang Wenqing, 73, 73n127

Wang Xianzhi, 47, 51n66, 70, 70n115, 86

Wang Xing, 56, 57–58

Wang Xizhi, 47, 51–52n66, 70, 70n115, 86

Wang Yuan (Fangping). *See* Wang, Lord, of the Western Citadel

Wang Zideng (Perfected of the Heaven of Lesser Existence), 164n152

Wang Ziqiao, 112, 128. *See also* Perfected of Mount Tongbo

Wang Zun, 143, 144

Water and Earth Offices, 11, 97n191

Watson, Burton, 105n30

way of retaining the black and the white, 50n64, 118n41

Way of the Buddha, 19, 22n66, 124, 145, 147, 148, 149n78, 150, 150n82. *See also* Buddhism

weft texts, 36, 36n25

Wei Huacun (Lady Southern Marchmount): association with *Scripture of Yellow Court*, 76, 76n140; bestowal of Shangqing scriptures, 38, 44–45, 54; biography of, 59, 59n82; compared with Pheneas, 18n46; composition of *Inner Traditions of Wang [Bao]*, 73n126; human existence of, 9–10, 9n18; on human life, 170–71; interactions with Yang Xi, 10; living son of, 72n122, 94; as Master of instruction, 43; as Master in the Heavens, 44–45, 45n49; residence of, 150; service to Yang Xi's Master, 59n82; titles of, 9, 54; writing box and ritual robes of, 77

Wei Xin, 71

White Horse Monastery, 144

White Jade Ale, 149, 149n77

White Prime (governing spirit), 75n134

white-souls, 152, 165

Winding Immaculate, 75, 75n137

wu ("shamanism"), 11n24, 16

Wu Tanba, 74

Wucheng zi, 115n18

Wushang biyao, 18–19, 136n37; expurgation of Buddhist elements, 19, 21, 19n54

Xia dynasty, 23, 147, 147n70, 148n72

Xiang, Prince of, 93, 120. *See also* Sima Yu

xianren. See Transcendents

Xiao Daocheng (High Thearch of the Qi), 67

Xiao Yan (Martial Emperor of Liang), 20, 32

Xie An, 82, 84, 84n162, 89

Xie family of Yongxing, 77

Xie Lingyun, "Rhapsody on Residing in the Mountains," 106n38

Xie Xuan, 84, 84n162

Xie Yi, 82

Xin'an, Princess of, 109

Xiwangmu. *See* Queen Mother of the West

Xu Chao, 83, 85

Xu Chisun, 89–90

Xu Daofu (Mingzhi), 88

Xu Ehuang, 85, 85n164, 91

Xu Fen, 83

Xu Fengyou, 88

Xu Fu (father of Xu Jing), 81

Xu Fu (Zhongxian, father of Xu Mi), 82, 85; daughters of, 85; sons of, 83–85, 87; wives of, 82–85

Xu, Grand Mistress (Daoyu), 92, 95

Xu Guang (Shaozhang), 78–79, 78n144, 80, 81; tomb of, 81; wife of, 81

Xu Guiwen, 67, 72

Xu Huangmin (Xuanwen): adopted Wang Lingqi's corpus, 61; biography of, 55n72, 92; birth and death of, 62, 92; collected scriptures after death of Xu Hui, 54–56; disciples of, 76; edits in autograph manuscripts, 46; predictions for, 95; scriptures in the possession of, 62–63, 74–75; sons of, 92–93; transmission of scriptures, 56, 58–59, 95; and the Xie family of Yongxing, 77

Xu Hui: as Accounts Clerk, 26; achievement of Dao, 54; biography of, 90; birth and death dates of, 41n41, 52, 54, 91; calligraphy of, 47; communications through Yang Xi, 5, 41, 41n42; death of, 90–91; inability to receive transmissions from Perfected, 13, 41; as "Lord," 34, 34n18; Master of, 44–45, 44n48; names for, 26, 90; notes and letters, 34; prediction of ascent, 32, 41n41, 90, 90n176, 95; receipt of scriptures from Yang Xi, 44, 54; residence on Mount Leiping, 54; son of (Huang Min), 92; text mentioned in a dream, 76n140; transcriptions of, 41, 42n43, 49, 54, 73, 75, 76, 118; visionary capability of, 15; visits from Yang Xi on Mount Leiping, 94; wives of, 91–92

Xu Huizhi, 83, 86
Xu Jie (uncle of Xu Que), 84
Xu Jing, 78, 78n144, 79–81, 79nn147,149, 80n152
Xu Jingtai (Yuanbao), 88
Xu, Lesser Mistress (Xu Shener), 93, 95
Xu Lian, 5, 95; wife of, 11, 89
Xu Ling, "Letter to Li Na," 106n37
Xu Lingbao, 85
Xu Lingzhen, 70, 70n114, 88, 88–89n173, 93; son of, 88–89n173, 95, 95n183
Xu Mai (Xu Xuanyou): achievement of the Dao, 63, 86, 109; asked about progeny by Sima Yu, 109, 111; birth and death of, 86; genealogy of, 83; Libationer/Master of, 95; names of, 86; as Prior-born, 51, 86, 95; prediction of ascent, 95; predictions attributed to, 95, 95n181; Traditions of, 51–52, 51–52n66; transcriptions forged by Xu Rongdi, 63; wife of, 86
Xu Maoxuan, 84
Xu Mi (Senior Officer to the Defensive Army): ancestors of, 78–93; calligraphy of, 41, 47; communications from departed wife, 165n153, 172n181; copied record of method for retaining the black and the white, 118n41; correspondence with Middle Lord Mao, 39, 95; correspondence with Perfected, 45; Daoist practice, 54, 87; dates for, 41n41, 52, 54, 87–88; descendants of, 88–93; father of, 82, 84; inability to receive transmissions from Perfected, 13, 41; as "Lord," 34, 34n18; marriage of, 43–44; Master of, 44–45, 44n48; messages transmitted by Hua Qiao, 40; names for, 26, 87; notes and letters, 34, 52; offer from Azure Lad, 138; offices and residence on Mount Leiping, 54, 94; and the "Poems of Dependence and Independence," 140n48; prediction of ascent, 32, 41n41, 95; previous life of, 160n133; quest to stop his old age, 9; relationship with Sima Yu, 54n70, 87, 99, 111; revelations from Perfected transmitted to, 4–5, 40–41, 44, 54; service of, 87; seventh-generation ancestor of, 78, 79; seventh-generation descendant of, 88–89n173, 95, 95n183; as Shangqing Perfected, 87; sons and daughters of, 88–90, 92; spiritual marriage to Lady Right Blossom, 99, 113, 123, 123n3, 130, 136n38;

transcriptions of, 41–42, 42n43, 49, 54; transmission of writings to Chen Lei, 71; use of revelations to raise his status, 99; visionary capability of, 15; wives of, 8, 88, 89, 112; Yang Xi's offer to pursue the Dao, 9
Xu Mu. See Xu Mi
Xu Qing, 92–93
Xu Quan (son of Xu Mi), 88, 93
Xu Que (Jiyou), 81
Xu Que (Yixuan), 84
Xu Qun (Taihe), 83
Xu Rongdi (Yuzhi), 46, 62–63, 92, 95
Xu Shang (Yuanfu), 82
Xu Shao (Zijiang), 78n144, 80, 80n153
Xu Shener (Qionghui), 93, 95
Xu Shengqing, 80
Xu Shubiao, 67, 72, 125n8
Xu Sixuan. See Xu Mi
Xu Suxun, 92
Xu Xiang, 78, 80
Xu Xiu (Wenlie), 81–82
Xu Xun, 78, 80
Xu Yan (Xiaoran), 80, 80n154
Xu Yiwu, 83, 85
Xu Zhao (Xingming), 83
Xu Zhao (Zi'a), 79
Xuan Guang, "Disputing Deceptions," 58n80
Xuanji, 35, 35n22. See also Big Dipper
Xuanxuan (Celestial Coach), 115, 115n22
Xu family, 4–6; autograph manuscripts of, 6, 31, 46, 54, 76; correspondence and jottings, 7, 8; and the death of Tao Kedou, 8, 95; family names used by, 95; genealogy of, 29, 30, 52, 55n73, 78–93; received transmissions through Yang Xi, 13, 125, 152, 152n98; relationship with Sima Yu, 98, 107n43; residence of, 78–79, 79n145, 80, 82, 95n184; spiritual marriages of, 135; those who will ascend and those who will pass out of this world, 95; women of, 11, 85. See also Xu Huangmin; Xu Hui; Xu Jing; Xu Lingzhen; Xu Mi

Yan Qiu, 73
Yan Yuan, as Brilliant and Pure Bodhisattva, 148n73
Yan Zhitui, 70n114
Yan Zun, Daodejing zhigui, 170n176
Yang Chen (Changru), 98, 99n5, 107
Yang Quan (Daoyu): connection with Sima Yu, 107, 107n43; connection with Yang

Yang Quan (continued)
Xi, 107; descent of Elühua to, 102, 107; as Elühua's prospective mate, 101; family of, 98, 99, 107; gifts and proposal from Elühua, 98–99, 101, 102–3; given drug for *shijie* by Elühua, 99, 99n4, 100, 103; poems and teachings from Elühua, 98, 101, 102, 102n13; leaking of celestial secrets, 102; name erased in *Declarations* account of Elühua, 100, 101–2, 102nn15,17, 103nn19,23, 105n29; political career, 98; reference to, as ram, 106, 106n40; as student, 105, 105n29

Yang Xi: account of emperor's dream, 141; appearances of Lady Wang the Central Watchlord to, 134; appointment by Sima Yu, 54, 54n70; ascension of, 32; autograph manuscripts, 6, 31, 49; biography of, 29, 30, 93, 94; calligraphy of, 6, 45, 47, 101, 114n17, 122, 154, 172; and the Buddhist *Scripture in Forty-Two Sections*, 15, 23, 32, 123, 126, 141, 142; as Daoist medium channeling deities, 1–2, 4–5, 11–13, 54, 112; and Chi Yin, 152n98; death of, 40, 94; descent of Perfected to, 12–13, 94, 154, 156, 156n117, 158; disdain for sexual practices, 65n95; and the "eight pages of lined text," 122, 127–28, 165–72; instructions for Daoist practice, 15–16; interactions with Perfected, 12–13; knowledge of Eastern Buddhism of Fangzhu, 22–24, 142–43, 145; as "Lord," 32, 34, 34n18; meditation chamber on Mount Mao, 1, 2, 13, 31; as medium for Xu Mi's departed wife, 112; notes and letters, 7, 8, 34; Perfected revelations written out by, 67, 73–74; and the "Poems of Dependence and Independence," 140, 140n48; predictions from Perfected on Sima Yu progeny, 108, 111; post promised to, 94, 150; receipt of *Five Talismans of Lingbao* from son of Wei Huacun, 72n122, 94; receipt of palindromes, 118; records of dreams, 13; records with and without copies, 42, 42n43; relationship with Sima Yu, 125n8; relationship with Xus, 9, 93, 94; as replacement for Hua Qiao, 40, 96; scholarship on, 2n1; scriptures orally bestowed on, by Perfected, 12, 53–54, 94; Shangqing scriptures of, 3–4, 38;

slips written by, 41n39, 107, 107n42, 118, 120; spiritual marriage to Consort An, 41n39, 43n45, 99, 131, 136, 136n38; talismans received from Perfected, 74n130; as teacher of Xus, 44, 44n48; terminology of, used in later works, 26–27; transmission of revelations to Xus, 4–5, 40–41, 44, 54, 125, 152, 152n98; visions of, 14–15, 14n39; visits of Right Blossom, 164n152

Yang Xi of Hongnong, 60, 60n85
Yang Xin, 98, 98n2, 99n5, 105n29, 107, 107n44
Yellow Emperor, time of, 74n130
yin and yang, 10, 119n43
Ying Laizi, 82
Ying Shao, *Ceremonials of Han Officialdom*, 79, 79n149
Ying Yanhui, 82
Yongcheng jixian lu (Du Guangting), 117n36
Yongxing, Xie family of, 77
Yoshikawa Tadao, 25
Yu Jianwu, *Shupin*, 99n5
Yu, Mount, 88
Yu Tan, 83
Yunji qiqian: account of Elühua, 100–101, 101n11; biography of Tao Hongjing, 99n5; "Three Poems Presented to Yang Quan by Elühua," 102n13
Yuwen Yong, Emperor, 20

Zacchetti, Stefano, 149n81
Zhang Dao'en, 47, 47n54
Zhang Kan, 144
Zhang Lingmin, 75, 77
Zhang Lu, 91
Zhang Qian, 143, 144
Zhang Yin, 144
Zhang Yujing, 65
Zhangsang Gongzi, 36, 36n27
Zhao Yi, 124n6
Zheng Xuan, 105n31, 115n20
Zhen'gao. See Declarations of the Perfected
Zhengtong daozang, 25, 173
Zhi Qian, translation of *Vimalakīrtinirdeśa sūtra*, 136n37
zhiguai (strange tales) genre, 5
Zhong Fuguang (daughter of Zhong Xing), 69, 69n113, 71
Zhong Xing, 69, 69n113
Zhong Yishan of Yanguan, 66, 66n96, 68, 69n113, 70–71, 76

Zhonghua daozang, 25
Zhou Yishan, Lord (Perfected of Purple
    Yang), 22n66, 97n192, 148n73
Zhou Ziyang, 96, 97
Zhou dynasty, 80
Zhouli, 105n31, 147n71
Zhu Quan, 145, 148–49, 149n78
Zhu Sengbiao, 59, 59–60n84, 67n104, 69,
    74, 76
Zhu Xi, 126
Zhuangzi, 36n27, 140, 105, 105nn30–31.
    See also *Zhuangzi*

Zhuangzi, 43, 132n23, 137, 172n180; on
    Liezi's ability to fly, 106n39, 129;
    division into seven chapters, 29, 35, 36,
    36n26; *Inner Chapters,* 35, 35n22,
    36n26; three-word titles, 33n14;
    Zhuangzi and Huizi's discussion of
    fishes, 105n30
zi gui (return of themselves/naturally), 140
Ziyou (Wang Huizhi), 86
zong huiwen (plaited palindrome), 113–14,
    114n16, 118–19
zongjing (set phosphors free), 135n33

Founded in 1893,
UNIVERSITY OF CALIFORNIA PRESS
publishes bold, progressive books and journals
on topics in the arts, humanities, social sciences,
and natural sciences—with a focus on social
justice issues—that inspire thought and action
among readers worldwide.

The UC PRESS FOUNDATION
raises funds to uphold the press's vital role
as an independent, nonprofit publisher, and
receives philanthropic support from a wide
range of individuals and institutions—and from
committed readers like you. To learn more, visit
ucpress.edu/supportus.